Beyond Foucault: Excursions in Political Genealogy

Beyond Foucault: Excursions in Political Genealogy

Special Issue Editor

Michael Clifford

MDPI • Basel • Beijing • Wuhan • Barcelona • Belgrade

MDPI

Special Issue Editor
Michael Clifford
Mississippi State University
USA

Editorial Office
MDPI
St. Alban-Anlage 66
Basel, Switzerland

This is a reprint of articles from the Special Issue published online in the open access journal *Genealogy* (ISSN 2313-5778) from 2017 to 2018 (available at: http://www.mdpi.com/journal/genealogy/special_issues/After_Foucault)

For citation purposes, cite each article independently as indicated on the article page online and as indicated below:

LastName, A.A.; LastName, B.B.; LastName, C.C. Article Title. *Journal Name* **Year**, *Article Number*, Page Range.

ISBN 978-3-03897-244-0 (Pbk)
ISBN 978-3-03897-245-7 (PDF)

Cover image courtesy of Michael Clifford.

Contents

About the Special Issue Editor

Michael Clifford is a Professor of Philosophy in the Department of Philosophy and Religion at Mississippi State University. Specializing in Political Philosophy and Michel Foucault, he is author of two other books on political genealogy, Savage Identities: Political Genealogy After Foucault, and Empowerment: The Theory and Practice of Political Genealogy.

genealogy

MDPI

Editorial

Introduction: Beyond Foucault: Excursions in Political Genealogy

Michael Clifford

Department of Philosophy and Religion, Mississippi State University, Mississippi State, MS 39762, USA; Mrc4@msstate.edu

Received: 30 August 2018; Accepted: 5 September 2018; Published: 5 September 2018

The essays in this volume were submitted for a special issue of the new journal, *Genealogy*, on the theme, "Political Genealogy After Foucault." Inspired by the work of Michel Foucault, this volume includes articles from scholars employing political genealogy as a methodology and model of theoretical inquiry representing a wide range of disciplines, from the social sciences to the humanities, from philosophy to medicine to economics to political and cultural theory. The goal of this volume is to publish some of the best and most current work in political genealogy, showing how this work invites us to rethink many of the key concepts in political theory as well as cultural types of expression that we do not routinely think of as political, such as dance, romantic movies, and literature. Broadly conceived, this volume contains essays—excursions, explorations, experimentations—into how political genealogy helps us to understand what Foucault calls "the history of our present," while at the same time looking to our future, to what being a political subject will look like in the 21st century.

The geographical diversity of the authors is remarkable. They come from the United States, Canada, England, Finland, Lithuania, Australia, and Hong Kong. This diversity reflects not only the international influence of Foucault, but, more importantly, the intellectual range of the authors, their ability to mine the potential of political genealogy and to generate their own unique contributions and creations. The topical diversity of the papers is equally impressive—on Trump and Trumpism, popular culture and ideology, political identity and personhood, sovereignty, genealogy and ethics, heroism and cowardice in 21st century warfare, governmentality and chronic illness, even intellectual property. This is a testament to the potential and real fecundity of political genealogy.

This is not a homage to Foucault. Nor a critique of Foucault. It is certainly not a Baudriallardian attempt to "forget" Foucault (Baudriallard 2007). These are excursions, from the Latin, *excurrere*, or "running out", not in the sense of exhausting something, but of finding a new path. Going *beyond* Foucault means finding new paths, new outlets, sorties exploring the potential of genealogy, as understood and elaborated upon by Foucault, ones which deviate from the usual routes in order to find new pathways, new avenues of exploration, of finding and addressing issues and concerns not yet investigated.

Inspiration is never *sui generis*. Sometimes it springs from the beautiful, the sublime, or the merely practical. Sometimes, it arises from something latent, not quite realized. The authors in this volume have at least this much in common: they are all inspired by the mode of enquiry that stems from Foucault's work on political genealogy.

Elsewhere I have argued that a viable methodology, one whose main focus is on political genealogy, could be generated by bringing together the three main movements of Foucault's thought (Clifford 2001). Although there is no clear separation between these movements either chronologically or thematically, they include his early "archaeological" analysis of discourse and discursive regimes (Foucault 1972, 1973), his later work, a more explicitly "genealogical" study of power/knowledge relations and governmentality (Foucault 1979), and finally his examination of processes of subjectivation, a move he often referred to, somewhat idiosyncratically, as "ethics," focusing on sexuality (Foucault 1982, 1985). With respect to the application of the latter, in his essay here entitled, "Heroes and Cowards: Genealogy, Subjectivity and War in the Twenty-First Century," Peter Lee conducts a study of the ethical subjects of war, specifically, the hero and coward, and how they are self-constituted in the contemporary era in the forms of the drone operator vs. the jihadist (Lee 2018). Genealogy makes it possible to better understand the ethical subjectivity of Islamic terrorists by concentrating on the "moral basis of their actions; their justifications for killing non-combatants and the relationship between" religion and violence. By the same token, genealogy reveals "a deeper understanding of the subjectivity of the drone operator who conducts lethal operations." There is a certain mutuality of self-constitution on the part of the jihadist and the drone operator, an agonistic relationship through which the heroism or cowardice of the other is seen through their respective prisms of what constitutes a just war and of how they understand themselves as respective participants in such a war.

Lee's analysis is similar to that conducted by Engin Isin on the relational character between citizens and non-citizens (Isin 2002). Says Isin, "Citizenship and its alterity always emerged simultaneously in a dialogical manner and constituted each other." According to Isin, what we call groups, whether dominant or dominated, are better understood as "projects" of citizenship. These projects involve strategies which are solidaristic, enjoining individuals under a mantle of likeness and identity, or antagonistic, wherein these same individuals orient themselves to others as outsiders or strangers. But the dialogical character of this process means that *both* the dominant group and the dominated group are mutually constituted through the very same gestures. Like Lee, Isin sees these projects of identity formation as reflective of what Foucault's calls technologies of the self. These technologies, says Isin, enable "individuals to effect by their own means or with others a certain number of operations on their own bodies and souls, thoughts and conduct, so as to transform themselves." Through such processes, individuals transform themselves into identities, such as the citizen and the non-citizen, or, for example, "the heroic war-hero of the Greek polis" and the slave boy, who helps the charioteer in his rigorous training but who himself is not allowed to take part in such training—or, as Lee demonstrates, the jihadist and the drone operator.

The question of identity is central to Foucault's work and to genealogy more generally. Rather than assuming a metaphysically given Cartesian self or identity, genealogy brings about "the systematic disassociation of identity," says Foucault (Foucault 1977). The purpose of genealogy, if we can characterize it that way, "is not to discover the roots of our identity, but to commit itself to its dissipation." Nevertheless, effecting this kind of deconstruction involves tracing the "roots" of identity, not in the sense of discovering its ontological origin, but of revealing the historical contingencies of its emergence. Here, in her essay, "Persons and Sovereigns in Ethical Thought," Ladelle McWhorter does exactly that with her analysis of the notion of personhood (McWhorter 2017). She reveals the historical emergence of personhood in the 17th century, and how it was originally used as a tool of oppression. Like Foucault, she anticipates a future when personhood will disappear and thereby open up new possibilities for ethical and political selfhood.

From the cult of personality to the origins of personhood itself, McWhorter's and Bruce Knauft's essays are like bookends enclosing the vexing problem of modern political identity. In his essay here called, "On the Political Genealogy of Trump After Foucault," Knauft discusses how Trump and Trumpism have cast a huge shadow over the political and cultural landscape (Knauft 2018). Trumpism has taken or coincided with many forms, which include a rabid populism, xenophobia, and anti-intellectualism, observes Knauft. In what Time magazine has called a "post-truth" era, in which "fake news" and "alternative facts" have gained unprecedented traction, the very discourse of political engagement has been transformed at a dizzying rate. At the time of this writing, Trump has been implicated in illegal campaign contributions, but it is not clear what the outcome will be for the Trump presidency or the country, given that the norms of political discourse and political practice have been altered so dramatically. Knauft traces out the potential ramifications for this new era.

Donald Trump is a mask, the mask of "Donald Trump," a simulacrum, the image of an image(s)—of the billionaire, of the brand, of a television celebrity playing the billionaire, who fires people, the act itself an embellishment of the brand, now, however unlikely, the President of the United States, or the simulacrum of such, like the auto-animatronic figures in Disney's Hall of Presidents. In some ways, Trump is not unlike the figure of Jeremy Bentham, who sits in a huge mahogany box in the hallway at the University of London. This "auto-icon" is witness to the parade of students on their way to class. Imagine if a wax figure (actually only the head is made of wax—the clothes cover Bentham's actual bones) like this were to come to life, orange-faced, hair plastered over in a yellow mash, raised to the pedestal of the highest office in the land. How could we not be transfixed, with reverence or revulsion, by this figure, this personage, this auto-icon? What does this say about the inter-emersion of the cultural "colonization of consciousness," as Knauft puts it, of kitsch personified, to extend Bielskis's analysis reprinted here, as well (Bielskis 2018), of the infiltration and mutual empowerment of neo-liberalism into the media, of 21st century subjectivity itself. We are tempted to say that our identities have been co-opted, but that presupposes a pre-given, foundational self, as McWhorter shows, something which is revealed to be a kind of illusion, a kind of mask, by the harsh, subversive light of genealogy.

Political genealogy can also be deployed to illuminate the political dimensions of aesthetic aspects of the cultural landscape, such as dance and literature. Genealogies, of course, render the past intelligible in ways that are disruptive of the present and which thereby alter our future. In a sense, there is a kind of dance between what Heidegger and Sartre called the "temporal ekstases" of past, present, and future. And the genealogist is the choreographer. This metaphor of the dance informs Julian Reid's political genealogy here of actual dance, focusing on the groundbreaking work of such dancers as Loïe Fuller, in his essay, "A Political Genealogy of Dance: The Choreographing of Life and Images." (Reid 2018)

This brings to mind Nietzsche's exhortation that one needs to have chaos in one's soul to give birth to a dancing star. Dance plays with the chaotic, gives it shape and form. As such, the chaotic is chiaroscuric. It plays with light and darkness, with absence and presence, movement and stasis, birth and death. There is also form, a tenuous unity in chaos/chiaroscuro—that form is necessarily political in the way that Reid describes it. Dance "can be understood to be deeply political," says Reid, because it "transform[s] by creating time for a belief in the impossible." Dance is a discourse of sorts, a discourse with a history, with a set of norms and rules, "aims and practices," which at once demand compliance, but in so doing herald their own transgression. Along the way its suspends and elevates, "reawakening [the] political imagination in times of crisis and neoliberal hegemony."

Foucault had an ambiguous relationship/attitude toward neoliberalism. It is against this backdrop that Riccardo Baldissone stages a "re-reading" of Foucault's formative essay, "Nietzsche, Genealogy, History." (Foucault 1977). In his essay reprinted here, "Foucault and Foucault: Following in Pierre Menard's Footsteps" (Baldissone 2018), Baldissone adopts a gesture similar to that taken up by Borges, in his "recomposition" of Cervantes' *Don Quijote*. In so doing, Baldissone offers a reading of Foucault that demonstrates the equivocal character of Foucault's relationship toward neoliberalism that compels us to re-think the Foucauldian, and Nietzschean, consequences for the political, and genealogy, more generally.

What is meant by "political genealogy" as a methodology and a form of historical critique? (See Clifford 2013) It is genealogical in the sense that Nietzsche and Foucault use the term: an historical critique that traces the forgotten origins of our present, including, but not limited to, the institutions of government and the forms of identity constructed therein. There are at least two senses in which genealogy is political. One is with respect to the object of inquiry, in that it focuses on the established ideas and institutions of traditional political theory, namely, government, power, freedom, representation, rights, justice, and so on. However, as I said, it also focuses on areas not immediately recognized as political. Genealogy questions the privilege of these ideas by suggesting that there are areas of inquiry, as demonstrated in this collection, that have not only been overlooked or discounted by conventional political theory, but that in fact have dramatic consequences for the traditional areas mentioned above. In this sense, the aim of political genealogy is, to use the words of Nikolas Rose, "to reshape and expand the terms of political debate, enabling different questions to be asked, enlarging the space of legitimate contestation" (Rose 1999).

Political genealogy is political, secondly, in its effects. By revealing the historical contingency of established values and practices, genealogy destabilizes the mechanisms through which we are governed. Genealogy empowers modes of contestation not previously available to political subjects. For this reason, Nietzsche thought of genealogy as "therapeutic" in that it exposes the decadence of entrenched value systems. Similarly, Foucault describes a kind of "counter-memory" that emerges from genealogical critique, through which the power of a given set of beliefs about, for example, how things should be done or the nature of our identity as political subjects, is suspended. In the space opened up by this suspension, a certain kind of freedom is made possible, minimally the recognition that things might be *otherwise*, which can serve as an impetus to political change. (See, McWhorter 2017)

The project—or more appropriately, projects—in the larger sense, of which the essays published here are exemplars, of political genealogy is to piece together a critical methodology based on the genealogical model that can be applied to the political, both the conceptual and the practical. This methodology is strictly speaking neither Nietzschean nor Foucauldian, although it draws from both thinkers as its conceptual wellspring. Or rather, it is Nietzschean *and* Foucauldian in that both represent the source of the methodology, and to the extent that the methodology cannot be separated from the corpus of either thinker. Yet it is not meant as a simple recapitulation of their views; nor is it primarily, or even secondarily, a critical analysis or evaluation of their respective genealogies.

The projects here might be referred to as examples of "poligen studies" (see Clifford 2013). The term "poligen" comes from the collapse into a single term of political genealogy. The term is analogically connected to its cousin in biology, the polygenic. In biology, the polygenic refers to the inheritance of traits from multiple, often unknown factors. Similarly, the history of the present conducted by genealogy attempts to reveal those hidden multiple factors contributing to the identity of the present, and to the identities populating the present.

Moreover, as Réal Fillion shows in his essay reprinted here, "Situating Poligen Studies: Between Moral Enquiry and Political Theory", (Fillion 2017), there is both a moral and political aspect to poligen studies. Says Fillion, "Another way to say this is that situating the pursuit of poligen studies between moral enquiry and political theory is to recognize that these struggles and resistances themselves express the moral refusal of the ordering constraints being imposed on the struggling and resisting agents subject to them." This moral dimension of poligen studies is not just an exploration of the historical constitution of the self through what Foucault calls an ethics of subjection, which is meant to be neutral with respect to understanding the identities that are formed through the self-appropriation of values. There is a normative dimension to political genealogy that Foucault may or may not have been happy with supporting. Nevertheless, poligen studies have the effect of disrupting established modes of subjection, empowering subjects to resist, with the implied assumption that things, even one's very identity, might be different than they presently are. Difference, differing is itself intrinsically political and inherently moral, by virtue of the stance it makes possible in the face of entrenched power relations. This means in part acknowledging and to some degree facilitating the potential of a genealogical critique on the practical lives of individuals. Moreover, the genealogical emphasis on local knowledge and experience forces us to contend with real-world instantiations of justice, power, and freedom. In so doing, these ideas typically undergo a transformation sometimes at odds with their traditional ideological and philosophical meanings. That is, on the ground, in the trenches, genealogical analysis reveals the true meaning, the meaning in *praxis*, of justice, power, and freedom for those whose very identity is a product of practices, policies, and institutions that operate according to a different logic, a different agenda than that prescribed by the traditional juridical discourse of political representation.

Despite the diversity of approaches, these essays have two very important things in common. One, a certain understanding of political genealogy as a method and what it can facilitate and, second, a commitment to the application of that method to real issues and problems beyond a critique of Foucault, to the extent that the two can be separated. To wit, with regard to method, Wendyl Luna says, in his essay here on intellectual property, "Foucault's genealogy provides a useful and still relevant approach to analyzing rights and power, especially in the specific context of [intellectual property]" (Luna 2018). Lee echoes this sentiment: "Political genealogy after Foucault can open up a conceptual space that will provide a more nuanced understanding of subjectivity in modern war." Ann Reich and Margo Turnbull bring a Foucauldian -inspired methodology to the understanding of the power relations related to disease, saying that, in their project "the genealogical approach informed by Foucault facilitated a unique tracing of the dominant discourses and practices circulating in the local, national and global contexts and linkages to the day-to-day lives of the clients with chronic diseases," (here in "Using Foucault: Genealogy, Governmentality and the problem of Chronic Illness," (Reich and Turnbull 2018)).

On the other hand, to say that Foucault has a method which can be straightforwardly adopted and applied should be tempered with a healthy degree of caveats and cautions. Says Andrius Bielskis, "We should not understand Foucault's genealogy as a heavy-handed theoretical methodology with deductively established first principles, which are then applied to the analysis of existing power relations and social institutions." ("On the Genealogy of Kitsch and Critique of Ideology: A Reflection on Method," (Bielskis 2018); reprinted here.) As Foucault himself says, observes Bielskis, he considers himself more of an "experimenter" than a theorist. Applying political genealogy is more of an experiment, an excursion, if you will, into areas of the political, social, and cultural in ways that have previously been overlooked or never considered. Reich and Turnbull are even more blunt about the limitations of political genealogy as a method: "As a 'method' for analyzing contemporary problems, readings of Foucault's work have revealed that there is no clearly stated, well-defined or prescribed methodology for investigations."

Generally speaking, when it comes to theory/methodology/application, there is no clear demarcation. Thinkers as diverse as Leo Strauss and Baudrilliard have questioned the distinction between theory and it is application. The mediator between the two is arguably considered to be methodology, but here, too, the lines are blurred, such that it is not clear where one leaves off and the other begins. In one sense, this is not all surprising, since the mediation between theory and practice—notably understood as "praxis" in Marxist camps and beyond—is fluid. Not surprisingly, Foucault is suspicious of the separation between theory and practice. For him, the distinction is another of the numerous dichotomies shaping Western thought. Which puts the projects of the essays in this collection in something of a precarious position, since they ostensibly rely on these very dichotomies. Perhaps we need to allow the authors their points of departure, their modes of execution, their conclusions, and sort out the differences between theory, methodology, and application later. After all, what counts with genealogies is not so much the truth of their expositions (since "truth" itself is problematized and historicized by genealogy), but the effects of these excursions on how we think and how we live.

Funding: This research received no external funding.

Conflicts of Interest: The author declares no conflicts of interest.

References

Baldissone, Riccardo. 2018. Foucault and Foucault: Following in Pierre Menard's Footsteps. *Genealogy* 2: 19. [CrossRef]

Baudriallard, Jean. 2007. *Forget Foucault*. Los Angeles: Semiotexte.

Bielskis, Andrius. 2018. On the Genealogy of Kitsch and the Critique of Ideology: A Reflection on Method. *Genealogy* 2: 9. [CrossRef]

Clifford, Michael. 2001. *Political Genealogy after Foucault: Savage Identities*. New York and London: Routledge Press.

Clifford, Michael. 2013. *Empowerment: The Theory and Practice of Political Genealogy*. Lanham: Lexington/Rowan & Littlefield.

Fillion, Réal. 2017. Situating Poligen Studies: Between Moral Enquiry and Political Theory. *Genealogy* 2: 2. [CrossRef]

Foucault, Michel. 1972. *The Archaeology of Knowledge and the Discourse on Language*. Translated by A. M. Sheridan Smith. New York: Pantheon.

Foucault, Michel. 1973. *The Order of Things: An Archaeology of the Human Sciences*. New York: Vintage Books.

Foucault, Michel. 1977. *Language, Counter-Memory*, practice, ed. Edited by Donald Bouchard. Ithaca: Cornell University Press.

Foucault, Michel. 1979. *Discipline and Punish: The Birth of the Prison*. Translated by Alan Sheridan. New York: Vintage Books.

Foucault, Michel. 1982. On the Genealogy of Ethics: An Overview of Work in Progress. In *Michel Foucault: Beyond Structuralism and Hermeneutics*, 2nd ed. Edited by Hubert L. Dreyfus and Paul Rabinow. Chicago: University of Chicago Press.

Foucault, Michel. 1985. *The Use of Pleasure: Volume 2 of the History of Sexuality*. Translated by Robert Hurley. New York: Pantheon Books.

Isin, Engin F. 2002. *Being Political: Genealogies of Citizenship*. Minneapolis: University of Minnesota Press.

Knauft, Bruce M. 2018. On the Political Genealogy of Trump after Foucault. *Genealogy* 2: 4. [CrossRef]

Lee, Peter. 2018. Heroes and Cowards: Genealogy, Subjectivity and War in the Twenty-First Century. *Genealogy* 2: 15. [CrossRef]

Luna, Wendyl. 2018. Emancipating Intellectual Property from Proprietarianism: Drahos, Foucault, and a Quasi-Genealogy of IP. *Genealogy* 2: 6. [CrossRef]

McWhorter, Ladelle. 2017. Persons and Sovereigns in Ethical Thought. *Genealogy* 1: 24. [CrossRef]

Reich, Ann, and Margo Turnbull. 2018. Using Foucault: Genealogy, Governmentality and the Problem of Chronic Illness. *Genealogy* 2: 13. [CrossRef]

Reid, Julian. 2018. A Political Genealogy of Dance: Choreographing of Life and Images. *Genealogy* 2: 20. [CrossRef]

Rose, Nikolas. 1999. *Powers of Freedom: Reframing Political Thought*. Cambridge: Cambridge University Press.

genealogy

MDPI

Article

Situating Poligen Studies: Between Moral Enquiry and Political Theory

Réal Fillion

Department of Philosophy, University of Sudbury, Sudbury, ON P3E 2C6, Canada; rfillion@usudbury.ca

Received: 13 November 2017; Accepted: 24 December 2017; Published: 27 December 2017

Abstract: In this article, I argue that we can best appreciate those works that appeal to the notion of "political genealogy" as distinct forms of study by situating them between moral enquiry and political theory. They draw from moral enquiry the concern with how we ought to live but are not themselves prescriptive. They address the political constitution of our social lives but not as a theoretical object. Reversing the relation between enquiry and truth, political genealogies are historiographical studies motivated by forms of resistance that expose the will to truth of the present ordering of discourses, thereby releasing the hold such orderings have on what we think, say, and do to their on-going agonistic relations.

Keywords: discourse; ordering; truth; enquiry; subversion; Foucault; MacIntyre; historiography; resistance; possibility

---

Joining my colleagues on the picket line in support of their work action (my own federated university has its own administration and, though we teach the same students, we are under a different collective agreement), I was afforded an interesting opportunity to appreciate what brings us together as academics, even as it divides us. This particular strike was occasioned by the declaration of an "impasse" in negotiations by the administration just before the strike deadline. As universities are increasingly administered by organizational principles and people only tangentially connected to the performance of academic work per se (defined in North America as research, teaching, and community service), such declarations of "impasse" should no doubt be expected, as both parties increasingly are faced with forging workable language to continue doing what each thinks it is its job to do. Given the administration's apparent conception of the relation between research and teaching (proposing that ostensibly measurable lower research output should be redressed with increased teaching loads), for faculty the hugely diverse character of what counts as actual academic work took second place to a rallying resistance. But, of course, as conversations amongst ourselves eventually moved beyond the immediate circumstances, the differences within academic work resurfaced, and the divisions within the academy and its various discourses reconfigured the conversational partners along familiar lines even as we all walked and stood the line, solidarity sporadically reaffirmed by the honking of passing cars.

This was especially marked for me because I was not myself on strike—that is, I continued to be paid my regular salary, as opposed to strike pay—and yet all classes on campus were suspended, effectively putting a stop to my own teaching, and releasing me to my other duties, which for most of us meant our research which may or may not include contact and communication with various communities. This is not as simple a situation as it sounds, given the various ways academics can divide up the time to pursue these different activities, blocking research around particular periods of the year, outside of the teaching schedule, for example (as often happens in largely undergraduate institutions like my own). As it turns out, the suspension of my teaching did have the fortuitous effect of allowing me to focus my attention on this particular article. But thrown together on the picket line, I was reminded how peculiar it is to explain to my (immediately) fellow academics the kinds of lines of enquiry I pursue. Walking alongside some of my colleagues from the sciences and engineering, saying that I was working on an article on Foucault would pretty much cover the extent of my explication, unless they were polemically informed and inclined. Pockets of colleagues from other disciplines, already self-selected into groups by interdisciplinary projects and concerns, might be receptive to the particular focus on political genealogy and questions might be asked, some of them still slightly polemical, but others more engaged and substantial.

Indeed, as I chatted with various colleagues and scanned the assembled group, I realized that the work that many of them do might very well be implicitly allied with what Clifford (2013) has termed "poligen studies," that is, a distinct mode of study which, albeit with various points of departure, can be discerned through asking the following questions: "does [the work in question] give us a plausible understanding of the historical origins of the area it is examining? Furthermore, is this understanding disruptive of the way that we have heretofore understood ourselves and the world? Does it point toward the possibility of being other than we currently are?" (Clifford 2013, p. 123). I say that some of their work might be *implicitly* allied because their own discursive commitments might not lead them to characterize their efforts as explicitly *genealogical*, though they would no doubt appreciate their *political* character, and this along the lines proposed by Clifford, that is, as "disruptive" and "other" to the prevailing discursive commitments of many of their colleagues in the university and society at large. What then would be required for their work explicitly to participate in "poligen studies"? The most obvious thing to say, if we reference the questions posed above, is that they would need to pay explicit attention to something like the "historical origins" of what concerns them. That is, they would need to see that their concerns fall within the historical parameters of a distinctly constituted dissatisfying *present*, a present that contains and maintains features that *ought not to be* the way they are and that are nevertheless somehow sustained in their being as they are. We can see, then, that such studies have an implicit *moral* concern with what ought to be, with how we ought to live; however, as forms of *study* the explicit concern is with the historically determinable conditions of how we do in fact live with and within the terms of this present.

With this focus on a distinctly constituted dissatisfying *present*, my suggestion will be that we can situate poligen studies between moral enquiry and political theory. I say "between" because, though the kinds of study that we might qualify as political genealogies do address the moral questions of how we ought to live, they do so indirectly. As such, they themselves are not strictly speaking moral enquiries but rather investigations or studies that challenge or disrupt the discourses and practices that arguably do provide answers to those moral questions of how we ought to live. As well, though these investigations or studies are deemed "political," their object is not the political understood as some kind of timeless feature of social life and as such their objective is not to produce nor to rely on a "theory." Like the moral (or morality), the political is approached indirectly, not through theoretical elaboration as an object, but through a studious disruption of the discourses and practices that are said to constitute it as the *present*, a discernably distinctive historically specific configuration of relations of power.

The sense of the "between" here is thus spatially imagined. Such studies situate themselves as distinct from, though related to, both moral enquiry and political theory. However, there is another reason for situating them here, perhaps "betwixt" is the better word, as their distinctiveness nevertheless depends on these contrasting concerns and, I will be arguing, they are subject to the pull of both. The resultant tension is creative, but also difficult to sustain, with the danger of the relevance of such studies giving way to mere moral exhortation or being replaced by largely politically ineffective theorizing.

That poligen studies should be akin to political theory should be obvious given their explicit qualification as political. Such explicitness serves to inflect their genealogical approach from Nietzsche (2006) original study (and targeting) of morality, expanding its scope to discursive formations more generally conceived (and, once again following Clifford (2001, 2013) following Foucault, as these discursive formations connect to power relations and practices of self-formation) and favoring an approach that is perhaps less polemical in presentation and more focused on illuminating the conditions of the intelligibility of the present. That is, while Nietzsche (1997) meant to show us the "uses and disadvantages" of the appeal to history for *life*, including a critical history that serves life by sometimes being "clear as to how unjust the existence of anything—a privilege, a caste, a dynasty, for example—is, and how greatly this thing deserves to perish" (Nietzsche 1997, p. 76), the focus of political genealogy is less on "life" than on the *present*. However, the intention to "disrupt," indeed to *subvert*, remains central, though if we think of subversion here not merely as undermining an established order, but etymologically as a kind of "overthrowing," a "throwing over from below," we might consider its genealogical version as a "throwing off" of the constraints definitive of our present discursive ordering. This subversive intent is no doubt what links Nietzschean and Foucaultian genealogy. Before exploring the particular political inflection of Foucaultian genealogy further, I suggest we consider genealogy as a mode of moral enquiry for a moment so that we can better discern the distinctiveness of an explicitly political genealogy, but also so that we can better discern the pull and purpose that moral enquiry will continue to exert on the situating of poligen studies.

Alasdair MacIntyre (1990) qualifies genealogy as one of three rival versions of moral enquiry, the other two being "encyclopedia" and "tradition." While this might appear to be a somewhat idiosyncratic parsing of the field of moral enquiry, it is actually quite illuminating, especially as I think back to the conversations with my colleagues on the picket line. All of my academic colleagues are engaged in enquiries of some sort. This is what we mean when we say we are engaged in "research." Not all of them, indeed perhaps not many of them, would qualify their enquiring engagement as "moral," and yet it is not implausible to do so, given that what they do is connected to the question of how we ought to live. If they were on strike, it was because their conception of the work that they do contributes to the way they believe we ought to live, which includes "the pursuit of knowledge" through their research, and that subordinating that research to administratively determined financial priorities was morally unacceptable (i.e., not how we ought to "pursue" knowledge). That such an appeal to the morally unacceptable should remain largely implicit is part and parcel of the particular mode of moral enquiry MacIntyre calls "encyclopedia," arguably the typical or predominant mode informing the discursive practices that make up the academy, inasmuch as the academy as a whole—and insofar as it considers itself as a coherent whole, as my striking colleagues surely did, at least under the circumstances—commits itself to something it calls "rationality" or rational enquiry.

MacIntyre calls this particular mode of moral enquiry "encyclopedia" because "morality" is treated not (explicitly) as something that informs our lives as a whole but rather qualifies certain judgments we might make within the broader context of a "rational" appreciation of ourselves and the world: that appreciation, ideally-conceived, would be captured "encyclopedically," divided into various entries as it were, and serving as the common reference of our knowledge. Something like this common "encyclopedia" of knowledge is what unites all enquirers in their endeavors, in their common "pursuit of knowledge." As MacIntyre puts it: "The encyclopedist's conception is of a single framework within which knowledge is discriminated from mere belief, progress towards knowledge is mapped, the truth is understood as the relationship of our knowledge to the world, through the application of those methods whose rules are the rules of rationality as such" (MacIntyre 1990, p. 42).

Moral judgement—determining what is right or wrong—within this broader context of rational enquiry is for each of us to make and, if it is to be assessed, then it is to be assessed by rational criteria, theoretically devised: how the action it proposes contributes to the greatest good of the greatest number, or how it respects an imperative that is categorical, for example. The problem with this approach, which MacIntyre (1984, 1988) has long been at pains to point out, is that the rational tests proposed by "morality" theoretically conceived do not yield agreement but rather intractable *dis*agreement, albeit in a way that curiously does not expunge the conception of rationality that informs them. Part of the reason for this, I would argue, is that on the encyclopedic conception of ourselves and the world, rationality remains the explicit reference, and lives governed by explicit rules and laws (the articulation of which are the hallmarks of rationality) prove themselves to be sufficiently orderly and stable to allow for such merely "moral" disagreements.

Not all of my colleagues on the picket line would subscribe to this account of "morality," other than—and this should be emphasized—recognizing that the determination of right and wrong is a judgment for each of us to make. Many of them would see in the rational ordering of explicit rules and laws much to condemn from a moral point of view (of how we ought to live) and would appeal, not to rational tests, but to various forms of action (including forms of study) protesting the so-called rational ordering in question. It is this subversive intent with regard to the dominant ordering of the social world that opens the possibility of connecting the work of these colleagues to a different conception of moral enquiry, one that MacIntyre describes as "genealogy" and distinguishes it from "encyclopedia" and its relation to (rational) truth and the world. Privileging Nietzsche's account, this approach "takes there to be a multiplicity of perspectives within each of which truth-from-a-point-of-view may be asserted, but no truth-as-such, an empty notion, about the world, an equally empty notion. There are no rules of rationality as such to be appealed to, there are rather strategies of insight and strategies of subversion" (MacIntyre 1990, p. 42)[1]. What makes these approaches radically different (and *rivals* on MacIntyre's view) is how they relate enquiry and truth. For encyclopedia, enquiry purportedly subordinates itself to truth; for genealogy, truth is subordinated to enquiry, truth revealed upon investigation to be in effect supported by the *will* to truth through the imposing of particular discursive orderings (including determinations on how we ought to live). Showing this to be the case requires strategic interventions within those discursive orderings.

But what, if anything, might be seen to guide such strategic interventions? Simply another will, Nietzsche's will to power? One might be tempted to see in my example of striking colleagues precisely this, less a moral judgment about how we ought to live, and more a question of the relative power of faculty and administration when it comes to determining the conditions of what each does. But this is to oppose moral judgment and power relations, an opposition that builds on the isolating of "morality" from the unfolding of our lives, something promoted by the rational (encyclopedic) appropriation of the term, which MacIntyre reminds us does not have this independent status in pre-modern languages, the moral being folded into the descriptive comprehension of social life (*mores, ethos*). I agree with MacIntyre that this opposition should be resisted. My striking colleagues were indeed engaged in power relations, but their moral judgment of how we ought to live was no less present in their actions and their actions a function of their agency. What "genealogy" does, at least as practiced by Foucault, is precisely to focus on the power relations involved in these interactions between various agents, where their "freedom" as agents shows itself to be inflected in distinct ways.[2] This distinctiveness becomes apparent from the point of view afforded by the presence of resistance within these power relations. As Foucault (1982) puts it, a genealogical approach "consists of taking the forms of resistance against different forms of power *as a starting point*. . . . it consists of using this resistance as a chemical catalyst so as to bring to light power relations, locate their position, and find out their point of application and the methods used. Rather than using power from the point of view of its internal rationality, it

---

[1] Clearly not all of my colleagues critical of the dominant political ordering of the world will see themselves in such a genealogical perspective, many preferring instead to reference the notion of human rights. How the notion of human rights fits into either MacIntyre's parsing of moral enquiry or how it relates to political genealogy more generally is beyond the scope of this paper. For an interesting discussion of the paradigm of human rights, cf. Moyn (2010).

[2] That, for Foucault (1982), the exercise of power and agency as freedom mutually imply each other is clear in the following oft-cited passage: "Power is exercised only over free subjects, and only insofar as they are free. By this we mean individual or collective subjects who are faced with a field of possibilities in which several ways of behaving, several reactions and diverse comportments may be realized. Where the determining factors saturate the whole, there is no relationship of power; slavery is not a power relationship when man is in chains. (In this case it is a question of a physical relationship of constraint.) Consequently, there is no face-to-face confrontation of power and freedom, which are mutually exclusive (freedom disappears everywhere power is exercised), but a much more complicated interplay. In this game freedom may well appear as the condition for the exercise of power (at the same time its precondition, since freedom must exist for power to be exerted, and also its permanent support, since without the possibility of recalcitrance, power would be equivalent to physical determination)" (Foucault 1982, p. 790).

consists of analyzing power relations through the *antagonism* of strategies" (Foucault 1982, p. 780, my emphasis). Therefore, to the question of what guides strategic genealogical investigations, the answer is to be found in actual resistances within the discursive orderings of our present society. As Foucault immediately suggests (where we recognize his own work): "to find out what our society means by sanity, perhaps we should investigate what is happening in the field of insanity. And what we mean by legality in the field of illegality" (Foucault 1982, p. 780).

But here is where I would suggest that specifically Foucaultian genealogical investigations are something other than MacIntyre's "rival version" of *moral* enquiry. MacIntyre's basic claim (MacIntyre 1984) is that moral enquiry today is a fractured affair, that the development of "morality" as a distinct dimension of human life (captured in moral judgments about how we ought to live) was a consequence of its severance from the unfolding of our whole lives (whose wholeness Aristotelian philosophy and then Christian theology had better captured). On MacIntyre's account, this severance has resulted in a truncated "rationality" confronting an indifferent world grasped through observed regularities with its "morality" of (dis)agreement on the one hand, and a rejection of any graspable "timeless" truth in favor of a project of disordering subversion on the other. Thus "encyclopedia" and "genealogy" are rivals to each other in their distinct relating of enquiry and truth but also rivals to a conception of moral enquiry as integral to the living wholeness that MacIntyre calls "tradition." For MacIntyre, "tradition" names the argumentative context within which a moral *enquiry* into how best to realize the Good takes place, a Good that the potential enquirer first takes as given (as real) and thus, in becoming an actual *enquirer* into that Good, only then seeks to know it. In MacIntyre's account of this rival version of moral enquiry, the real object becomes the enquirer him or herself and his or her relation to the Good and the authoritative tradition that creates an argumentative space for this enquiry to take place, where disagreements are articulated against a background of agreement. The critique of genealogy from the perspective of this rival version of moral enquiry thus targets the genealogist whose subversive purpose is not accounted for, even on his or her own terms, given the lack of recognition of any authoritative context within which one can make sense of it; such enquiry can only appear, again on MacIntyre's view, even to the genealogist him or herself, as arbitrary.

However, I would argue that this apparent arbitrariness is not a function of the genealogist's *own* subversive purpose, but the very real effect of ordering discourses themselves as seen from the perspective of that which resists them. It is in this sense that a genealogy that focuses on the present does not pretend to be a form of specifically moral enquiry, interestingly largely because, like MacIntyre's account of "tradition," it can be said to treat "morality" not as its own distinct sphere (and tied to discreet judgments) but as incorporated into social life more generally. Unlike "tradition," however, it does not see the "good" that is realized through the practices of social life as having a "timeless" source and an independent "truth." MacIntyre's critique of the genealogical project, with its focus on the genealogist's accounting for him or herself of the very point of his or her enquiry, is not without merit, as far as conceptions of the moral self are concerned (something to which Foucault, for example, turns his attention in his discussions of self-formation in his later works); however, this critique does not address the fact that the ordering discourses of social life are resisted and that such resistances open up a possible perspective on their character as distinctly constituted *and imposed* ordering discourses. These real resistances to the imposed character of ordering discourses are the real and actual sources of the possibility of genealogical subversion, and not the arbitrary purpose of any given genealogist. Or so I would suggest, following Foucault's development of a more *political* genealogy.

What distinguishes genealogy as a form of enquiry, then, is that it reverses the relation between enquiry and truth: enquiry is not subordinated to an independent truth, truth itself becomes subject to enquiry. In this reversal, truth becomes "truth" and its effects come under scrutiny. "Truth" circulates in the ordering of discourses and it impacts on what is thought, said, and done. It has effects. As mentioned above, such effects as effects are evidenced in the resistances to the ordering of discourses, especially as these discourses coalesce around those kinds of knowledges meant to intervene into the workings of social life. Such interventions count as *political* insofar as they actively contribute to the on-going constitution of our social order; and as such, they become subject to a distinct form of genealogical enquiry from the perspective opened by attention to the resistances to those interventions. To qualify such enquiry as "genealogical" is to underscore the eventfulness of that which it is investigating, its historically determinable constitution at the confluence of discursive practices and their effects. Thus, genealogical enquiry proposes itself as a form of historiography, where history here must be understood not in terms of its object (i.e., the past), but etymologically as what it is itself, its own distinct form of "enquiry,"[3] an investigation meant to provide an account of the goings-on of human affairs in their eventfulness and "impactfulness," as it were. But what makes this form of historiography "genealogical" remains the subversive intent. It is not an enquiry whose findings are meant to *culminate* into an account of an ordered establishing of the facts. It is not a judicial enquiry into a *past* event or series of events. It is a genealogical enquiry into the constituting of a *present* ordering that reveals its historical distinctness and *lack* of necessity. That is, the present order of things is discernably intelligible not because it rests on a true grasp of them but because of the discursive regularities it exhibits and maintains.

I have been privileging in this discussion the notion of discourses and more specifically the ordering of discourses. I am taking as central Foucault's *L'ordre du discours* (Foucault 1971), his inaugural lecture at the Collège de France. Translated into English, somewhat curiously as "The Discourse on Language," and appended to the translation of *Archaeology of Knowledge* (Foucault 1972), I would argue that this text can now, with the publication of all of Foucault's subsequent lectures at the Collège de France, take its central place as inaugurating the mode of enquiry he would continue to develop as "genealogy" throughout the 1970s and should be, in my view, a key textual reference for situating poligen studies themselves. In it, we find a clear expression of the subversive intent of inverting truth and enquiry, by showing how "truth" rests on both a will to truth and a will to know and to knowledge that operate by *ordering* discourses. Thus, the "order of discourse" is an *ordering*, an imposing of order *through* discourse, supported by a will to truth and a will to knowledge, truth and knowledge themselves given distinct status by this (willful) ordering of discourse. Foucault, near the opening of this inaugural speech (the opening of the opening discourse/lecture of the lectures he will henceforth be giving from the space of this newly self-designated Chair of the History of Systems of Thought—the Collège de France is an extraordinary institution), after fretting about this auspicious but nevertheless imposed need to begin, wonders about the institutionalized and institutionalizing, established and establishing ordering function of discourse and asks, quite simply: "What is so perilous, then, in the fact that people speak, and that their speech proliferates? Where is the danger in that?" (Foucault 1972, p. 216).

In asking this simple question, Foucault is pointing to a divide within discourse between a speech that proliferates and largely disappears or dissolves after its enunciation, and speech that, through certain forms of repetition and attention, organizes itself into discourse, into discursive formations that can be seen to operate in fact (evident when attention is paid to that which resists them) as systems of *exclusion* which he categorizes briefly as follows: that of prohibiting certain forms of speech (*la parole interdite*), that is, recognizing and reinforcing that not everything can be said; that of rejecting certain forms of speech as outside the bounds of sense and reason (*le partage de la folie*); and then finally that of the divide insisted on by the will to truth itself, that between *the* true and *the* false (Foucault 1972, pp. 216–19). This last divide, Foucault tells us, needs to be appreciated (if we want to account for a present that continues to insist on subordinating enquiry to an independent truth) as actually *historically* situated within Greek culture when, through philosophical appropriation in the fifth century, true discourse was separated from its distinct conditions of enunciation as act, as

---

3   "History is a Greek word, meaning simply an investigation or inquiry ... It is the use of this word, and its implications, that makes Herodotus the father of history. The conversion of legend-writing into the science of history was not native to the Greek mind, it was a fifth-century invention, and Herodotus was the man who invented it." Collingwood (1946, pp. 18–19).

assertion (as oath and ordeal[4]) and subordinated to formalized discourse; that is, "the highest truth no longer resided in what discourse was, nor in what it did: it lay in what was said. The day dawned when truth moved over from the ritualized act—potent and just—of enunciation to settle on what was enunciated itself: its meaning, its form, its object and its relation to what is referred to" (Foucault 1972, p. 218). The effect of this relation to the "truth" as the "enunciated" (within ordering discourse) creates a distance between the conditions of enunciation and what is enunciated. Sustained and continued attention to the enunciated ends up concealing from such ordering discourse its own willful conditions of enunciation, its own desire and exercise of power, and the point of genealogical investigations is to have us confront their continued workings within discourse. That is, as Foucault writes: "True discourse, liberated *by the nature of its form* from desire and power, is incapable of recognizing the will to truth that pervades it; and the will to truth, having imposed itself upon us for so long, is such that the truth it seeks to reveal cannot fail to mask it" (Foucault 1972, p. 219, my emphasis). The willful conditions that sustain the enunciation of truth, by becoming the discursively enunciated formally maintained, are systematically obscured and covered over, but nevertheless remain at work.

The genealogical task before us, then, is to challenge the order of discourse and to show on the one hand the workings of desire and the exercise of power within the ordering of discourses and their delimiting or policing function of what can legitimately be said. This task is a political one, inasmuch as the ordering of discourses it addresses contributes to the constitution and the maintenance of the particular *present* social order. But, as political, it is not direct political *action* (though of course part of its point is to have its enquiries resonate within political action or political movement) but a subversive engagement with and within the *given* ordering intelligibility of the present; however, while this engagement with the conditions of intelligibility of the present points to political *theory*, the intelligibility it lays bare is not that of a discursively determined *object* (the constitution of the political, timelessly conceived). It is the result of historiographical enquiry aimed at disrupting the hold the ordering of discourses has on what we think, say, and do in the present and specifically the hold it has by masking the "will to truth" that sustains this ordering function. This masking does not only operate in terms of systems of exclusion, however. As Foucault goes on to say in *L'ordre du discours*, there are "many other systems for the control and delimitation of discourse," such as those of "internal rules, where discourse exercises its own control; rules concerned with the principles of classification, ordering, and distribution" (Foucault 1972, p. 220). He groups these systems according to distinct principles for limiting discourse (which we can find throughout the academy): those linked to key texts and producing "commentary"; a linked but distinct principle coalescing texts around the notion of the "author"; and, finally, the principle of limitation most relevant to this effort of situating "poligen studies," that of "disciplines."

According to Foucault, "disciplines are defined by groups of objects, methods, their corpus of propositions considered to be true, the interplay of rules and definitions, of techniques and tools"

---

[4] Which the subsequent lectures will explore (Foucault 2013). Cf. also many years later the discussions of truth-telling in Foucault (2014). It is interesting to note how Foucault, in both series of lectures, themselves separated by ten years, appeals both to the same example (Antilochus' challenge to Menelaus) and sets up the discussion by quoting the same passage from Georges Dumézil's *Servius et la Fortune* (quoted in (Foucault 2013, p. 84)); " 'As far back as we go in the behavior of our species, the 'true utterance' is a force to which few forces resist ... very early on the Truth appeared to men as one of the most effective verbal weapons, one of the most prolific seeds of power, one of the most solid foundations for their institutions.'" Quoted in (Foucault 2014, p. 28), translated as: "'Looking back into the deepest reaches of our species' behavior, 'truthful speech' [*la parole vraie*] has been a force few could resist. From the earliest moments, truth was one of man's most formidable verbal weapons, most prolific sources of power, and most solid institutional foundations.'") In the lecture on 3 February 1971 (Foucault 2013, p. 85), he provides an illuminating contrast. First, there is what we easily recognize today as the uttering of truth in the form of bearing witness to something we have observed, thus serving the function of revealing to others something that has already taken place. Here the "non-verbal equivalent" of uttering the truth "is perception: showing things as if one was there, as if one was seeing them." A kind of distance is placed between the utterance and the truth of what is said. This contrasts with the earlier (Homeric) relation with truth through utterance where "the non-verbal equivalent for the word of truth is the ordeal, the test: being exposed or exposing someone to undefined danger." Here the relations between the truth, the occasion of its utterance, and the one who is challenged to utter it are much more intimate. The will to truth is more immediately present.

(Foucault 1972, p. 222), ultimately creating the conditions for "the possibility of formulating, and reformulating indefinitely, new propositions" (Foucault 1971, p. 32, my translation). They are thus both productive and restrictive—productive of new propositions and restrictive of what can actually be said. But they are also many and arguably poligen studies also circulate amongst—and between—such disciplines, not because such studies do not wish to be pinned down but precisely because their *political* aim is disruptive and subversive in its attempt to capture what the ordering discourses themselves do, the effects that they have as seen from the perspective of their imposition on what we think, say, and do, the imposed ordering of the present in its contingent particularity.

How effective are such studies in disrupting the imposed ordering of present discourses? This question seems to arise here, given the stated aim. But the asking of it might be coming from the distinct discursive space of normative political theory, with its own concern of identifying and articulating the appropriate conditions of political and social order conceived theoretically, placed at a distance from the ordering function itself. Political genealogies challenge this self-distancing; they do not seek to *establish* nor to delimit (theoretically) such conditions, they seek to show the contingent hold such conditions actually have on what we think, say, and do and part of their purpose is to contribute to releasing us from their imposed character. Any effectiveness they might have in that regard should be measured by their ability to allow us to think, say, and do *otherwise*, despite and against the ordering of discourses all around us. And what that might be cannot be pre-said. That is, indeed, the point: to open the possibility of enunciation in terms other than the enunciated.

I have argued that we should situate "poligen studies"—the various studies that have engaged many scholars in a certain kind of historiographical enquiry aimed at disrupting or subverting the hold that the present ordering of discourses has on what we think, say, and do—between moral enquiry and political theory. Such studies, like moral enquiry, address how we ought to live but do so not by prescription or rational assessment but by enquiring into and exposing the contingent formation of the discursive conditions delimiting how we are actually made to live. They are thus dissatisfied historiographical studies of a distinctly constraining present. In this, their object is not the past, but the present constitution of our social order and, like political theory, they question the normative character of that constitution; however, this is done not from the space of a theoretical elaboration (which presupposes the very distance that needs to be overcome) but from the perspective opened up by the struggles and resistances that manifest themselves against the imposed character of that constitution. Another way to say this is that situating the pursuit of poligen studies between moral enquiry and political theory is to recognize that these struggles and resistances themselves express the moral refusal of the ordering constraints being imposed on the struggling and resisting agents subject to them and that this motivates the study of the emergence of such constraining orderings, understanding them to be discursively constituted in a way that masks their own disciplinary willfulness. Exposing that willfulness loosens the constitutive hold those orderings have on what we are made to think, say, and do and opens up the possibility of equally willfully (agonistically) being otherwise within and against them.

My striking colleagues were not on the picket line very long. A settlement was reached and classes resumed. Thus, in appearance the disruption was reabsorbed into the disciplinary ordering and functioning of the university, as deadlines were extended, exam periods were contracted, and work discursively re-ordered itself. But this settlement, like all settlements, is in fact a contingently constructed reality, and the disruption that occasioned it also throws light on that disciplinary ordering, exposing its present delimiting powers to further and on-going contestation, a renewed wariness of willful constraints masquerading as "necessary." It is not an easy thing to sustain such wariness, to sustain a space of contestation to the exposed willful ordering of discourse that is not merely moral outrage or critical political theorizing, but it is possible. And it is to this possibility that political genealogy commits itself.

Conflicts of Interest: The author declares no conflicts of interest.

References

Clifford, Michael. 2001. *Political Genealogy after Foucault: Savage Identities*. New York and London: Routledge.

Clifford, Michael. 2013. *Empowerment: The Theory and Practice of Political Genealogy*. Lanham: Lexington Books.

Collingwood, Robin George. 1946. *The Idea of History*. Oxford: Clarendon Press.

Foucault, Michel. 1971. *L'ordre du Discours*. Paris: Gallimard.

Foucault, Michel. 1972. *The Archaeology of Knowledge and the Discourse on Language*. Translated by A. M. Sheridan Smith. New York: Pantheon.

Foucault, Michel. 1982. The Subject and Power. *Critical Inquiry* 8: 777–95. [CrossRef]

Foucault, Michel. 2013. *Lectures on the Will to Know: Lectures at the College de France, 1970–1971*. Edited by Daniel Defert. Translated by Graham Burchell. New York: Palgrave Macmillan.

Foucault, Michel. 2014. *Wrong-Doing, Truth-Telling: The Function of Avowal in Justice*. Edited by Fabienne Biron and Bernard E. Harcourt. Translated by Stephen W. Sawyer. Chicago: The University of Chicago Press.

MacIntyre, Alasdair. 1984. *After Virtue: A Study in Moral Theory*. Notre Dame: University of Notre Dame Press.

MacIntyre, Alasdair. 1988. *Whose Justice? Which Rationality?* Notre Dame: University of Notre Dame Press.

MacIntyre, Alasdair. 1990. *Three Rival Versions of Moral Enquiry: Encyclopedia, Genealogy, and Tradition*. Notre Dame: University of Notre Dame Press.

Moyn, Samuel. 2010. *The Last Utopia: Human Rights in History*. Cambridge: The Belknap Press of Harvard University Press.

Nietzsche, Friedrich. 1997. *Untimely Meditations*. Edited by Daniel Breazeale. Translated by R. J. Hollingdale. Cambridge: Cambridge University Press.

Nietzsche, Friedrich. 2006. *On the Genealogy of Morality*. Edited by Keith Ansell-Pearson. Translated by Carol Diethe. Cambridge: Cambridge University Press.

genealogy

MDPI

Article

On the Political Genealogy of Trump after Foucault

Bruce M. Knauft

Department of Anthropology, Emory University, Atlanta, GA 30322, USA; bruce.knauft@emory.edu

Received: 7 November 2017; Accepted: 10 January 2018; Published: 15 January 2018

Abstract: How would Foucault have viewed Trump as President, and Trumpism in the US more generally? More realistically, how can we discern and insightfully apply genealogical insights after Foucault to better comprehend and act in relation to our current political situation in the US? Questions of factuality across a base register of asserted falsehoods are now prominent in American politics in ways that put assertions of scholarly objectivity and interpretation in yet deeper question than previously. The extent, range, and vitriol of alt-Right assertions and their viral growth in American media provoke progressivist resistance and anxiety, but how can this opposition be most productively channeled? This paper examines a range of critical perspectives, timeframes, and topical optics with respect to Trump and Trumpism, including nationalist, racist, sexist, class-based, and oligarchical dimensions. These are considered in relation to media and the incitement of polarized subjectivity and dividing practices, and also in relation to Marxist political economy, neoliberalism/neoimperialism, and postcolonialism. I then address the limit points of Foucault, including with respect to engaged political activism and social protest movements, and I consider the relevance of these for the diverse optics that political genealogy as a form of analysis might pursue. Notwithstanding and indeed because of the present impetus to take organized political action, a Foucauldian perspective is useful in foregrounding the broader late modern formations of knowledge, power, and subjectivity within which both Rightist and Leftist political sensibilities in the US are presently cast. At larger issue are the values inscribed through contemporary late modernity that inform both sides of present divisive polarities—and which make the prognosis of tipping points or future political outcomes particularly difficult. As such, productive strategies of activist opposition are likely to vary under alternative conditions and opportunities—including in relation to the particular skills, history, and predilection of activists themselves. If the age of reason threatens to be over, the question of how and in what ways critical intellectualism can connect with productive action emerges afresh for each of us in a higher and more personal key.

Keywords: Trump; Foucault; genealogy; politics; modernity; critical theory

---

1. Introduction

How would Foucault have viewed Trump as President, and Trumpism in the US more generally? More realistically, how can we discern and insightfully apply genealogical insights from Foucault to better comprehend our current political situation in the US? The present contribution is both a research paper and a scholarly editorial, a practical application that draws on my previous article in *Genealogy* (Knauft 2016).

In this presentation, I sketch alternative perspectives and temporal scales or periodicities for a genealogical construction of Trump's Presidency. Drawing on Foucault's tendency to deepen our understanding through alternative historical reading, I explore complementary issues of knowledge, power, and subjectivity that are suggested by different genealogical framings of Trump/ism. Aspects of political economy are then engaged to augment the analysis and to put it in larger theoretical as well as historical and genealogical context. Finally, toward the end of the paper, I address the limit points of Foucault, including with respect to engaged political activism and social protest movements, and I consider the relevance of these for the multiple and multiperspectival optics that political genealogy as a form of analysis could be encouraged to pursue.

My tone and register of presentation throughout are informed by the very nature of the Trumpist beast, the circumstances of our present immediate time, in which the very issue of multiperspectival understanding begs the counter-assertion of 'alternative facts.' These are now employed with political effectiveness on the American alt-Right in ways that postmodernists could hardly have imagined several years ago—and in ways that Foucault himself might have found both understandable and ironic.

Questions of factuality or facticity—what it is for a portrayal to be taken as a valid depiction of something that objectively occurred, that actually happened—now confront an unprecedented base register of patently false assertions by the President, his advisors, and his supporters (e.g., Leonhardt 2017). Climate change doesn't exist, Trump won the popular vote as well as the Electoral College, Barack Obama wasn't born in the US, Trump didn't say what he actually did say, and on and on. Among other things, this aspect of Trumpism risks putting any scholarly assertion into deeper question—and subject to further de-funding as a public good or collective resource. To a degree that we should not underestimate, all of us so-called liberal or leftist academics are now subject more generally to the politics of de-legitimation. A reasoned factual account that builds on objectivist assertion of presumed facts as buttressed by scholarly documentation can be thrown into question to begin with. The debunking of realistic comprehension or effective analysis as conspiratorial, globally dominating, satanic, or simply irrelevant and beside the point brings to a newly poignant register the question, "What Is to Be Done?" (Lenin 1902).

Challenges to intellectual understanding are not just conceptual. A PEW poll found that 58% of Republicans and Republican-leaning independents in the US now think that college education has an overall negative impact in America (Fingerhut 2017). Accordingly, the federal tax changes now passed by the U.S. House are projected to penalize college and university students by $65 billion over the next decade (Hess 2017). Provisions include a new federal tax, the first in history, on the endowment income of elite private colleges and universities—while creating windfall tax benefits for businesses and the wealthiest (Green 2017; Hartocollis 2017; Meyers and Read 2017). Though the present bill may or may not proceed to Presidential approval without modification, its bellwether is clear.

Meanwhile, amid the deepening investigation of Trump campaign collusion with Russian interests, the Trumpist state of exception confronts its opposition with escalating cycles of Presidential lashing out, misinformation, and political precarity. The string of ongoing national political crises can seem so omnipresent, entrenched, and refractory to reasoned argument that there may seem little solid ground on which to gain critical intellectual leverage; each response we might consider seems dated already by the exceptionalist turn of events in the following day's national political news. At current writing, Trump is at war with MSNBC, through which the escalating edge of liberal media drives as well as reflects presidential outrage—including thinly veiled threats by Trump to rescind MSNBC's federal broadcasting license. CNN may also be at risk: following Trump's complaints about its media coverage, the Justice Department has pressured its parent companies to sell it—which would put the CNN news service at the potential mercy of the political proclivities of a new owner (NY Times Board 2017). Echoing Breitbart News and FOX, the alt-Right billionaire Koch brothers are spending mega-millions for new media acquisitions (Ember and Sorkin 2017; Mayer 2016). Per FCC approval, alt-Right Sinclair news is poised to reach 72% of American households via *local* TV news channels (Kroll 2017a; 2017b). Where this will lead by the time the present paper is published is impossible to know. Eighty-three percent of Republicans presently give Trump a favorable approval rating, an increase over the previous two months (Gallup News 2017). In this context, analysis beyond transient captivating details seems as difficult as it is important.

2. Trumpism and Foucault

Where, as progressive liberals and potential radicals might ask, is the tipping point beyond which Trump's Presidency, much less his general Bannonist politics now outsourced and unleashed and orchestrated beyond himself, might cause what used to be called a revolution: the decline or crashing down of government in its previous form? On one hand is the campaign for Trump's impeachment—which in just two weeks gained almost a million and a half petition signatures (Tolan 2017; Steyer 2017). But this merely ratifies for conservatives their distain for liberalism, as pumped up in conservative social media. A case in point is Sean Hannity, whose radio show has 13.5 million weekly listeners—the highest of talk radio except for Rush Limbaugh, at 14 million—and his *TV* program, which is, as of fall 2017, the most highly watched cable news show in the US (Bauder 2017). It is no longer possible to dismiss Hannity's views as those of a fringe crackpot. A catch-of-the-day illustration is his extended plumping of the book recently published by Edward Klein (Klein 2017): *All Out War—The Plot to Destroy Trump.* Chapter One on "The Cornerstone of American Democracy" begins:

> In America you are entitled to your own opinion, but you are not entitled to overthrow the democratically elected president of the United States .... That, however, is what Donald Trump's enemies on the Left and Right are doing. Through a variety of underhanded tactics—lies, leaks, obstruction, and violence—they are waging an all-out war to delegitimize President Trump and drive him from office before he can drain the swamp and take away their power. Who are these determined and ruthless villains?

Various chapters of the book consider "This is What a Coup Looks Like", "A Breach of Public Trust", "The ISIS Connection", "The Vulgarians", "A Red Flag", and "Villains' Report Cards". As reflected in these titles, many of the chapters are striking inversions of liberal critiques themselves, mocking the various criticisms of Trump—"Fake News", "The Trump Derangement Syndrome", "A Nationwide Orgy of Rage and Spite"—as themselves a malignant and traitorous conspiracy against which an all-out war must be waged by taking up arms.

Accordingly, intervening segments of Hannity's broadcast warn that "the Democratic Party shoots people" and urge listeners not just to own a concealed gun but practice with a free instruction manual how to most proactively use it. Sixty-five percent of American gun owners already believe that the purpose of their right to bear arms is, "to make sure that people are able to protect themselves from tyranny" (Lankford 2016b, p. 189). The CDC reports that rising American gun deaths now annually claim more than 33,000 lives (Hauser 2017). The mass gun killings that have also been escalating in the US (e.g., Rounds 2017; New York Times 2017) powerfully and convincingly correlate with the massive number of guns that Americans presently possess: 270 *million* (Fisher and Keller 2017; Lankford 2016a). It does not take a conspiracy theorist to worry that growing political tension in the US could foment increased civil violence. No other country in the world has more than one-sixth the number of guns—or more than one-fifth the number of mass shootings—as does the U.S. Though American mass shootings are overwhelmingly by whites, blacks and persons of color are enormously overrepresented in the prison population. And the incarceration rate in the US is the highest in the world, 50% highere than any other country. Foucault might have appreciated books by Jordan Camp (Camp 2016) and Michelle Alexander (Alexander 2012), among others, that document the growth of the American carceral state through its persecution of racial minorities, opponents, and protest movements.

Beyond a criminal war against underclass opponents, an explicit goal of Trump is the casting out of liberal government, including by systematically dismantling and hollowing out previous government functions and their personnel (e.g., Friedman et al. 2017). The larger question may thus not be the demise of Trump himself, or an irreversible change in governance, but social divisiveness on a scale that the US has not seen since ... when? The 1960s? The US Civil War? If a Democrat were again elected President, not to mention following a Trump impeachment, one can only imagine the resistance to federal authority among dedicated Red states and alt-Right conservatives.

How should we engage in, attack, or refuse, this climate of divisiveness? I contend here, in line with Foucault, that the terms of asking such questions have themselves become problematic and should be reconsidered. Even across the May 1968 fulcrum in France, even in the throes of what was perhaps the most viable Western political Marxism of the 20th century, Foucault refused it, refused Marxism, refused the fanciful specter of revolution, the organized pursuit of institutional opposition in hopes of decisive change. In large part, this is because it risked becoming not a sea change but the older kind of revolution, the revolving around and return to what came before. Change easily reinstates what it seems to oppose—another false guise, the siren of utopia reinscribing another version of the same, Marx's 18th Brumaire of Louis Bonaparte (Marx 1851), tragedy now trumped as farce.

In retrospect, how could we have thought that the challenges of postmodernism in relativizing knowledge and maligning truth would stay cloistered within an academic or philosophical closet? As if the revenge of the Political Right would not invent a radical performance theory far more propagandist to serve its own regressive agenda (cf. Williams 2017; Wilber 2017)? We are now well beyond the neoliberal statism of Reagan's and Thatcher's 1980s "The Empire Strikes Back" (CCC—The Centre for Contemporary Cultural Studies 1982). The colonization of consciousness has taken a more 21st-century media savvy and subjectively insidious turn, as if recasting Lukács (1923), Horkheimer and Adorno (1947), and even Harvey (1989, 2007).

Perhaps just because of this, the present seems a time for more rather than less caution about the limits of what we can currently "know." We do not yet have the luxury of history to put the significance of the present in context—what kind of transition the present is enacting or portending or merely pretending to augur from one or another imagined past. Foucault would warn us strongly on this point.

3. Time and Periodicity

How long is the political generation that Trump is upending (or upholding) and what optic do we take to view its line of nominal descent; what time frame of genealogy should we choose? One presidential cycle versus another—comparing Trump's Presidency to others; and if so, over what period of time?

A single cycle foregrounds Trump's ultra-Right whiteness as the racist backlash against Obama's reasonable center-left multiethnicity, with its Black Lives and even Puerto Ricans who might actually matter. (Against this are Trump's disparaging comments about Caribbeans and what he has called the"shithole countries" of Africa (Davis et al. 2018)). Following the presently chaotic Trump-after-Obama cycle, should we expect a middling out between their post-facto polarity, or another concertedly backward-looking attempt to make America *liberal* again—what Zygmunt Bauman (Bauman 2017) would call yet another recourse to retrotopia? Like Trump's pining for a glorious American past that has been abandoned as nonexistent but not yet dead, this would be a retreat from advancing modernity not by rejecting it but by embracing the nostalgia of yet another version of its past projected facsimile. It is hard to imagine that deep American divisions—now ricocheting and reinforcing across so many cultural, religious, and politcoeconomic registers—will be easily papered over much less dissolved by a subsequent return to "government as usual". Rather, Trump's Presidency seems integral to the larger "The Great Regression" of our times (Geiselberger 2017)—a world that seems to be suddenly moving backwards across so many progressive or at least liberal fronts—politically, ethically, environmentally, culturally, and in economic equality (cf. Luce 2017).

Within this regressive panoply, should we be foregrounding the racism of Trump's incitement—or its sexism and homophobia? Comparison of Trump with Obama would emphasize race; comparison with Hillary Clinton, sex and gender. Clearly, Trump's white exceptionalism cannot be divorced from a larger and deeper history of American racism, as Coates (2017a, 2017b) and Rosa and Bonilla (2017) have emphasized. The same could also be said of his resurgent sexism and homophobia, amid which Trump seems immune from the "reckoning" that is currently bringing down powerful male sexual harrassers and abusers (e.g., Twohey and Rutenberg 2018). As Ruiz (2017) asks, "*Now* can we admit sexism was a factor in the 2016 election?" Yet, more than half of white women voters in the US cast their ballots for Trump. How do we mediate, orchestrate, and analyze the gendered dimensions of Trump and Trumpism—and their deeper punitive history in the US (e.g., Lancaster 2011)—vis-à-vis racial, religious, class-based, and other discriminations?

Should we be considering Trump's election and tenure historically against the caustic politics, dirty tricks, and deceptions of 19th-century American elections and presidencies, which until recently seemed so far behind us? Social movement theorist Doug McAdam (McAdam 2017) documents that US Congressional polarization is now greater than at any point in the past 135 years. Should we compare Trump to non-establishment Presidents like Andrew Jackson and his acolyte James Polk, the former banishing Native Americans from their own land and the latter conquering and stealing one-third of what was then Mexico? Jackson is still lionized in American history, enshrined on the twenty-dollar bill.

Or should we take a yet longer optic to consider the *longue durée* of political economy in relation to social media and subjectivity? To be late Gothic, we could take as both parallel and inversion of our tumult the challenges of 16th–17th century central Europe during the Reformation (Gorbis 2017). These included the explosion of alternative social media via the printing press and Luther's Bible, virulent divisiveness of alternative beliefs, the strategic stoking of these by competing political interests, a refiguration of cultural status and authority, and ensuing chaos of prolonged cultural-cum-civil war (Osnos 2016). What changes in consciousness and politics are now informed by mind-melded devices and apps through which we see the world, facsimiles of facts from a never-ending stream of niche posts and twitter feeds? Should we follow César Rendueles (Rendueles 2017) and see in the current politics of social media the sociophobia and dystopia of our present digital era?

The Economist (2017) recently analyzed how new social media drive and reinforce political polarization. Based on a viewer's own viewing history, addictive-by-design media employ sophisticated algorithms in tandem with iterative targeting to keep viewers riveted to their devices through a reinforcing chain of emotion-laden connections. These, in turn, channel, shape, and reinforce a particular sense of subjective identification and, ultimately, identity. Bots drive this process by generating content that is taken as true or genuine. (In the 2016 presidential campaign, one of every five political opinions or commentaries posted on Twitter was generated by a bot (ibid., p. 20). One should expect this frequency to increase in the future.) To a growing extent—including per the recent rescinding of net neutrality laws by Trump's FCC (e.g., Kang 2017)—social media seems increasingly influenced and dominated by the money of moguls and oligarchs (e.g., Mayer 2016). Especially on the alt-Right, these explicitly cast the issues and stances taken to inform what it means or should mean to be "American".

In presidential politics but more widely, how can we connect developments to the political incitement of reactionary white nationalism and sexism, not just in rural or suburban America but in the West more generally, including the alt-Right in growing parts of Europe and Brexit in the UK (Gusterson 2017a; Polakow-Suransky 2017a, 2017b)? Or, perhaps we should reach yet deeper in history and compare the American shift from democracy to autocracy to the ancient Roman transition between Republican and spectacularist Imperial eras, auguring the latter's banality of power (cf. Mbembe 1992).

4. Taking Exception to Exceptionalism

Foucault would warn us against viewing the above alternatives as mutually exclusive—as if we could find "the right optic" to establish the best and most critically "true" history of the present. Rather, we would be better advised to question the deeper assumptions that inform framings of political genealogical to begin with, to interrogate not only how different optics themselves differ but, at least if not more importantly, what they share—what they share by way of fundamental assumptions about progress and human development and entitlement, notwithstanding and even especially amid the seemingly ironclad opposition between Rightist and Leftist views.

A non-Hegelian *longue durée* that transcends the chimera of diametric polarizations (much less their synthesis) was indispensable for Foucault; as a genealogical historian, this was one of his greatest strengths. As such, he likely would not privilege one or another scale of temporal analysis, and certainly not one or another event or specific grand or terrible person of influence. He looked in a different register, for ways to expose more fundamental assumptions of worldview by looking at specifics that push our envelope from its margins.

How, then, would Foucault view the fact that we now find social media seeding alternative world-views as conspiracy theories of ostensible fact? Do we see these as a violently emergent genie from the 21st century bottle of angry alterities, perhaps strong enough to rip apart the US as we know it—or *thought* we knew it? Or is this view itself short-sightedly alarmist—as if we could identify "the problem" and then "avoid" or "prevent" it if we pushed strongly and effectively enough in one or another strategically crafted political direction? Should we support or join American antifa (anti-fascist) protest movements to combat the rise of neo-fascist nationalism (e.g., Bray 2017; cf. Hawkins 2017)? But more immediately, as if trumping this very question, how do we respond to the way such antifa initiatives are themselves portrayed in the alt-Right press—an interspliced dimension of actual Intifada terrorism and ISIS beheadings germinating in the heart of America (e.g., DeLisi 2017)? Alt-Right portrayal by Alton (2017), among others, asserts that newly dubbed American Anti*fa*-da aims for not just the "extermination of non-progressive expression" but a terrorist "extermination of people". How does one respond to the paranoid projections of Rightist violence that legitimize their own, especially as these views gain audience?

On the other hand, polarization includes ratcheting up fearful Leftist as well as alt-Right perspectives. Each of these serve as the punching bag of the other's Otherness—and pump up the viewer ratings of both in the bargain. Perhaps in spiraling result we really *are* experiencing a continuing crisis in the MSNBC mode—each day a newly-fanned flame of political outrage, a crisis of one hurricane upon another that portends some Armageddon of political collapse. And *then* what, on Trump's tattered coat-tails? Michael *Pence* as President? The state of exception may become not so exceptional after all. In this regard, reconsidering new dimensions of critical theory from the Frankfurt School is especially timely (e.g., O'Kane 2017; Ross 2016; see Knauft 2013).

One a larger scale, we could view the presidential present as cultural and social rather than narrowly political: Trumpism beyond Trump, Bannon as Robespierre, the hollowing out of modernity's cultural *zeitgeist* from the inside—at once Luddite, socially mediatized, conspiracy on steroids, post-factual, post "news", and virulently anti-liberal across the board. But does this portend a new dark age of divisive, pernicious anti-humanism, a new variety of the Thirty Year's (Osnos 2016), either in the US, in the West, or more generally? Or are we merely witnessing a transient revenge of self-interest against liberal communitarianism—a regressivism that will, in the longer run, be outrun by the larger benefits of liberalism, ultimately yielding a neo-Westphalian acceptance and management of polarized diversity?

In about three decades from now given current trends, the racial composition of the US will be dominantly non-white: the present minorities will be a collective majority (Census Bureau 2015). Will American politics hence become more liberal over time, fueled by changing racial demography and the thriving fiscal dominance of Blue state economies (cf. Burns and Johnson 2017)? Are we overweighting the significance of the present? Will the reactionary Right effectively sap and tax Democratic states, making them part of a yet more apartheid national formation, inscribed, among other things, by greater racial and political bias in electoral procedures amid selective cross-ethnic conservative alliances? It is difficult to know.

5. Political Economy

From one vantage point, the Trump presidency is simply the logical culmination of cutthroat capitalism at its most unfettered, subjectively insidious, digitized, and manipulated—controlled not by feudal lords but by capitalist oligarchs as overlords, now including Trump in the US.

Indeed, it seems that what Trump really pursued was not the Presidency itself but the uber-oligarch status that a hotly contested and highly lucrative but failed presidential bid would afford (see Wolff 2018a, 2018b). This would have provided an enormous and even more unfettered anti-liberal media pulpit plus gargantuan new influxes of money to Trump personally (against which he refused to give away even a single cent of his own money to fund his campaign—or release his tax returns). For Trump and his team, high-price economic and cultural goals seemed more important than the mere political prize of the Presidency itself. Accounts of Trump's election night and its aftermath suggest not only how amazingly unprepared he was for the Presidency but that he and his team had a palpable and shocked sense of cost if not catastrophe in the final results. By winning the election, they felt they had unexpectedly lost—and were saddled with the onus of the Presidency itself (Wolff 2018a, 2018b; cf. Martin 2018; Kruzel 2018).

To pursue a Marxist perspective, we can re-theorize the larger links between economics, politics, and media in Trump and Trumpism, including how newly dominant modes of digital production galvanize not just new means of production but new *relations* of socially mediated production. Influential control over mediated self-production insinuates and incites subjectivity in new ways that are easily reinforced by virulent ideologies and paranoid lies. These intensify and escalate highly profitable cycles of *ressentiment*. The result is not just a technological change but a change of political economy: the accumulation through dispossession of a subjective *attention* economy.

With the average American clicking on his/her smartphone more than 2600 times a day and having the TV on five hours a day, notions such as "ideology", "propaganda", "hegemony", "identity", and "truth" beg critical reformulation. In the same way that Marx saw through the veneer of "free wage labor", the ostensible freedom and democracy of digital social and mass media, now increasingly influenced by capitalist oligarchs, can be critically reconsidered. As the ability to channel our attention becomes the ultimate capitalist commodity, potentials for more considered critical understanding, especially among the underclass, are easily obliterated—and the insights of progressive intellectuals masked, trashed, and de-funded.

In a more conventional geography of global political economy, we can see present developments as an escalated internal backlash against America's declining international hegemony (see Knauft 2007).

Whether or not the US hit its high-water mark as a neo-imperial power in 1989, with the Soviet collapse, or earlier, in the 1970s, the 1990s and since have seen a groundswell of counter-hegemonies against America and its Western allies. These have come most obviously from China but also of course from Russia, Muslim extremists, and other venues. Even the *Economist* (title story, 11 November 2017), now considers the US to be endangered as a global power. Following the pattern of past world powers, the fomenting of divisive conflict could now be considered expectable in the US, as it supplies a ready means of intensifying nationalist fervor and attempting to reclaim an imagined glorious past. However, detailed analysis of previous world powers passing their peak reveals that such fomenting of conflict does not work: its heavy economic and social costs accelerate rather than forestall hegemonic decline (Arrighi 1994; Arrighi and Silver 1999; for 20th century Europe, see Ferguson 2006).

Accordingly, Wallerstein writes in his *Decline of American Power* (Wallerstein 2003, p. 27) that, "the real question is not whether US hegemony is waning but whether the United States can devise a way to descend gracefully, with minimum damage to the world and to itself". From a world systems perspective, the biggest beneficiary of the current turmoil in the US is China—and yet moreso insofar as China's ascendancy is backgrounded by America's self-preoccupation (cf. Frank 1998; Arrighi et al. 2003; cf. Rudolph and Szonyi 2018). In this respect, it is particularly remarkable that Trump in his recent state visit to the Middle Kingdom "projected an air of deference to China that was almost unheard-of for an American President. Far from attacking Mr. Xi on trade [as he had done relentlessly during the electoral campaign] Mr. Trump saluted him for leading a country that he said had left the United State 'so far behind.'" (Landler et al. 2017).

Declining American hegemony has already included extremely costly and unprofitable Gulf Wars I & II as well as the escalating hyperbola of its "war on terror" (see Ali 2002; Harvey 2003; Knauft 2007). Unsurprisingly, Bauman's "retrotopia" (Bauman 2017) is commonly found in failing hegemonic or imperial states. More generally, as Appadurai (2017) suggests, loss of economic sovereignty in current nation-states increases their compensatory emphasis on *cultural* sovereignty—which in turn fuels the rise of authoritarian populism. In the US, the sense of failed national prowess is marked clearly if not enshrined in Trump's reactive attempts to "Make America Great Again".

In fact, from the standpoint of global political economy, Trump is doing just the reverse—burning down the world's largest-ever superpower from within by deconstructing, de-legitimating, and imploding its own government. This both by explicit curtailing and cutting back of government services and fomenting the resignations and retirements of career national employees (e.g., Harris 2017; Friedman et al. 2017). From *that* perspective, the really committed postcolonial radical might ask whether we should be *supporting* Trump's deconstruction of American government, speeding its descent. In the mix, however, Leftist radicalism then stands alongside pernicious White nationalism: the Leninist circle closes.

In larger register, it could be argued that current events actually signal continuity rather than rupture between conservatism and neoliberalism (cf. Harvey 2007). In this critical view, their apparent differences merely ratchet to a higher amplitude their combined oscillation. Some of us are old enough to remember how retrograde the US electorate seemed to be in electing Richard Nixon, including a second time, or Ronald Reagan, including a second time, or George W. Bush, including a second time—interspersed with Jimmy Carter, Bill Clinton, and then Barack Obama. What exactly is now different, and worse, in the continuing specter of Trump and his aftermath?

One difference is the increasingly virulent disaffection with progressivist values among those parts of the US left economically and culturally behind, our own Weimar curse. Popular support for Trump—and the key electoral votes that enabled him to win the Presidency—came especially of course from economically depressed swaths of the US that have been systematically left aside by advanced education and income growth, especially in rural and struggling urban areas. The anger of those underemployed, less educated, less urbane, and viewed as regressive by the progressive elite now seems as malignant as it was previously overlooked.

6. The American Postcolony

In some ways, what we now see are the geopolitics of third world failure and resistance, however twisted, among the attempted and failed bourgeoisie within the US itself. Many parts of rural and undereducated America now experience life under liberalism as their own "Desert of the Real" (Zizek 2002): deeply felt economic despair, cultural abjection, and political meaninglessness (e.g., Kendzior 2015/18; cf. Hochschild 2016). Are these now so deeply inscribed and stoked as *ressentiment* as to be reminiscent of the paranoid desperation experienced so poignantly in 1930s socialist Germany? Pushing yet further, what, if any, similarities are there, amid huge differences, to the despondency of the world's bottom billion—and the anti-establishment revolts of the wretched of the earth (Collier 2008; Fanon 2005)?

The very point here is *not* to equate the economic plight of left-behind Americans with those who are truly immiserated in so many developing countries—not to occlude chasms of difference in privilege, wealth, and opportunity. The so-called poverty level in the U.S. is still an individual annual income of $12,060—as opposed to those many in the world's poorest countries who earn less than two dollars or even one dollar a day. The point is rather to underscore that oppression as a *felt* and *perceived* condition is importantly cultural and psychological.

The subaltern middle class that Pandey (2015) finds operative among both African Americans and Indian *dalits* also seems applicable in some ways to rural white Trump supporters, including just how and why in a neo-liberal world "the cultural and class markers of the subordinated have been particularly difficult to shed" (ibid., p. 340). Writing prior to the election of Trump, Ortner (2016, p. 53) presciently suggests that, "the American working class [has] basically collapsed, economically and politically". Further, she sees, "beyond deindustrialization a kind of active war on the poor", including "a kind of contemptuous attitude toward the working classes and the poor beyond the necessity for profit" (p. 54). This selective similarity to the subaltern is poignant even though and perhaps just because the reactions and politics of underprivileged American whites have become so warped and regressive (compare also afflicted *dalit* politics in some parts of India).

At issue is whether and how the threads of modest privilege amid relative deprivation beg *ressentiment* that is or can be driven to deeper and more pernicious levels of reactionary lashing out. An extreme example can be taken by considering the increasing incidence of mass shootings in the U.S. (e.g., New York Times 2017). If mass shooting is defined as the firearm killing of four or more people, then whites, blacks, and Latinos commit mass murders no more or less frequently than their proportion in the population. But while blacks are more likely to kill multiply in robberies or crimes, white mass shooters are much more likely to kill far larger numbers of people indiscriminately in public. As Lankford (2016a) suggests, it is the structural *advantages* of disaffected and disillusioned subaltern whites—benefits of agency, means, sophisticated weapons, and opportunity—that seem to explain this racial difference. We can be tempted to rethink Mamdani's *When Victims Become Killers* (Mamdani 2002), in a radically new guise. The revenge of reactive modernity is no less and can indeed be greater when those in positions of modest privilege who deem themselves deserving and destined to be highly successful ... are not.

We can consider, then, how the risks of the empowered subaltern rebound and are co-opted so regressively in the world's most powerful superpower—Mbembe's (Mbembe 2001) postcolony come home to roost in the heart of the hegemon. At a minimum, there seem selective resonances between geo-capital inequality *within* the US and the spatial geographics of inequity internationally—complementary sides of Capital Difference (cf. Harvey 2001).

7. Modernity Is Dead, Long Live Modernity

Given the indeterminacy of eventful specifics, a larger view is warranted. This can lead us to reconsider in a new key the *zeitgeist* of our broader epistemic regime, the *longue durée* of its continuity beyond fanciful diagnoses or tactics for its presumed end or transformation. This was one of Foucault's most important and enduring interests. In our present circumstance, it is hard to avoid or ignore the power of opposition between humanist and anti-humanist modernism. Yet both of these seem unable to give up tropes of ultimate or deeper or greater progress against which the present is hopelessly unfulfilled—whether due to retrograde rightist politics, on the one hand, or liberal leftist pandering, on the other. In his day, Foucault was confronted with seemingly analogous stark choices—between the "establishment" and one or another shade of 1960s and 1970s Marxism—and then, in the later 1970s and early 1980s, between his private sexual proclivities and his refusal to publicly identify with a Gay identity or political agenda. He consistently refused categorical alternatives and the choice between them.

Ultimately, Foucault was an empirical continualist rather than a categorical absolutist. Though he identified in hindsight the portent of big epistemic breaks and ruptural transformations—especially classic to modern regimes of European knowing in the late 18th and 19th centuries—Foucault shied from the hubris of claiming or portending major cleavages in the present. Such claims easily become another version of "crisis news", the mechanical reproduction of the very cataclysmic change that is lamented and resisted as caused by those "on the other side". Amid the drumbeat of daily crises, it is now all too easy to be riveted to and ultimately co-opted by their flow. How and when do we cut the network and turn off our devices—suppress our fear and curiosity and excitement that today's crisis or tomorrow's may be yet bigger and more calamitous than yesterday's—addicted to a daily fix of Trumpist contestation? How do we turn down the volume, stop, and find a stable fulcrum of external perspective? And in the bargain, how do we do something more than just symbolic or ignorantly short-sighted?

Using genealogy against history, Foucault did not attempt to predict or project whether, when, and how May '68 would or could or should turn into political revolution—or what its outcome could otherwise be. His answer was not to become a Leftist champion or Marxist, even and perhaps especially at its apparent high tide ever in Western Europe. To him, the fight was to put one's own personal actions on the line (including on the very literal line of protest) in ways that did not seek grand publicity or assume or validate the pleas or paradigms of one or another political movement or party. An ultimate anarchist (cf. Graeber 2004, 2014), Foucault did not ask the Marxist or even the Gramscian question of when the time would be right to mobilize the pilot light of critical intellectualism, its own small war of position, into one of frontal opposition or political maneuver.

Especially in his later work on ancient Greek and Greco-Roman subjectivity, but also consistently earlier, Foucault kept the freshness of a more deeply refractory view in focus, not recoursing to claims and projections of some then-current or now-current crisis, of proclaiming the end of history or the limit point of current political structures and economic structures. Against this, he continually warns us Other Victorians against projecting a historical trajectory of meaning or value or crisis that augurs to validate some grander prediction or design, intending to transform the present, but concluding in fact by reinscribing it in yet another false guise. Indeed, "modernity" for Foucault was itself "often characterized in terms of consciousness of the discontinuity of time, a break with tradition" (Foucault 1984, p. 39).

As such, Foucault might well dodge the Trump in Trumpism altogether. In viewing tectonic shifts of epistemic regime, he deemphasized the role of supreme rulers, prominent intellectuals, or canonical thinkers. He was more interested in the myriad features of the overlooked, the details of personal accounts and institutions that revealed the contours not only of epistemic *zeitgeist* but of the subject's self-relationship, what he latterly called subjectivation. Rather than slavishly following the daily news, he might have been more interested in the oppositional *mentalité* of J.D. Vance's *Hillbilly Elegy* (Vance 2016), or Kathleen Stewart's *A Space on the Side of the Road* (Stewart 1996), or Sarah Kendzior's *The View from Flyover Country* (Kendzior 2015/18). Or some apparently random overlooked detail in the life or actions of Stephen Paddock, the Las Vegas mass shooter who has been so refractory to psychological or cultural understanding (cf. Goldman and Medina 2018). What are the facets, lineaments, and depth of modern anti-modernism in the US? And how does this resonate with Christian Evangelicalism, the sense of identifying with Jesus in direct communication with God (e.g., Luhrmann 2012; cf. Hochschild 2016, chp. 11)?

Beyond this, Foucault might ask how the current political tumult and its progressivist opposition *both* draw upon a bedrock faith in the entitlements of modernity—that we all deserve not just the right to *pursue* happiness but the right to *be* happy, to have a continually better, more developed, and more actualized future. As if having favorable conditions that actually bring about personal happiness are themselves a core political right. This is arguably a precondition for the retro-regressive tendency to move backward through divisiveness, to seek forward glory by refraction from an imagined perfect past by debunking the present. In the mix, one finds an inability to give up the entitlements of continual betterment despite and even because of their experienced absence and seemingly hopeless future.

Everyone happy, and happier all the time. Stepping back, how, even in God's name, could we ever expect such an odd and frankly irrational system of cultural value—with all its accumulated capitalist political power—to become an actual reality, much less save us from the existential dilemmas of being human? In the US, at least, a major revision to Weber's *zeitgeist* of capitalism in relation to current Protestant ethics seems sorely needed (cf. Weber 1958). No amount of economic growth, no reduction of unemployment and underemployment, can ever topple such a curse of value; we will always be hopelessly deprived against our inflated holy grail of capital desire. In social terms, we may always be impoverished, in relative deprivation, against those who are richer and better off. Conversely, we may always be vulnerable to regressive co-optation, the stoked *ressentiment* that is all the deeper and pernicious because it can never be ameliorated, much less contravened, by objective improvements in empirical or economic terms.

Against our entitlement to a continually better future, we arguably now have at once, simultaneously, the spiraling failure and yet inescapable desire for the modern after the modern, the after-modern, the yet better and yet less and less actually feasible beyond any present horizon of expectation or knowability. Maybe this is what links rather than divides us all: the expectation of endless improvement and betterment that can neither be actualized nor given up, either by those of us in the degraded cultural elite or by the oligarchs and underclass of less well-educated, poorer, rural, and generally discontented white and white-associated Americans.

8. Critical Theory, Social Movements, and the Limits of Foucault

In one or another form, the past century and more of critical Western intellectualism has identified, problematized, and theorized many if not all of the above issues. In the Western academy, such critical understanding increased importantly following World War II and especially during the 1960s, 1970s, and early 1980s. (Following this, critical Marxist and political economic perspectives were increasingly confronted—and often superceded, sidelined, or hybridized—with hyper-relativizing postmodern sensibilities and their sequelae (see Knauft 1996).) In this sense, a present view much less a Foucualdian one has no privilege of original discovery concerning the intricate workings of industrial and post-industrial capitalism, nationalism, racism, sexism, class-based oligarchy, and the degradation of both social life and the physical environment on which it depends. And yet, this is somehow just the point: many decades of keen and critical intellectual work seem somehow now at risk of disconnection from our present political moment. This seems the case specifically as well for our understanding of modernity and its alters, which were so actively and critically explored during the late 1980s and 1990s (e.g., Harvey 1989; Gaonkar 2001; Knauft 2002), but which seem so relatively left aside today (e.g., Povinelli 2016; Tsing 2017).

Recursively, this can lead us to more actively consider the relationship between critical theory and engaged social action—which leads us in turn to the limit points of Foucault.

Though Foucault was a political activist in personal terms, his actions were fairly ineffectual in a practical sense. To be uncharitable, one could even say that the power and contribution of his critical thought were inversely related to its lack of pragmatic application. In a shorter-term perspective, this was perhaps Foucault's intention, as intimated further above. But in the longer term, this risks reinscribing a rarefied intellectualism divorced from practical engagement. In anthropology, at least, the tendency to shun rather than seek practical engagement runs against the field's dominant current trend, which is the critical exposure, examination, and amelioration of inequity and other challenging human problems (e.g., Low and Merry 2010; Robbins 2013; Ortner 2016). And yet, as is also widely noted, these objectives are seldom met beyond cultivating critical intellectualism per se. As such, they risk tacitly demurring against the agendas critiqued by Gusterson (2017b, p. 455) whereby academic work in fields such as economics and international studies extend as if naturally the political and policy agendas of the rightest American state.

Much has been written of late about the handmaiden capitalism of the contemporary neoliberal university (e.g., Gusterson 2017b; Tejani 2017; Cottom 2017; Caanan and Shumar 2011; cf. earlier work by Readings 1997; Bourdieu 1988; Bourdieu and Passeron 1990). This includes how money and power configure the construction of value in knowledge; the gatekeeping, reinforcement, and reproduction of valued knowledge and skills; and how these reflect and reinforce inequities if not firewalls of socioeconomic division by means of differential debt, advancement, and highly paid professional success. Increasingly, the war over the university is also a war of explicit politics. To take just one example, the George Mason University Law School received $10 million from the Charles Koch Foundation in 2016—following a decade in which the university received more than $95 million from the Foundation. Simultaneously, an anonymous $20 million donation was received—contingent on the school being renamed "The Antonin Scalia School of Law" (Kotch 2017).

In the 1960s, universities, including elite universities such as Columbia, Berkeley and Michigan, were hotbeds of widespread social protest and opposition. This is far from the case today.

The causes and conditions under which social movements effectively grow and develop is widely debated. Progressive political scientists such as McAdam (e.g., McAdam 2017) suggest that a scaffolded triumvirate of structural, political, and emotionally activated motivation are in play, including conducive or unconducive political opportunities, the availability or viability of mobilizing organizational structures, and affective priming such as anger at perceived injustice or fear of perceived threat. Key here is the perception that collective social action has a realistic chance of redressing or overturning current trends or practices. As such, McAdam (McAdam 2017; McAdam and Kloos 2014) suggests, based on historical research, that progressive social movements in the US are *less* likely to develop at times such as the present when the Republicans control Congress, as opposed to when an at least relatively-more-sympathetic Democratic party is in power.

A more critical view is taken by Cini et al. (2017, pp. 429–30), who argue that social movement studies have "not paid enough attention to the dynamics of capitalist transformations". More generally, they suggest that social movement studies emphasize meso and micro-practices that tacitly assume the presence and continuation of political institutions and regimes in their present form—rather than considering the larger-scale and longer-term trends (especially those of capital dispossession and differential accumulation) that presage and provoke movements of opposition if not transformation.

Negri (2017) goes so far as to suggest that the definition of social movements in our contemporary era is itself changing and malleable—not conditioned or constrained by received organizational parameters. Rather, contemporary social upheavals mark a "liberation process" of subversion against larger capitalist conditions. He thus suggests transforming Marxist notions of class struggle into ones of "entrepreneurial opposition" based not on wage labor but on "living labor" that is often immaterial. As such, expressions of resistance are changing and not necessarily repeatable as an identifiable social movement over time.

Culminating this line of thought is perhaps the work of anarchist activist and anthropologist David Graeber (e.g., Graeber 2004, 2014). For Graeber, the *lack* of a social movement's achievement as an organization actually indicates its larger success: "As an anarchist, he believes in what he calls 'prefigurative' politics; protests are not meant to extract concessions from the existing system, but to give people an idea of what the world would be like if there was no system and individuals were free to make their own choices" (Runciman 2013). As such, the Occupy Wall Street movement that Graeber helped foment "showed that real democracy can break out almost anywhere given the chance" (ibid.) even though the movement itself has spawned little organized or institutional legacy.

Amid the diverse perspectives above—from a structured theory of social movements that borders on being historically static or tautological, to the privileging of undefined and ephemeral expressions of protest that leave little legacy—there seems little ground on which to stake a strong current claim to social activism by means of organizational or institutional commitment. This is not to say that newly progressive social movements (e.g., MoveOn.org) are unlikely to be possible or important in the American future—nor that such developments should be considered misguided or unfruitful. It is rather to suggest, as with the genealogy of politics more generally, that alternative productive strategies are likely to vary under different specific conditions and opportunities—including in relation to the particular skills, history, and predilection of individual activists themselves. This does not eulogize the particular kinds of action (and inaction) that happen to have been favored by Foucault, but neither does it debunk the potential that all of us have for pushing as assertively and consistently as possible in the directions we find ourselves most critically and productively poised to pursue. If the age of reason threatens to be over, the question of how and in what ways critical intellectualism can connect with productive action emerges afresh for each of us in a higher and more personal key.

9. Political Genealogy

A genealogical rather than a historical view would urge or at least allow for perspectives that do not and should not add up to a singular view of political periodicity or political commitment, including with respect to our present crises and what we can expect or realistically hope to change. As Michael Clifford (Clifford 2013, pp. 33, 123) suggests, political genealogy not just encompasses but necessitates a wide diversity of lenses and fames to trace the lineaments of power, knowledge, and subjectivity. At the same time—and this is perhaps the more important point of a truly genealogical analysis in the Foucauldian sense—*this is not at all a mandate much less a license for nihilism or giving up.* It is not at all an excuse or a rationale for doing nothing personally or politically. It is rather a deeper commitment, critical fascination, and radical curiosity for newly creative understanding. This is, as Clifford (2013, pp. 12–13) suggests, a deeper kind of empowerment.

Perhaps this is the grounding for what Gramsci (1971) would call a continuing war of position in a more strongly subjectified sense—one that understands more intricately the terms and conditions of knowledge, power, and self-relationship even as one does not pretend to know or forecast their immediate temporal outcome. Pessimism of the intellect, optimism of the will. In the practical mix, an embrace of diverse routes and sensibilities of critique and activism seems appropriate. Intellectually, we can incubate juices of critical sensibility more productively and profoundly. During the 1960s and 1970s, this is certainly what occurred in French intellectual life across a range of registers, including in the work of Foucault himself.

As factuality is itself increasingly contended, it is important to employ what might otherwise be a depressive view of the present to fuel rather than dampen our own best objective and subjective potentials (cf. Latour 2004). As Marxists would say, crises are also opportunities to see laid yet more bare the underlying contradictions of the era. These presently include the continuing role of modernity, an epistemic regime whose ideology draws upon destructive creation as well as creative destruction in the context of 21st century digital capitalism and political power (cf. Berman 1982; Knauft 2002).

Political genealogy allows us to gain both broader and more specific purchase on the diverse optics, lineaments, transitions, and periodicities of this power. This includes for American politics how to view our current chaotic situation across different temporal scales of genealogy that may variously compare millennia, centuries, decades, ongoing four-year cycles, and politics as an American institution vis-à-vis the political economy of a portended after-modernity that we can barely yet glimpse much less know. This includes but is not reducible to the current regressive recourse to American white racism, sexism, and overclass domination. These continue to darken the contours of modernity's owl-of-Minerva horizon in ways that beg more than simple intellectual or conceptual critique.

Foucault and the genealogy of the political as applied in the American present should allow an opening of larger questions that have strong traction, both intellectually and practically (see Appendix A). These can be engaged without being mortgaged to one or another definitive view of when and in what form political change will take place or should be pursued. This, I think, is Foucault's contribution to the present. Amid competing voices and increasingly chaotic alternatives, this to me provides an ironically important stabilizing force for those who would cultivate a seriously critical set of optics to actively engage what is presently going on and to configure, in our various ways, what we can actually do about it.

> [G]enealogy retrieves an indispensable restraint: it must record the singularity of events outside of any monotonous finality; it must seek them in the most unpromising places, in what we tend to feel is without history—in sentiments, love, conscience, instincts; it must be sensitive to their recurrence, not in order to trace the gradual curve of their evolution, but to isolate the different scenes where they engaged in different roles .... Genealogy ... requires patience and a knowledge of details, and it depends on a vast accumulation of source material .... In short, genealogy demands relentless erudition ... [I]t rejects the metahistorical deployment of ideal significations and indefinite teleologies. It opposes itself to the search for 'origins.' (Foucault 1984, pp. 76–77)

Conflicts of Interest: The author declares no conflicts of interest.

Appendix A

If one wanted to be categorical—taking on board the caveats that categorical divisions carry, especially for Foucault—genealogies of the American political present could be parsed into perspectives reflecting his major emphases (cf. Clifford 2013, pp. 26–34), including the following:

1.   Knowledge—explore the margins of transition between modern and after-modern sensibilities. Document and analyze present regimes of asserted truth and untruth, and how these contest each other vis-à-vis objectively discernible facts of history and the present. Analyze the attempted reformations and counter-reformations that both reinscribe a self-interested Western modernity of indefinite betterment and progress. Explore the overlooked margins of alternative as well as mainstream and ostensibly subaltern subjectification, including in areas of media, sex, religion, art, and culture—as well as in politics and political economy per se.

2.   Power—how subjects are incited through evolving forms of sovereignty, governmentality, and social media; how altered types of self-relationship are fomented, including in relation to newly-reinforced dividing practices concerning race, sex, religion, and nationality. Investigate how diverse corporate and political institutions of power and influence—and their increasing connection—canalize and fuel social divisiveness, including across differentiated spaces of capitalism that grate against each other so rawly in current American polarization. Consider how and through what means of capital and political reinforcement the interests of overclass America are linked with underclass vulnerabilities and anxieties. Consider these in relation to counter-hegemonies that contend to provincialize America vis-à-vis other world areas, peoples, and countries. Analyze how institutions of power, social media, and the trail of corporate money classify, stigmatize, and sequester differently ascribed categories of people and personhood.

3.   Self-relationship—examine emerging vis-à-vis received regimes of subjectivity and subjectivation, including in relation to social media and money. How and in what way are reifications of selfhood newly reconstructed and reinforced, including through digital social media; what are the larger patterns through which new identities and rigidities are forged, asserted, reinforced—and divided? What informs opposition between differently asserted forms of subjectivity, including modern and anti-modern, progressive and reactionary? How can we attend to the dynamism and impact of contended subjectivity without bleaching their differences or reifying larger prognoses, either cataclysmic or ultimately utopic? And how, in the process, can we push against or beyond the false hope for greater dialectical improvement and "progress"?

References

Alexander, Michelle. 2012. *The New Jim Crow: Mass Incarceration in the Age of Colorblindness*. New York: New Press.

Ali, Tariq. 2002. *The Clash of Fundamentalisms: Crusades, Jihads, and Modernity*. London: Verso.

Alton, Joe. 2017. The Left's "Antifa-Da" against America. *The Daily Caller*, May 15.

Appadurai, Arjun. 2017. Democracy Fatigue. In *The Great Regression*. Edited by Heinrich Geiselberger. London: Polity.

Arrighi, Giovanni. 1994. *The Long Twentieth Century: Money, Power, and the Origin of Our Times*. London: Verso.

Arrighi, Giovanni, and Beverly J. Silver. 1999. *Chaos and Governance in the Modern World System*. Minneapolis: University of Minnesota Press.

Giovanni Arrighi, Takeshi Hamashita, and Mark Selden, eds. 2003. *The Resurgence of East Asia: 500, 150, and 50 Year Perspectives*. New York: Routledge.

Bauder, David. 2017. *Fox News Channel's Sean Hannity Tops Cable News Rankings*. New York: Associated Press.

Bauman, Zygmunt. 2017. *Retrotopia*. Cambridge: Polity Press.

Berman, Marshall. 1982. *All That Is Solid Melts into Air: The Experience of Modernity*. New York: Penguin.

Bourdieu, Pierre. 1988. *Homo Academicus*. Stanford: Stanford University Press.

Bourdieu, Pierre, and Jean-Claude Passeron. 1990. *Reproduction in Education, Society, and Culture*, 2nd ed. Thousand Oaks: Sage Publications.

Bray, Mark. 2017. *Antifa: The Anti-Fascist Handbook*. Brooklyn: Melville House.

Burns, Alexander, and Kirk Johnson. 2017. Poised for West Coast Dominance, Democrats Eye Grand Agenda. *The New York Times*, November 4.

Joyce E. Caanan, and Wesley Shumar, eds. 2011. *Structure and Agency in the Neoliberal University*. New York: Routledge.

Camp, Jordan T. 2016. *Incarcerating the Crisis: Freedom Struggles and the Rise of the Neoliberal State*. Berekeley: University of California Press.

CCC—The Centre for Contemporary Cultural Studies. 1982. *Empire Strikes Back: Race and Racism in 1970s Britain.* London: Routledge.

Census Bureau. 2015. New Census Bureau Report Analyzes US Population Projections. *United States Census Bureau*, March 3.

Cini, Lorenzo, Daniela Chironi, Eliska Drapalova, and Federico Tomasello. 2017. Towards a Critical Theory of Social Movements: An Introduction. *Anthropological Theory* 17: 429–52. [CrossRef]

Clifford, Michael. 2013. *Empowerment: The Theory and Practice of Political Genealogy.* Lanham: Lexington Books.

Coates, Ta-Nehisi. 2017a. *We Were Eight Years in Power: An American Tragedy.* New York: One World Publishing.

Coates, Ta-Nehisi. 2017b. The First White President: The Foundation of Donald Trump's Presidency is the Negation of Barack Obama's Legacy. *The Atlantic.*

Collier, Paul. 2008. *The Bottom Billion: Why the Poorest Countries Are Failing and What Can Be Done about It.* Oxford: Oxford University Press.

Cottom, Tressie M. 2017. *Lower Ed: The Troubling Rise of For-Profit Colleges in the New Economy.* New York: New Press.

Davis, Julie H., Gay Stolberg, and Thomas Kaplan. 2018. Trump Alarms Lawmakers with Disparaging Words for Haiti and Africa. *The New York Times*, January 11.

DeLisi, Bejamin. 2017. What is 'Antifa'? and Why is the Liberal Media So Reluctant to Cover it? *Project Republic*, May 19.

Ember, Sydney, and Andrew Ross Sorkin. 2017. Meredith Bid for Time Inc. Said to Be Backed by Koch Brothers. *The New York Times*, November 15.

Fanon, Frantz. 2005. *The Wretched of the Earth.* New York: Grove Atlantic.

Ferguson, Niall. 2006. *The War of the World: Twentieth-Century Conflict and the Descent of the West.* New York: Penguin.

Fingerhut, Hannah. 2017. Republicans Skeptical of Colleges' Impact on U.S. *PEW Research Center*, July 20.

Fisher, Max, and Josh Keller. 2017. What Explains U.S. Mass Shootings? International Comparisons Suggest an Answer. *The New York Times*, November 7.

Foucault, Michel. 1984. *The Foucault Reader.* Edited by Paul Rabinow. New York: Pantheon.

Frank, Andre Gunder. 1998. *ReOrient: Global Economy in the Asian Age.* Berkeley: University of California Press.

Friedman, Lisa, Marina Affo, and Derek Kravnitz. 2017. E.P.A. Officals, Disheartened by Agencies Direction, Are Leaving in Droves. *The New York Times*, December 22.

Gallup News. 2017. Presidential Approval Ratings, 30 October–5 November 2017. Available online: http://news.gallup.com/poll/203198/presidential-approval-ratings-donald-trump.aspx (accessed on 12 January 2018).

Dilip Parameshwar Gaonkar, ed. 2001. *Alternative Modernities.* Chapel Hill: Duke University Press.

Heinrich Geiselberger, ed. 2017. *The Great Regression.* London: Polity.

Goldman, Adam, and Jennifer Medina. 2018. Las Vegas Gunman Took Elaborate Steps to Hide His Tracks, New Documents Show. *The New York Times*, January 12, (online).

Gorbis, Marina. 2017. Our Gutenberg Moment. *Stanford Social Innovation Review*, March 15.

Graeber, David. 2004. *Fragments of an Anarchist Anthropology.* Chicago: Prickly Paradigm Press.

Graeber, David. 2014. *The Democracy Project: A History, a Crisis, A Movement.* New York: Spiegel & Grau.

Gramsci, Antonio. 1971. *Selections from the Prison Notebooks of Antonio Gramsci.* Edited by Quintin Hoare and Geoffrey Nowell-Smith. London: Lawrence and Wishart.

Green, Erica L. 2017. House G.O.P. Tax Writers Take Aim at College Tuition Benefits. *The New York Times*, November 15.

Gusterson, Hugh. 2017a. From Brexit to Trump: Anthropology and the Rise of Nationalist Populism. *American Ethnologist* 44: 209–14. [CrossRef]

Gusterson, Hugh. 2017b. Homework: Toward a Critical Ethnography of the University. *American Ethnologist* 44: 435–50. [CrossRef]

Harris, Gardiner. 2017. Diplomats Sound the Alarm as They Are Pushed Out in Droves. *The New York Times*, November 24.

Hartocollis, Anemonia. 2017. Swelling College Endowments Tempt Lawmakers Looking for Dollars. *The New York Times*, November 4.

Harvey, David. 1989. *The Condition of Postmodernity.* Oxford: Basil Blackwell.

Harvey, David. 2001. *Spaces of Capital: Towards a Critical Geography.* London: Routledge.

Harvey, David. 2003. *The New Imperialism.* New York: Oxford University Press.

Harvey, David. 2007. *A Brief History of Neoliberalism.* Oxford: Oxford University Press.

Hauser, Christine. 2017. Gun Death Rate Rose Again in 2016, CDC Says. *The New York Times*, November 4.

Hawkins, Derek. 2017. A Dartmouth Antifa Expert Was Disavowed by his College President for "Supporting Violent Protest", Angering Many Faculty. *The Washington Post*, August 29.

Hess, Abigail. 2017. Here's How the House GOP Tax Plan Could Affect Students, Parents, and Universities. *Make It*, November 17.

Hochschild, Arlie Russell. 2016. *Strangers in Their Own Land: Anger and Mourning on the American Right*. New York: New Press.

Horkheimer, Max, and Theodor Adorno. 1947. *Dialectic of Enlightenment*. New York: Continuum.

Kang, Cecilia. 2017. F.C.C. Repeals Net Neutrality Rules. *The New York Times*, December 14.

Kendzior, Sarah. 2015/18. *The View from Flyover Country: Dispatches from Forgotten America*. New York: Kindle/Flatiron Press.

Klein, Edward. 2017. *All out War: The Plot to Destroy Trump*. Washington: Regnery Publishing.

Knauft, Bruce. 1996. *Genealogies for the Present in Cultural Anthropology*. New York: Routledge.

Knauft, Bruce. 2002. Critically Modern: An Introduction. In *Critically Modern: Alternatives, Alterities, Anthropologies*. Edited by B. Knauft. Bloomington: Indiana University Press, pp. 1–54.

Knauft, Bruce. 2007. Provincializing America: Imperialism, Capitalism, and Counter-hegemony in the Twenty-first Century. *Current Anthropology* 48: 781–805. [CrossRef]

Knauft, Bruce. 2013. Critical Theory. In *Theory in Social and Cultural Anthropology*. Edited by R. Jon McGhee and Richard Warms. Thousand Oaks: Sage, pp. 139–42.

Knauft, Bruce. 2016. What is Genealogy?: An Anthropology/Philosophical Investigation. *Genealogy* 1: 1–16.

Kotch, Alex. 2017. Charles Koch Ramps up Higher Ed Funding to Fuel 'Talent Pipeline'. *PR Watch*, February 2.

Kroll, Andy. 2017a. Ready for Trump TV? Inside Sinclair Broadcasting's Plot to Take over Your Local News. *Mother Jones*, November/December.

Kroll, Andy. 2017b. Thanks to the FCC, Christmas Comes Early for Pro-Trump Sinclair Broadcast Group. *Mother Jones*, November 17.

Kruzel, John. 2018. Did Fire and Fury Author Michael Wolff have Access to the White House? *Politifact*, January 5.

Lancaster, Roger N. 2011. *Sex Panic and the Punitive State*. Berkeley: University of California Press.

Landler, Mark, Julie Hirschfeld Davis, and Jane Perlez. 2017. Trump, Aiming to Coax Xi Jinping, Bets on Flattery. *The New York Times*, November 8.

Lankford, Adam. 2016a. Public Mass Shooters and Firearms: A Cross-National Study of 171 Countries. *Violence and Victims* 32: 187–99. [CrossRef] [PubMed]

Lankford, Adam. 2016b. Race and Mass Murder in the United States: A Social and Behavioral Analysis. *Current Sociology* 64: 470–90. [CrossRef]

Latour, Bruno. 2004. Why Has Critique Run Out of Steam?: From Matters of Fact to Matters of Concern. *Critical Inquiry* 30: 225–48. [CrossRef]

Lenin, Vladimir I. 1902. *What Is to Be Done?* Beijing: Foreign Language Press.

Leonhardt, David. 2017. Trump's Lies vs. Obama's. *The New York Times*, December 17.

Low, Setha M., and Sally Engel Merry. 2010. Engaged Anthropology: Diversity and Dilemmas. *Current Anthropology* 51: 203–26. [CrossRef]

Luce, Edward. 2017. *The Retreat of Western Liberalism*. London: Verso.

Luhrmann, Tanya M. 2012. *When God Talks Back: Understanding the American Evangelical Relation with God*. New York: Vintage.

Lukács, Georg. 1923. *History and Class Consciousness: Studies in Marxist Dialectics*. Cambridge: MIT Press, First published 1971.

Mamdani, Mahmood. 2002. *When Victims Become Killers: Colonialism, Nativism, and Genocide in Rwanda*. Princeton: Princeton University Press.

Martin, Jonathan. 2018. From 'Fire and Fury' to Political Firestorm. *The New York Times*, January 8.

Marx, Karl. 1851. The Eighteenth Brumaire of Louis Bonaparte. In *Karl Marx: Selected Writings*. Edited by David McClellan. Oxford: Oxford University Press, pp. 300–25.

Mayer, Jane. 2016. *Dark Money: The Hidden History of the Billionaires behind the Rise of the Radical Right*. New York: Penguin.

Mbembe, Achille. 1992. The Banality of Power and the Aesthetics of Vulgarity in the Postcolony. *Public Culture* 4: 1–31. [CrossRef]

Mbembe, Achille. 2001. *On the Postcolony*. Berkeley: University of California Press.

McAdam, Doug. 2017. Social Movement Theory and the Prospects for Climate Change Activism in the United States. *Annual Review of Political Science* 20: 189–208. [CrossRef]

McAdam, Doug, and Karina Kloos. 2014. *Deeply Divided: Racial Politics and Social Movements in Post-War America*. New York: Oxford University Press.

Meyers, Ben, and Brock Read. 2017. If House Republicans Get their Way, These College Would See Their Endowments Taxed. *The Chronicle of Higher Education*, November 2.

Negri, Antonio. 2017. Living Labour and Social Movements: A Dialogue with Antonio Negri—Interview by Daniela Chironi. *Anthropological Theory* 17: 518–25.

New York Times. 2017. Mass Shootings in the U.S. *The New York Times*, October 2.

NY Times Board. 2017. Mr. Trump Casts a Shadow over the AT&T-Time Warner Deal. *The New York Times*, November 15.

O'Kane, Chris. 2017. "A Hostile World": Critical Theory in the Time of Trump. *Logos* 16: 1–2. Available online: http://logosjournal.com/2017/a-hostile-world-critical-theory-in-the-time-of-trump/ (accessed on 15 January 2018).

Ortner, Sherry B. 2016. Dark Anthropology and Its Others: Theory since the Eighties. *Hau* 6: 47–73. [CrossRef]

Osnos, Evan. 2016. The Far Right Revival: A Thirty-Years War? *The New Yorker*, January 12.

Pandey, Gyan. 2015. Can There Be a Subaltern Middle Class?: Notes on African American and Dalit History. *Public Culture* 21: 321–42. [CrossRef]

Polakow-Suransky, Sasha. 2017a. White Nationalism Is Destroying the West. *The New York Times Sunday Review*, October 12.

Polakow-Suransky, Sasha. 2017b. *Go Back to Where You Came from: The Backlash against Immigration and the Fate of Western Democracy*. New York: Nation Books.

Povinelli, Beth A. 2016. *Geontologies: A Requiem to Late Liberalism*. Chapel Hill: Duke University Press.

Readings, Bill. 1997. *The University in Ruins*. Cambridge: Harvard University Press.

Rendueles, César. 2017. *Sociophobia: Political Change in the Digital Utopia*. New York: Columbia University Press.

Robbins, Joel. 2013. Beyond the Suffering Subject: Toward an Anthropology of the Good. *Journal of the Royal Anthropological Institute* 19: 447–62. [CrossRef]

Rosa, Jonathan, and Yarimar Bonilla. 2017. Deprovincializing Trump, Decolonizing Diversity, and Unsettling Anthropology. *American Ethnologist* 44: 201–8. [CrossRef]

Ross, Alex. 2016. The Frankfurt School Knew Trump Was Coming. *The New Yorker*, December 5.

Rounds. 2017. Timeline: The "Worst" Mass Shootings in Modern U.S. History. *Rounds*, October 4.

Jennifer Rudolph, and Michael Szonyi, eds. 2018. *The China Question: Critrical Insights into a Rising Power*. Cambridge: Harvard University Press.

Ruiz, Michelle. 2017. Now can we admit Sexism was a factor in the 2016 election? *Vogue*, May 16.

Runciman, Daivd. 2013. The Democracy Project—A Review. *The Guardian*, March 28.

Stewart, Kathleen. 1996. *A Space on the Side of the Road: Cultural Poetics in an "Other" America*. Princeton: Princeton University Press.

Steyer, Tom. 2017. [Political Ad]. Watch the Impeachment Ad that Sent Trump Into a Twitter Melt Down. *Polityke: The Damage Report*. October 17. Available online: https://www.polityke.com/archives/2017/10/27/watch-the-impeachment-ad-that-sent-trump-into-a-twitter-melt-down (accessed on 27 October 2017).

Tejani, Riaz. 2017. Professional Apartheid: The Racialization of US Law Schools after the Global Economic Crisis. *American Ethnologist* 44: 451–63. [CrossRef]

The Economist. 2017. How the World Was Trolled: Once Considered a Boon to Democracy, Social Media Have Started to Look Like Its Nemesis. *The Economist*, November 4, 19–22.

Tolan, Casey. 2017. Trump-Tweet Target Tom Steyer's Impeachment Campaign Tops 1.4 Million Signatures. *The Mercury News*, November 1.

Tsing, Anna. 2017. *The Mushroom at the End of the World: On the Possibility of Life in Capitalist Ruins*. Princeton: Princeton University Press.

Twohey, Megan, and Jim Rutenberg. 2018. Porn Star Was Reportedly Paid to Stqy Quiet About Trump. *The New York Times*. January 12. Available online: https://www.nytimes.com/2018/01/12/us/trump-stephanie-clifford-stormy-daniels.html (accessed on 12 January 2017).

Vance, J. D. 2016. *Hillbilly Elegy: A Memoir of a Family and Culture in Crisis*. New York: Harper.

Wallerstein, Immanuel. 2003. *The Decline of American Power*. New York: New Press.

Weber, Max. 1958. *The Protestant Ethic and the Spirit of Capitalism*. New York: Scribner's.

Wilber, Ken. 2017. *Trump and a Post-Truth World*. Boulder: Shambala.

Williams, Casey. 2017. Has Trump Stolen Philosophy's Critical Tools? *The New York Times*, April 17.

Wolff, Michael. 2018a. Donald Trump Didn't Want to Be President: One Year Ago: The Plan to Lose, and the Admistration's Shocked First Days. *New York*, January 3.

Wolff, Michael. 2018b. *Fire and Fury: Inside the Trump White House*. New York: Henry Holt & Co.

Zizek, Slavoj. 2002. *Welcome to the Desert of the Real: Five Essays on September 11 and Related Dates*. London: Verso.

genealogy

Article
Persons and Sovereigns in Ethical Thought

Ladelle McWhorter

School of Arts and Sciences, University of Richmond, Richmond, VA 23173, USA; lmcwhort@richmond.edu

Received: 18 August 2017; Accepted: 16 November 2017; Published: 20 November 2017

Abstract: Contemporary concepts of moral personhood prevent us from grappling effectively with contemporary social, political, and moral problems. One way to counter the power of such concepts is to trace their lineage and shifting political investments. This article presents a genealogy of personhood, focusing on the crisis of both personhood and sovereignty in seventeenth-century England. It demonstrates the optionality of personhood for moral thinking and exposes personhood's functions in political dividing practices.

Keywords: Foucault; sovereignty; personhood; Levellers; Hobbes

---

1. Introduction: Moral Anguish

In Western traditions, at least since the turn of the eighteenth century, ethical action and responsibility have been thought to lie with persons—that is, with free, independent initiators of pre-meditated or deliberate action. To be an ethical person means not only to perform good acts, but, in the first place, to provide oneself with a set of carefully chosen values or rules by which to live. An ethical person thus wields the powers of judgment, legislation, and execution within his or her sphere of influence much as a sovereign exercises those powers over a territory. Although prior to the late eighteenth century, thinkers did not use the term *sovereign* in their accounts of moral selfhood, their successors have not hesitated to do so. According to Paul Fairfield, all of the classical liberal thinkers hold that the self in general (and not merely in its ethical practice) "is a sovereign chooser which assigns to itself its own plan of life together with a set of values, principles, and beliefs without having to take direction from any higher authority" (Fairfield 2000, p. 16).

The idea that human beings are or ever can be "sovereign"—independent, or even psychically unitary in the requisite ways—has not lacked for criticism. In particular, it has been contested by psychoanalysts and feminists for many decades. Human subjectivity is an historical and always less than complete and stable achievement, such theorists maintain; it emerges in networks of meaning and relationships of power, and it shifts as they shift. Insofar as Kant et al., require judgment and action to proceed from a fully rational, autonomous mentality, they unwittingly stymy their own normative projects; for no one can be what such theorists say we must be if we are to judge and conduct ourselves morally. Yet the idea lives on.

Michel Foucault famously asserted that "[i]n political thought and analysis we still have not cut off the head of the king" (Foucault 1978, pp. 88–89). The same is true in moral philosophy. But the idea lives on not just in esoteric philosophical literature but in everyday experience. We hold ourselves and each other responsible as if we have sovereign control over our moral lives. This is nowhere more apparent than in individuals' feelings of regret and guilt over poor judgments, injurious actions, and good works left undone. Psychoanalysts and feminists are surely correct; no individual holds sovereign power in his or her own moral realm. There are no "sovereign choosers". But in these moments of regret or guilt all the critical theory in the world seems not to have much effect on ethical experience. One still feels responsible.[1]

A few years ago, I spoke at a "debate camp", a summer program for high school debate teams and their coaches, who were preparing for a year's debate season on environmental issues. Conversation during my session turned to questions of responsibility for addressing big issues—such as climate change—in which almost everyone is implicated, perhaps as both wrongdoer and victim. Students and coaches expressed a deep sense of responsibility and at the same time frustration in their efforts not to worsen and maybe even to mitigate the problems. They all felt that they ought to be doing something and that not doing anything would be a moral failing. Yet they were aware that no individual's actions are likely to be effective at changing the overall situation. Their values compelled them not to behave in ways that harm people, but their everyday actions as American consumers and citizens do harm people, and of course not just people. In a very honest discussion, they acknowledged that they live with ongoing moral pain. I do not think those high school students were unique. If we believe that morality means at the very least conducting our lives in accordance with our values, we—at least we middle class and affluent North Americans—find ourselves in the present day at best in episodic ethical quagmires and at worst in perpetual moral crisis.

Take me, for example: I want to save the biosphere. I want everyone to have safe and sufficient drinking water. I want children not to starve to death or live homeless in the streets. I want world peace. And yet, every day, I make choices in full awareness that I am undermining those values, taking action that works against their realization. No matter what I say I want, what I actually do is use up resources faster than any human being before me in the history of humanity, emit more pollution than any human being before me in the history of humanity, and in the process of doing so directly threaten the lives and health of several billion members of the current population of human beings on this planet, not to mention untold trillions of other organisms. And the truly disturbing thing is that when I try to do otherwise, I find that despite all my legal rights and economic power, I seem unable to. I can make minor adjustments, but I cannot get off the grid, get out of the market, or erase my carbon footprint. I am free to choose—in the market, in the voting booth—but in the very exercise of that freedom, I experience some of my most anguished moments of unfreedom.

I suspect that this kind of moral anguish drives many people to numb resignation or blanket defensiveness. Consume or don't consume this or that, vote for this party or that party or don't vote at all; does it really make any difference? I suspect that many North Americans have just more or less given up their claim to sovereign moral personhood. And although some few may be content in their quiescence, I think many more feel adrift and empty, sovereigns in exile, suffering from a humiliation of selfhood so deep that they cannot even locate the wound, chronically desperate and not infrequently inexplicably enraged.

2. Taking the Measure of the Moral Trap: Genealogy as a Conceptual Tool

When it finds itself in a trap, a smart animal soon ceases its panicked and senseless struggle and examines the structure of the trap. Every trap—even a conceptual trap—is a configuration of forces, a material system, and an historical assemblage. Seeing how the elements of the trap come together—how those material forces interplay, reinforce, and oppose each other—is a first step toward finding a way out, a step toward being able to think again. What I seek in this project is not some sort of definitive moral solution but simply a new chance to think ethically without the severe limitation imposed by our particular conceptual trap.

---

[1] Obviously, there are people who rarely or maybe even never feel responsible; writing in the immediate aftermath of the white supremacist violence in Charlottesville, Virginia, and Trump's defense of the terrorists, I am acutely aware of this fact. I simply mean that many people do, and they often feel responsible for actions or inactions that were not fully within their control.

There are several elements to this modern moral trap. One is the concept of freedom as individual choice. Another is the way responsibility is bound to unilateral causality.[2] Another is the commitment to personhood as the nature of human being and the ground of moral value. All of these, and others, are worth investigating. In this essay, I take up personhood, just one aspect of the trap, and I examine it as a configuration of forces within the configuration of forces that is modern moral discourse.

I proceed genealogically, tracing the contingencies and conditions under which our ethical personhood arose. The prevailing assumption is that personhood is a fact of human life and a legally and morally recognized status to which we all are entitled. Our personhood is what makes us worthy of moral consideration and respect.[3] A genealogy casts personhood, on the contrary, as an historically emergent category rather than an ontological fact. By investigating the conditions of its emergence, genealogy exposes personhood's entanglements with networks of power. The power of personhood over our thinking—its role in our modern moral trap—depends upon our unwillingness to question it, our fear of thinking without it, a fear perpetuated by personhood itself. Part of the power of personhood is its attendant definition of its own "outside" as "thing". Eschewing or abandoning personhood, according to the moral logic of personhood, means exiling oneself to the category of unworthy, morally inconsiderable thing. Genealogy disrupts that logic by telling a story of personhood as a mechanism for the exercise of power.

To be effective, a genealogy need not claim to be true, but it must be plausible under accepted standards of evidence. What follows is a story—a story I believe is quite plausible—of how personhood came to be such a powerful aspect of our ethical lives, despite its historically emergent and changing political nature. I begin with the decades just prior to what I call the "birth" of modern moral personhood, England in the midst of political, social, economic, and religious crisis in the mid-seventeenth century, at the time of the Civil Wars. I choose this point in time not because it is the only credible starting point but because it was a moment at which sovereignty was in serious trouble and at which, I will argue, individual personhood was not attributed unequivocally to a majority of human beings. We may recall that, in 1649, the English did in fact cut off the head of their king and went without for a number of years thereafter. What is less often remembered is the fact that personhood was under attack at the same time. At this critical juncture, either one or both concepts—sovereignty and personhood—might have been lost to history.

They were not lost, as we know. They were salvaged, in great part I believe, by being welded together for mutual reinforcement, an innovation that bequeathed to us not only an enduring liberal political theory but also the moral assumptions and values that inform our daily lives. They are formidable concepts now, but in this seventeenth-century moment we can see their tenuousness, their optionality perhaps, and maybe even catch a glimpse of how people might have come to think and live otherwise—as non-sovereign nonpersons leading ethical lives. If so, to that extent our imaginations might be freed for our own potential differing from ourselves.

3. The Crisis of Sovereignty in 17th Century England: Civil War

Queen Elizabeth having died childless in 1603, her cousin James Stuart of Scotland took the English throne. Neither he nor his son and successor Charles was well liked. The Stuarts claimed to rule by divine right, placing the royal prerogative above all parliamentary law,[4] and they used their prerogative repeatedly in ways that angered a wide range of constituencies. Exhausting other avenues of influence, various and sundry factions placed their hopes in parliamentary intervention.

---

[2] Although not totally bound. For a discussion, see (Lavin 2008, pp. 4–6).

[3] There are, of course, some ethicists who want to broaden moral considerability to include nonpersons. And there are some who want to extend the status of personhood beyond the human. Neither group disputes the concept of personhood, however, to my knowledge.

[4] Not that Elizabeth did not believe she reigned by divine right. She simply did not comment on the matter, whereas James and Charles both made speeches and wrote tracts insisting upon the fact and using it as justification to defy parliamentary decisions.

Parliament had two powers that could be leveraged against the king: sole power to levy taxes and the power of impeachment, that is, the power to remove royal advisors from their offices. Within four years of Charles' coronation, Parliament was bent on using these powers to the utmost to check the king's authority and impeach his closest advisor, the Duke of Buckingham. To prevent these actions, Charles dissolved Parliament in 1629, determined to rule on his own from that time forward. Using a variety of financial schemes, he was able to maintain his court for eleven years without Parliament's aid, an era known as the period of "Personal Rule".

Then, however, upon the advice of the Archbishop of Canterbury, Charles attempted to impose the Book of Common Prayer upon the Scottish Church—that is, he attempted to force the Calvinist Scots to conduct their worship services in accordance with the decidedly more Catholic Anglican liturgy. In response, 20,000 Scots invaded northern England. Charles needed funds to repel them. He had no choice but to recall Parliament.

Back in session for the first time in eleven years, members of both Houses realized they had but one chance and one means of influencing royal policies; they had to refuse to raise taxes unless the king made major concessions. First, they abolished all the prerogative courts, the mechanisms the king had used to bully lower court judges into enforcing his will. Within a few months, they enacted sufficient legislation to ensure that control over all major sources of revenue were in Parliamentary hands, leaving the king with no alternative but to work with them in the future. In addition, they passed the Triennial Act requiring parliamentary elections every three years, regardless of the king's desire to convene a session. All of this, the desperate monarch agreed to. Finally, however, they had to deal with the question of the Scottish invasion. Fearing that if they approved a tax to support a royal army, King Charles would turn it upon his English enemies as well, Parliament passed the Militia Ordinance, in effect fabricating a right of the two Houses to raise an army themselves. This they proceeded to do, prompting Charles to flee from London to the Midlands where, on 22 August 1642, he officially summoned his loyal subjects to stand with him against his parliamentary enemies. As Charles' army marched toward London, they were met by Parliamentary troops at Edgehill. A bloody but entirely indecisive battle ensued, the first of the English Civil War.

The next four years were terrible ones. The war itself—as was true of all war in those days—was sporadic and crude. Armed clashes might occur weeks or even months apart. But whatever intermittent pains the battles themselves inflicted upon the populace were as nothing compared to the hardships inflicted by the near-destruction of the domestic economy. Times had been relatively hard for more than two decades, but the war years were the worst (Hill 1972, p. 108). Trade lines were severed for long periods, resulting in widespread bankruptcies; agriculture came to a virtual halt in many areas. Disease spread. People were hungry, homeless, displaced, and terrified.

Realizing that they could not defeat the king's army alone, Parliament entered into a treaty with the invading Scots. The Scots agreed to this alliance because they were under the largely mistaken impression that the English had consented not only *not* to impose the Anglican Book of Common Prayer on the Scottish Church but, further, to accept Calvinist doctrine and ritual into the English Church—in other words, to unify the national church under Presbyterian rather than Episcopalian principles.[5] In July of 1644, the Scottish army decisively defeated Charles in the north, but Parliament's army suffered a terrible defeat in Cornwall, making it apparent that they needed to reorganize. The result was the so-called New Model Army under Sir Thomas Fairfax as Lord General and Oliver Cromwell as his second in command. The new army broke with tradition by basing ranks on degree of training and competence rather than class status. It quickly became a formidable fighting force. By June of 1645 the Royalist army was in ruins, and Charles had effectively lost the war. It was

---

[5] Etymologically, Presbyterian means rule by elders, while Episcopalian means rule by bishops. Not only was the conflict over doctrines but, just as importantly, it was over the structure and seat of church governance.

his turn then, in May of 1646, to form an alliance with the still disgruntled Scots. They soon betrayed him, however, selling him back to the English for 400,000 pounds.

Charles was taken into parliamentary custody in early 1647 and was imprisoned for nearly ten months while his captor-subjects deliberated about what to do with him. Should they negotiate with him to reinstate him as king with more limited authority? Should they try him as a traitor? These deliberations revealed and most likely hardened the very real and sharp ideological differences between factions that had earlier united in opposition to Charles' reign. It was no longer a question of curbing a king's excesses; with its sovereign deposed, England itself was in question. How could the country be reconstituted after civil war? Despite all their differences, most of the principal players in this political drama agreed that the solution to the problem lay in unification under a sovereign authority. On the assumption that sovereignty was a necessary condition for or feature of statehood, they believed that England's very existence depended on answering the question of how to re-establish sovereignty after such a dramatic collapse.

The concept of sovereignty that prevailed at this time, however, was in fact fairly new, and its necessity would not have appeared self-evident at all to Englishmen just a few hundred years earlier. The word *sovereignty*'s first appearances in English date back only to the fourteenth century, when it had a cluster of related meanings: pre-eminence or excellence in general or supremacy of power or rank, as well as the more narrow and familiar meaning, the position of a monarch. However, even when it was used as a name for the power of a ruler, medieval thinkers did not conceive of it as seventeenth-century thinkers did, namely, as the right to make or give law. In the Middle Ages, kings were judges, not legislators (Church 1969, pp. 55–57). The "state" itself was conceived as static and thus in need of no legal innovation. When circumstances required, regional edicts could be made by landlords, barons, dukes, etc. (theoretically in accord with traditional values and the law of God), and disputes were resolved, if necessary, by appeal to the king as supreme judge. In the late Renaissance, legal theorists began to attribute some legislative authority to the king, but still only under the auspices of his primary duty as supreme adjudicator responsible for seeing that justice was done. Only when this notion of a static state was no longer tenable did a different way of conceiving of sovereignty emerge. Once the state itself had to change in response to changing circumstances, ruling could not be limited to its judicial meaning; the ruler had to do more than decide cases. In the sixteenth century, the supreme judge was set to become a supreme legislator as well.

However, non-canonical legislation had long been the prerogative of landowners in England, and they were not interested in giving it up. Sovereignty in this new sixteenth-century sense—the increasingly important legislative sovereignty—was held by the king-in-parliament, not by the king independently. A century later, therefore, with the king deposed, it was not hard for many Englishmen to imagine a sovereign parliament without a king. But who had the authority, who could command the popular obedience, to establish any such thing?

With Charles in custody, it was the New Model Army rather than Parliament *per se* that was in control of the country—insofar as anyone was. But the army itself comprised an unstable coalition. Its military superiority had been purchased at the cost of dismantling the feudal structures that had reinforced political distinctions between nobility and commoners. Commoners who had fought valiantly, suffered deprivation, lost what little property they might have had before the war, and who had done so at least in part on the promise of a better future for themselves and their communities were not content to recede into the political background once the war was won. They did not want a return to monarchy, however limited the king's powers might be, and they wanted to play a significant role in a new English government. Through the summer of 1647, while Cromwell and Commissary-General Henry Ireton negotiated with the captive king, the London-based Levellers gained great influence among an increasingly angry rank-and-file. As the year wore on, it was clear that no one faction, either within the Army or without, could exert enough force to claim sovereignty as it was then conceived.

It is easy to see why Michel Foucault was fascinated with this moment in English history. The clash of forces was intense and beyond anyone's control. Law shines forth revealed as the product not of reason but of war. Succeeding events would not be an inevitable unfolding of causal necessity. In the turmoil of these transformations, the future lay open.

One eventual outcome of this turbulent time was what Foucault in his Collège de France lectures called "liberal governmentality", which took shape gradually alongside social contract theory and political economy over the next two hundred years. Another was modern racism, then state racism, and then the Nazi Holocaust, as Foucault tells the story in Part V of *The History of Sexuality, Volume 1* and in *"Society Must Be Defended"*. But in none of these works does Foucault spend much time on Cromwell or King Charles. Instead, he focuses a great deal of attention on Thomas Hobbes' *Leviathan*, published in 1651, and on pamphlets issued by the co-called Digger colonies through the spring and summer of 1649. While he does not examine them in quite the same way I do in this essay, I believe his choice of texts is extremely apt. In Hobbes' work, we see how a jeopardized sovereignty will be rescued through the medium of personhood, and in the Diggers' writings we see intense and explicit rejection of personhood and a resistance to earthly sovereignty of any kind. Hobbes' text points to the path that subsequent history did take. The Diggers' texts show us a path that was deliberately blocked and obscured.

4. The True Levellers' Challenge to Seventeenth-Century Personhood

Section 4 told a story about the destabilization of sovereignty in English life and thought in the seventeenth century. This section shows that at the same time sovereignty was in question, so was personhood, but more importantly it demonstrates that personhood in seventeenth-century England was not the moral category that it is today. Section 6 goes on to trace the genealogy of seventeenth-century personhood. Then in Section 6 we see how Hobbes fused the two unstable categories in an attempt to protect them from political and conceptual assault and, thus, set the stage for the rise of modern moral personhood in the eighteenth century.

The First English Civil War ended in 1646, but the political and economic situation did not stabilize. Londoners starved to death in the streets as Parliament and military leaders deliberated and argued over how to move the country forward. Common soldiers became increasingly angry with noble members of the military hierarchy and the vision of England's future they saw unfolding in aristocratic hands. No one knew what might happen next.

In the fall of 1647, five cavalry regiments made up largely of Levellers elected a group of men they called "Agitators" to represent their views to the military leadership. These men produced a pamphlet called "Agreement of the People", which called for elections to Parliament every two years and for a redistribution of Parliamentary seats based on population rather than land-holdings.[6] While the pamphlet never used the words 'universal manhood suffrage', something close to it is implied in the document. Parliament's power was also to be restrained by written and guaranteed equal political rights and liberties, including religious toleration. In an attempt to stave off total factionalization, the military leadership agreed to discuss the Leveller demands before the General Council of the Army at Putney in October and November of 1647. Transcripts of these discussions were kept only for the first few days, so we do not have a full record what transpired.[7] We do know, however, that the deliberators, aristocratic leaders and Levellers alike, assumed that legislative sovereignty would reside in a parliament of some description. At issue was whether that parliament would consist of something like the old House of Lords and House of Commons or take some other form. Much of the discussion

---

[6] This in itself is noteworthy. At the time, Englishmen tended to think of a country literally in terms of land, not people. The idea of a *nation*-state, a people-state, just did not exist.

[7] Transcripts of the Putney Debates can be found at http://oll.libertyfund.org/pages/1647-the-putney-debates and at http://www.constitution.org/lev/eng_lev_08.htm (accessed on 16 August 2017).

focused on how parliamentary seats would be allotted across the counties and which classes of people would have the right to vote.

At times in the transcripts, Leveller representatives seem to say that simply living within the boundaries of England should be enough to give a man the right to vote; one need not hold a literal stake in the territory. Landholders countered that if the property-less could vote, they would soon vote for land redistribution, which would put England on a slippery slope terminating in an end to all real property rights. Levellers consistently denied the charge that they were opposed to the private ownership of property, but their opponents brought the charge over and over again. At a crucial point in the debate, the Levellers appear to agree that those who are truly property-less—namely, servants and wage laborers—should not have a vote but that property requirements should be set low enough to afford the franchise to any man who owned a small farm or a business. Despite their desire for military and political unity, Ireton and Cromwell had no intention of granting the Levellers' radically democratic demands. To stop the proceedings, Cromwell finally managed to get a motion passed to suspend the meetings of the Army Council and order all soldiers back to their regiments. The Putney Debates ended without conclusion.

Three days later, on 11 November 1647, King Charles escaped from parliamentary custody. It was feared that he would make it to France where he might raise a new army with foreign support, although in fact he made the mistake of entrusting himself to his supposed ally the parliamentary governor of the Isle of Wight, who immediately placed him under arrest. Nevertheless, the escape was the excuse that the military leadership needed to impose strict discipline in the New Model Army and put down the Levellers. On 15 November, Levellers mutinied at Corkbush Field, but the mutineers were executed. Widespread fear of a second civil war rallied many discontents to Cromwell, and the Leveller faction within the army was crushed.

The king's escape had another effect, however; it drove home to the military hierarchy that further negotiations with Charles would be futile. He could not be trusted to abide by any agreement they might reach. But what to do with him instead? Through 1648, Parliament dragged its heels on the question, until finally, that December, army officers purged Parliament of all members who had voted to continue negotiations with Charles. One hundred eighty members were turned out and an additional forty arrested. Seventy or eighty of the remaining one hundred sixty members formed what became known as the Rump Parliament, which on 4 January 1649, proclaimed itself the supreme power in the nation and established a High Court of Justice to put the king on trial.[8] Charles was quickly found guilty of treason and executed at Whitehall by decapitation. Within days, the Rump voted to abolish the House of Lords and the institution of monarchy.

That spring, desperate for means to feed themselves and their families, a small group of impoverished men staged an occupation of St. George's Hill. Despite having no legal right to the land, these men broke ground for cultivation of crops and put up huts, earning them the somewhat derogatory label "the Diggers". Three weeks later they issued a declaration entitled "The True Levellers Standard Advanced"—*true* Levellers, they called themselves, as opposed to the Levellers in London and the military who would deny the franchise to the property-less. That pamphlet, dated 20 April 1649, and signed by fifteen men, declares in part:

> The work we are going about is this, To dig up *Georges Hill* and the waste Ground thereabouts, and to Sow Corn, and to eat our bread together by the sweat of our brows. And the First Reason is this, That we may work in righteousness, and lay the Foundation of making the Earth a Common Treasury for All, both Rich and Poor, That every one that is born in the Land, may be fed by the Earth his Mother that brought him forth, according to the Reason that rules in the Creation. Not Inclosing any part into any particular hand, but

---

[8] Some of the information for this section on the Rump Parliament came be found online at http://www.british-civil-wars.co.uk/index.htm (accessed on 29 December 2012).

all as one man, working together, and feeding together as Sons of one Father, members of one Family; not one Lording over another, but all looking upon each other, as equals in the Creation; so that our Maker may be glorified in the work of his own hands, and that every one may see, he is no respecter of Persons, but equally loves his whole Creation ...
("True Levellers Standard Advanced" 1649, p. 7)

By May the occupation had become a village with families, dwellings, gardens, and livestock. Through the next year at least ten similar groups took over wasteland and commons in the south Midlands.[9]

We see in this first Digger pamphlet evidence that in seventeenth-century England, human beings were not necessarily persons, as they are generally taken to be now. People were not born persons but might become persons, depending on their acquisition of legal status and property rights. Property-less people were not persons at all. Clearly, this was not a mere quirk of legal terminology with no currency among common people. Common people knew they were not persons, and some of them, like the Diggers, not only did not aspire to be, but actively opposed the status of personhood altogether.

The claim that God is "no respecter of Persons" recurs in Digger pamphlets, as well as in Gerard Winstanley's 1652 monograph *The Law of Freedom* (Winstanley 1973, p. 283). The phrase comes from the 1611 King James translation of the Bible, where it occurs in the Acts of the Apostles 10:34–35: "Then Peter opened his mouth and said, Of a truth I perceive that God is no respecter of persons: but in every nation he that feareth him, and worketh righteousness, is accepted with him". Here Peter is preaching in the house of the Gentile Cornelius to a non-Jewish gathering. He is emphasizing that God does not favor any one nation over any other. The phrase in question is a translation from the Greek προσωπολημπτήσ [prosopoletes], which comes from προσωπολεμια [prosopolemia], commonly translated subsequently as *partiality*.[10] God shows no partiality; regardless of nationality, all are equal before God. But in the English of the seventeenth and eighteenth centuries (the phrase is retained in the 1769 King James translation), recognition of equality precludes recognition of persons. Clearly, personhood is understood in these texts as a classification of human being that excludes many people, including the impoverished authors of Diggers pamphlets. The Diggers were not persons, nor were they respecters of those who were.

The meaning of personhood is still contested today, as we know from abortion and end-of-life debates and some discussions of animal rights. But most of the time, we use the word as a synonym for human being. Personhood's history, however, ties it very closely to the ownership of property, including the ownership of human beings. As Section 6 will show, the Diggers' use of the term is continuous with that history.

5. A Brief Sketch of the Genealogy of Seventeenth Century Personhood

The True Levellers' conception of personhood was no anomaly. In the 1640s, personhood—or, more appropriately, its lineage—was already close to two thousand years old, and at least some of that lineage was common knowledge, as the True Levellers' pamphlets show. Personhood was a legal and social status designed to exclude and deprive many people of land and freedom. It was a tool of oppression. This section outlines a story of how it came to be so, of how seventeenth-century personhood was constructed.

---

[9] Hill informs us that the Diggers of 1649 were not the first to be so named. There had been a Digger (as well as a Leveller) movement in 1607. They opposed the enclosure movement. See (Hill 1972, pp. 117–18).

[10] Interestingly, this passage is not rendered in this way in the earlier Tyndale translation, which was begun in 1522, finished in 1524, and revised in 1534 and 1536. In that translation, God is simply not "parciall". The Revised Standard Version does not include the phrase, nor does any other translation I have come across except the Amplified translation of 1965. The Saint Joseph edition of the New American Bible (revised, 2010), for example, translates the passage thusly: Then Peter proceeded to speak and said, 'In truth, I see that God shows no partiality. Rather, in every nation whoever fears him and acts uprightly is acceptable to him". I am very grateful to my colleague Dr. Julie Laskaris for tremendous help in identifying these and other Greek sources and English translations.

The word *person* comes from the Etruscan *phersu*, which meant mask. In a famous (though dated) article on the concept of person, anthropologist Marcel Mauss asserts that there is some evidence that the Etruscan word is a garbled version of a Greek word for mask, πρόσωπον [prosopon] (Mauss 1985, p. 274).[11] Although in Homer the word πρόσωπον means face or countenance, by the fourth century BCE it did mean mask or portrait.[12] In any case, the Romans apparently absorbed the Etruscan word rather than the Greek into Latin as *persona*, also meaning mask or role or, sometimes, the wearer of the mask and player of the role. By the third century BCE, Roman grammarians were using the term *persona* to indicate different categories of pronoun—our first person plural, third person singular, etc.[13] Over the next two or three centuries, the word's meaning expanded considerably; *personae* came to designate not only categories of pronoun and theatrical roles, but social roles as well. One could be a son, a father, a military officer, a priest, etc. Such "roles" brought with them sets of duties, expectations, and privileges. Each individual might have several *personae*, and the number could increase or decrease as one's circumstances changed.

Cicero's *De Officiis* (*On Duties*) provides insight into its broadened philosophical meaning. There Cicero explains that everyone has a rational *persona*, which distinguishes human beings from "brute creatures". Here we see *persona* indicating something a bit more substantial than a changeable social role. In addition, each of us has an individual *persona* that distinguishes us from each other (Cicero 1991, p. 42). This latter seems to involve basic bodily and mental dispositions that might be referred to colloquially as one's "temperament" or "nature". A well-lived life involves expression of the common *persona*, the rational, but also the expression of the particular *persona*. Cicero also attributes two other types of *personae* to human individuals. One type includes that which one takes on in consequence of chance occurrences or contingent circumstances, and these may be multiple and shifting. The other includes those that we acquire as the result of our decisions. "Kingdoms, military powers, nobility, political honours, wealth and influence, as well as the opposites of these, are in the gift of chance and governed by circumstances. In addition, assuming a role [*persona*] that we want ourselves is something that proceeds from our own will; as a consequence, some people apply themselves to philosophy, others to civil law, and others again to oratory, while even in the case of the virtues, different men prefer to excel in different of them" (Cicero 1991, p. 45). In the Latin of Cicero's time, in sum, the individual was not a person; the individual was many persons (and presumably also exceeded his or her many persons).

It makes sense, then, that when Tertullian (160–220 CE) began to set forth arguments for the unity of God and the embodied Christ and then later for the divine *trinitas* he used the language of *personae*. Just as one human being may have multiple *personae*, some emanating from his nature and others acquired or produced at identifiable historical moments, so too may one divine being have multiple *personae*. *Persona* here is no longer a mask that may conceal but is something more like an aspect or particular manifestation.[14]

Meanwhile, and not surprisingly given concerns like those of Cicero to determine which duties adhered to which *personae*, a close connection between *personae* and duties or offices shows up in Roman jurisprudence through the first few centuries of the Common Era. Again, we see a shift in the

---

[11] *Phersu* is the transliteration most common in dictionaries, but Mauss spells it *farsu*. He lists his source as Meillet and Ernout's *Dictionaire Etymologique*. He says that he learned of the possible derivation from the older Greek word in a personal communication with M. Benveniste. See (Mauss 1985, p. 274).

[12] My source for this Greek etymological history is my colleague Dr. Erika Zimmerman Damer, personal communication, 7 August 2012.

[13] These grammatical categories correspond to the rules of ancient theatre. No matter how many characters there were in a play, there was only three actors, so there were never more than three characters on stage at a time. The first person was the actor/character who spoke first. The second person was the actor/character to whom the first person spoke. The third person was the actor/character about whom the first two spoke.

[14] Esposito (following the work of Adriano Prosperi) suggests that a significant moment of "integration between representation and reality" occurs in rituals involving death masks. Waxen masks were made of the faces of the deceased, preserving the "true face" in the mask. See (Esposito 2012b, pp. 75–76).

term's extension. Jurists' were concerned not so much with analyzing the various *personae* that one individual might have but, rather, with distributing or withholding rights to Rome's subjects based on their status within the Empire.

The word *persona* received a decisive and enduring legal meaning when Justinian undertook to revise and streamline the Roman codes with his *Institutes* in 535. Classicist J. B. Moyle discusses Justinian's and other Roman jurists' use of the term in his Introduction to Book I of the Latin edition of 1912.

> What did the Romans mean by 'persona'? It is clear there is some relation between persona and homo: for the leading division of the 'ius quod ad personas pertinet' (i.3.pr.) is that all men are either free or slaves. It is equally clear that they did not regard all men as persons; it is not said all persons, but all *men* are either free or slaves. [...] An essential element in the conception of 'persona' is the capacity of acquiring or possessing legal rights, and ... a slave could have no legal rights of any kind whatsoever. In other words, a persona is a man regarded as invested with legal rights, or as capable of acquiring them, so that our attention is drawn away from the man to the rights, or to the capacity of having them in virtue of which he is a persona. (Justinian 1912, pp. 85–86).[15]

By this point, depending on discursive context, not only was it possible for one human being to have several *personae*; it was also possible for some human beings to have no *persona* at all.

Commenting on Justinian's *Institutes*, Italian political philosopher Roberto Esposito writes, "[N]o one in Rome was a full-fledged person from the beginning of life nor did one remain a person forever. Some became persons, as *filii* became *patres*; others were excluded because they were prisoners of war or were debtors" (Esposito 2012a, p. 24).[16] An individual could be and then not be a person of one sort or another several times throughout life. As one's status changed, so did one's legal rights. But, Esposito maintains, the only way that some individuals could be legal persons at any time was for others not to be, either some of the time or all of the time. "A category defined in juridical terms, no matter how broad, becomes meaningful only thanks to the comparison and indeed the opposition with another category from which all other categories are excluded" (Esposito 2012a, p. 23). The function of the Roman category was, therefore, as much to depersonalize as it was to personalize. As a legal category, person functioned to preclude general, human equality. Acquisition of the status "person" brought with it rights denied to the vast majority of people.

This Roman concept of personhood as an exclusive status was retained in the natural rights tradition through the Middle Ages and Renaissance. English jurists and political philosophers of the seventeenth century were steeped in it.[17] As the Diggers well knew, personhood was still an exclusive category during the English Civil Wars.

Who were persons in seventeenth-century England? As we have seen, Diggers' pamphlets consistently denounce the landed gentry, whose rights and privileges over the common people they traced to the Norman Conquest. Their second pamphlet, issued 1 June 1649, in response to landowners' attacks, opens with these lines:

---

[15] Moyle's translation of the relevant passages in Justinian can be found in (Justinian 1912, pp. 7–9).

[16] For more extensive discussion of this point, see (Esposito 2012b, pp. 76–80).

[17] Esposito offers a few examples: "If, in the mid-sixteenth century, Hugues Doneau (Donellus, 1517–1591) noted that 'a slave is a man, not a person; man is term of nature, person is a term of civil law' (*servus homo est, non persona, homo naturae, persona iuris civilis vocabulum*), Hermann Woehl (Vulteius, 1565–1634) later limited personhood to 'a man possessing civil status, as it exists in the tribe, in personal freedom, in citizenship, and in the household' (*homo habens caput civile, quod positum est in tribus, in libertate, in civitate, in familia*). Finally, Arnold Vinnen (Vinnius, 1588–1657) brought the distinction to completion when he argued that 'a man is anyone for whom a human mind connects with a human body' (*homo dicitur cuicumque contingit in corpore human omens humana*), whereas 'a person is a man with a certain status, just as if he had been clothed in it' (*persona est homo statu quodam veluit indutus*). Not only is *homo*—the word generally reserved in Latin for a slave—not a *persona*; the word *persona* is the *terminus technicus* that separates the juridical capacity from the naturalness of the human being" (Esposito 2012b, p. 81).

We whose names are subscribed do in the name of all the poor oppressed people in England declare unto you that call yourselves lords of manors and lords of the land that in regard the King of righteousness, our maker, hath enlightened our hearts so far as to see that the earth was not made purposefully for you to be lords of it, and we to be your slaves, servants and beggars; but it was made to be a common livelihood to all, without respect of persons: and that your buying and selling of the fruits of it, one to another, is the cursed thing, and was brought in by war; which hath and still does establish murder and theft in the hands of some branches of mankind over others, which is the greatest outward burden and unrighteous power that the creation groans under. For the power of enclosing land and owning property was brought into the creation by your ancestors by the sword; which first did murder their fellow creatures, men, and after plunder or steal away their land, and left this land successively to you, their children. And therefore, though you did not kill or thieve, yet you hold that cursed thing in your hand by the power of the sword; and so you justify the wicked deeds of your fathers, and that sin of your fathers shall be visited upon the head of you and your children to the third and fourth generation, and longer too, till your bloody and thieving power be rooted out of the land. (Winstanley 1973, p. 99)

Forty-five men at St. George's Hill signed this Declaration, which ends by calling for a free commonwealth without division of land—a commonwealth where, consequently, there would be no persons.

Two other groups came in for strong criticism from the Diggers: lawyers, who charged exorbitant fees and conducted their legal business in Norman French, and clerics. Both groups were drawn from the landed gentry. The law of primogeniture precluded younger sons from inheriting their fathers' estates, so they were given Oxford educations and lucrative positions at court or in the national church hierarchy, positions that often brought with them land as well as income—in other words, property and personhood.

Parish priests were especially hated. Not only did they enforce the strictly hierarchical state religion at the local level, but they lived off the mandatory tithes of those who resided within their parishes. Many did no physical labor themselves, and quite a few neglected their official duties as well. The word *parson* actually derives from the same root as *person* and in the seventeenth century would have been pronounced and often spelled in the same way.[18] Not only is God no respecter of the distinction between commoners and lords of manors, then; he is also no respecter of parsons. No one is to be set above others. All are equal, and anyone who asserts otherwise offends against God, as is stated in the Epistle of James, 2:9: "But if ye have respect to persons, ye commit sin, and are convinced of the law as transgressors."

From the beginning, the persons in the vicinity of the Diggers' occupation at St. George's Hill were incensed. At first, landowners called upon military leaders to disperse the community, but after a brief investigation General Fairfax dismissed their concerns and told them to work through the courts. They did not follow this suggestion but instead launched a series of attacks against the colony, repeatedly pulling down huts, destroying crops, and killing animals. The Diggers responded by issuing their second pamphlet, just quoted, "A Declaration from the Poor oppressed People of England". In response to this declaration, landowners had the Diggers charged with trespass.

This legal action posed a new problem. In the 1640s it was not possible to enter a plea at court unless one hired an attorney; ordinary people (non-persons) could not simply appear and speak for themselves. Attorneys were expensive, however, and the Diggers despised them on principle, so they

---

[18] This would most likely be generally acknowledged, but for documentation, see (Maitland 1975, p. 226): "The thought that the 'parson' of a church was or bore the 'person' of the church was probably less distant from them than it is from us, for the two words long remained one word for the eye and for the ear".

did not hire one. As a result, they were sentenced without a hearing. They were fined ten pounds per man plus court costs, but of course they had no money, so their livestock were seized. Nevertheless the colony held its contested ground.

Landowners continued to press for decisive action to oust the occupation. In July of 1649 General Fairfax received instructions to arrest ringleader Winstanley to disperse the people by force. The group abandoned St. George's Hill and moved to Cobham Heath, but they were harassed there too, arrested, and fined. In November troops were called in, houses pulled down, crops destroyed, and participants beaten by landowners as soldiers stood by. Many Diggers were imprisoned. Similar events occurred at the other settlements through the spring of 1650, and by the beginning of 1651 the Digger movement was destroyed. That same year, Thomas Hobbes published *Leviathan*.

6. Hobbes' Solution to Instability: A Condition for Emergence of Modern Personhood

Hobbes had supported Charles I until his execution, after which he set his hopes on a reintroduction of the Stuart monarchy under the exiled Prince of Wales as Charles II. Like many of his contemporaries, though, he believed that what mattered most was unifying the country under a sovereign authority, however that could be brought about. A state would only have internal stability if there were a single or at least institutionally unified, supreme, well-armed, generally recognized legislative authority. Hobbes' solution to England's woes is the diametrical opposite of the Diggers'. Instead of the abolition of the legal person in favor of basic human equality, he describes and advocates for the creation of a sort of super-person to function as the repository of sovereignty, precisely in order to eradicate the natural equality that he believes leads to nothing but unending war.

Hobbes holds that people unite under an authority if and only if fear drives them to. They obey because the available alternatives put their lives and property at risk (either at the hands of that authority or at the hands of other people if that authority is undermined). He agrees with his sixteenth-century French predecessor Jean Bodin that sovereignty cannot be divided. A mixed system wherein the sovereign powers of legislation and execution are separated—as would take shape in Locke's *Second Treatise* and of course in the US Constitution—was untenable. It would never maintain internal stability, Hobbes believed, because people could play the components against one another. Since fear is the only thing that makes people governable, governmental unity and stability require that there be someone who is feared by everyone. That someone was, by definition, the sovereign, the source of legislation and the wielder of the sword of enforcement.

But Hobbes had to distinguish sovereign authority from tyranny. Otherwise the state and its laws would be, as anti-Norman radicals had long claimed (and as Foucault discusses at some length in "*Society Must Be Defended*"), nothing other than war by other means. To accomplish this, Hobbes needed a theory of representation, which he presents in *Leviathan*, chapter 16, entitled "Of Persons, Authors, and Things Personated". Here Hobbes undertakes to distinguish and clarify the concepts of person, actor, and author in order to explain how it is that an individual can be bound by a contract or covenant that his representative initiates. This is a necessary step in his argument that a multitude of individuals can be bound together into one person, that is, the sovereign, and bound to obey the sovereign's law.

Hobbes uses the ambiguity of the ancient notion of *persona* to explain the transfer of authority from one individual to another. What is transferred, he claims, is the personhood of one individual to another. He notes that the Latin word "signifies the *disguise* or *outward appearance* of a man, counterfeited on the stage, and sometimes more particularly that part of it which disguises the face, as a mask or vizard; and from the stage has been translated to any representer of speech and action, as well in tribunals as theaters. So that a *person* is the same that an *actor* is, both on the stage and in common conversation … " (Hobbes 1958, p. 132). There are two types of person, then, those who act on their own authority and who are thus both the owner of the action and the actor—these Hobbes calls natural persons—and those who act by prior covenant in the place of another, in which case the actor bears the personal authority of the owner but is a distinct individual—these Hobbes calls feigned or artificial persons. Personhood is a matter of authority, and in particular of the authority to make promises, covenants, or contracts. It is alienable and is not coextensive with selfhood or humanity.

To a great extent at least, Hobbes has in mind property owners and actions regarding property. He explicitly relates ownership of words and actions to ownership of goods and possessions (which he refers to in Latin as *dominus*), distinguishing the former as a type of ownership called authorship (Hobbes 1958, p. 133). In a case of authorized representation, the actor personates the owner or author, Hobbes says; the actor bears the person of the author, and, insofar as he does, he has the right to act. Persons are, quite simply, bearers of certain legal rights.

There are human beings without authority, human beings who are not "natural persons". Hobbes mentions "children, fools, and madmen" (Hobbes 1958, p. 134). Although they are not persons in themselves, the sovereign can authorize means by which they can be personated; the sovereign can create a person to act on their behalf. Hobbes notes, for example, that a legally authorized guardian can personate a child. This authorization does not confer personhood upon the child, however; it simply establishes a new "feigned" or "artificial" person borne by the guardian. Sovereign authority can create persons at will, wherever it sees a need for authorization to act. It can even cause inanimate objects to be personated. For example, Hobbes says, a rector can personate a church.[19] And it is easy to see how the currently controversial corporate person can arise. The sovereign power can grant the status of personhood—that is the authority and right to act—to groups of people united in a common enterprise. Corporate personhood did not begin with *Citizens United*; it stretches all the way back to Rome and was clearly recognized in English law. Corporations have virtually always been persons; it is people who are not always persons.

This power of civil law to grant authority for personation can even extend to the personating of non-existent things, Hobbes notes, such as the heathen personation of false gods. He is quick to assert, though, that Moses' personation of the One True God was duly authorized and nonfictional, and at that point in the text he digresses briefly into a discussion of the Doctrine of the Holy Trinity and the divine personhood of the Holy Spirit and Jesus Christ.

Hobbes' main purpose in chapter 16 is not to adumbrate an entire theory of personhood, however; as we have seen, the category was already well-established and generally accepted among his readership. Rather, it is to explain how a multitude of individuals can be unified under a single, undivided sovereign to establish civil authority in the first place. "A multitude of men are made *one* person when they are by one man or one person represented ... For it is the *unity* of the representer, not the *unity* of the represented, that makes the person *one*. And it is the representer that bears the person, and but one person ... " (Hobbes 1958, p. 135). This is the only way to establish security against foreign invasion and against injury by one's neighbors; everyone must "confer all their power and strength upon one man, or upon one assembly of men that may reduce all their wills, by plurality of voice, unto one will; which is to as much as to say, to appoint one man or assembly of men to bear their person ... " (Hobbes 1958, p. 142). This one person is Leviathan, who "has the use of so much power and strength conferred on him that, by terror thereof, he is enabled to form the wills of them all to peace at home and mutual aid against their enemies abroad" (Hobbes 1958, p. 143). Further, "he that carries this person is called SOVEREIGN and said to have *sovereign power*; and everyone besides, his SUBJECT" (Hobbes 1958, p. 143). This one sovereign person may be one individual or a collection of individuals as in a parliament. Hobbes discusses the advantages and disadvantages of each type of government, although he clearly favors the model of the single individual.

Regardless of the form it takes though, Hobbes insists, sovereignty once constituted cannot be challenged. Subjects are not to pass judgment on the decisions or actions of government, for subjection to a sovereign authority is incompatible with the exercise of personal judgment. Hobbes thus banishes

---

[19] Actually apparently there was a great deal of controversy over this in Hobbes' time having to do with the question of the status of a corporation sole. See (Maitland 1975, pp. 210–44).

private conscience from political life, calling the very idea "that every private man is judge of good and evil actions" a "disease of the commonwealth" proceeding "from the poison of seditious doctrines" (Hobbes 1958, p. 253). Whatever authority an individual might hold over his life and property was granted to him by the sovereign power and could always be revoked by it. Once sovereignty was established, all other legal and political authority—all other personhood—existed only by leave of that sovereign power.

Hobbes' absolutism did not prevail. But personhood as a conditional status dependent upon law remained, despite the Diggers' call for its abolition. No one who was not granted authority under the law was a person. And although over the succeeding four hundred years the law has in fact granted such authority to many more classes of people, including now even servants and day laborers, personhood remains a category of exclusion. Who or what is excluded from it is often a point of great controversy, but the fact that it excludes some human beings is uncontestable. The point of personhood has always been to demarcate. And—the mechanism of extended inclusion having been the liberal invention of property in one's body and in one's labor—the line of demarcation is still drawn where the law recognizes property and propriety. A person is a proprietor, if only of its flesh and energy, which is why human fetuses and nonhuman animals, for example, can be counted out.

In addition to this tight coupling of personhood and property, the close connection—amounting almost, though in the seventeenth century not quite yet an identification—of personhood with sovereignty has persisted as well. Hobbes to the contrary, sovereign power could be divided, late seventeenth and eighteenth-century thinkers maintained, and in fact it had to be divided in order to protect personal dominion, possession. In subsequent decades, not only did theorists and statesmen insist that sovereign power must be divided institutionally (between monarch and parliament, between houses of parliament, or in the United States between legislative and executive branches of government with various checks and balances built in), but they began to view the power that an author-actor, a person, withheld from government, which constituted the so-called private sphere, as that person's dominion. This limit to sovereign government suggested to subsequent thinkers that powers retained by individual persons were themselves sovereign powers.

At the close of the seventeenth century, John Locke avoided referring to individuals as sovereign; sovereignty arose in social contract as it had in Hobbes' view. Nevertheless, Locke's account of property in the body coupled with his carefully argued account of personal identity in the 1694 edition of *An Essay Concerning Human Understanding* paved the path that Hobbes' work indicated. Locke extended personhood—precisely as individual proprietorship—to almost all human beings, thus saving it from the True Levellers' challenge. In the process, he created a new way in which human beings would be made subjects of law and morality; as persons—that is, as consciousnesses—they would be owners of their acts and ideas and accountable for them to law and God. With the American and French Revolutions in the following century, however, governmental sovereignty underwent transformation; revolutionaries proclaimed the possibility of government of the people, by the people. As people assumed this new responsibility, it became possible to imagine even the individual person as a self-governing unit. It was almost inevitable, thereafter, that such beings would be identified explicitly as sovereigns, as they were at least by the early nineteenth century and have been since.[20]

7. Life beyond Personhood?

Near-sovereign personhood having been conferred upon us all—even us women, servants, and day laborers—we bear tremendous moral responsibility, but without the material independence for much, if any, genuine authority. This, I think, explains a great deal of present-day political and moral cynicism and ethical anguish. Take me, for example: I want to save the polar bears, but I am

---

[20] The "sovereign individual" is the center of a set of works by American utopian thinkers Josiah Warren and Stephen Pearl Andrews by the 1840s. See especially (Warren 1852; Andrews 1853).

part of a gigantic economic system that will eventually kill them all. Not only can I not save them from suffering and extinction, but I cannot even seem to disengage myself from that system so that I am not one of their killers. Against my will, I have polar bear blood on my hands—as well as the blood of child laborers, coal miners, migrant workers whose flesh is burned with chemical pesticides, and would-be immigrants dead in the deserts or shot at the borders of this great country of mine.

I find this intolerable. Equally intolerable is the idea that I should just accept my impotence, accept the reality that a truly ethical life is out of my reach. No. There has to be another way to think, another way to live.

"In political thought and analysis, we still have not cut off the head of the king", Foucault declared (Foucault 1978, p. 89), and he intimated that our failure to perform this conceptual regicide results in a fundamental inability to comprehend the relations and networks of power that constrain us and give shape to our world. As long we keep the concept of sovereignty at the fore, we maintain ourselves in political ignorance. And there are forces that reinforce that ignorance and keep us focused on the same futile issues and concerns. Government is not a matter of sovereignty, Foucault insists. Government is not even a matter of the State, although the last several centuries have seen a massive "statification" of governmentality. If we want to understand our present circumstances, we must rethink power without the king; we must rethink government without the state. And I believe we must likewise rethink ethics without the person.

I do not propose that we all go out and occupy the commons, although I did cheer on the people around the world who did something very like that around the world in 2011 and in North Dakota in 2016. I do not think the solution to global economic and environmental crises is to establish egalitarian agricultural communities without private ownership of land. I turn to the Diggers not because their material practices would work for us but because their undertaking proves that ethical non-personhood is possible. True Levellers could and did imagine and enact a way of life without personhood. Perhaps we could do so as well, if we could loosen the hold that personhood has on our self-understanding. Obviously, that is not easily done. Kant drew the line very starkly: If you are not a person, a being with dignity, then you are a thing, a chattel that can be bought and sold. We neoliberal self-entrepreneurs, we day laborers and servants, live very, very close to that line as it is; none of us wants to stray across it. To do so would be to cede our ownership of our selves.

What I propose, then, is dangerous. But everything is dangerous. All we can do is assess the current dangers and plunge ahead, one way or another. The greater danger for us lies, I think, in continuing to try to live the intolerable or in abandoning the ethical altogether to save ourselves from unending moral anguish. I do not yet see how to construct an ethical way of life in a globalized, neoliberal capitalist world; such a life can only be constructed in the living. But I believe the foregoing genealogical analysis demonstrates that personhood is a major component of the trap we find ourselves in. Foucault developed genealogical practice as a means of prying apart the jaws of such traps, loosening at least to some degree their hold on our lives. I hope that a genealogy of personhood can serve as a first step not toward losing ourselves but toward getting free of ourselves, free for lives beyond personhood and for selves that we have yet to imagine.

Conflicts of Interest: The author declares no conflict of interest.

References

Andrews, Stephen Pearl. 1853. Love, Marriage, and Divorce and the Sovereignty of the Individual. Available online: http://praxeology.net/HJ-HG-SPA-LMD.htm (accessed on 18 November 2017).

Church, William Farr. 1969. *Constitutional Thought in Sixteenth-Century France: A Study in the Evolution of Ideas.* New York: Octagon Books.

Cicero, Marcus Tullius. 1991. *On Duties.* Edited by M. T. Griffin and E. M. Atkins. Cambridge: Cambridge University Press.

Esposito, Roberto. 2012a. The *Dispositif* of the Person. *Law, Culture and the Humanities* 8: 17–30. [CrossRef]

Esposito, Roberto. 2012b. *Third Person: Politics of Life and Philosophy of the Impersonal*. Translated by Zakiya Hanafi. Malden: Polity Press.

Fairfield, Paul. 2000. *Moral Selfhood in the Liberal Tradition: The Politics of Individuality*. Toronto: University of Toronto Press.

Foucault, Michel. 1978. *The History of Sexuality, Volume 1: An Introduction*. Translated by Robert Hurley. New York: Random House.

Hill, Christopher. 1972. *The World Turned Upside Down: Radical Ideas during the English Revolution*. New York: Penguin.

Hobbes, Thomas. 1958. *Leviathan, Part I and II*. Edited by Herbert W. Schneider. Indianapolis: The Bobbs-Merrill Co., Inc.

Justinian. 1912. *Imperatoris Iustiniani Institutiones*, 5th ed. Edited by J. B. Moyle. Oxford: Oxford University Press.

Lavin, Chad. 2008. *The Politics of Responsibility*. Urbana: University of Illinois Press.

Maitland, Frederic William. 1975. *The Collected Papers of Frederic William Maitland, Downing Professor of the Laws of England*. Edited by Herbert Albert L. Fisher. Tokyo: Logos, vol. III. This book is a reprint of a 1911 publication by Cambridge University Press.

Mauss, Marcel. 1985. A category of the human mind: the notion of person; the notion of self. In *The Category of the Person: Anthropology, Philosophy, History*. Translated by W. D. Halls. Edited by Michael Carrithers, Steven Collins and Steven Lukes. Cambridge: Cambridge University Press, First published 1938.

Warren, Josiah. 1852. Equitable Commerce: A Development of New Principles as Substitutes for Laws and Governments, for the Harmonious Adjustment and Regulation of the Pecuniary, Intellectual, and Moral Intercourse of Mankind Proposed as Elements of a New Society. Available online: http://dwardmac.pitzer.edu/anarchist_archives/bright/warren/equcom.pdf (accessed on 16 August 2017).

Winstanley, Gerrard. 1973. *The Law of Freedom and Other Writings*. Edited by Christopher Hill. New York: Penguin Books. First Published 1652.

genealogy

MDPI

Article

Heroes and Cowards: Genealogy, Subjectivity and War in the Twenty-First Century

Peter Lee

Department of Strategy, Enterprise and Innovation, University of Portsmouth, Portsmouth PO1 3DE, UK;
peter.lee@port.ac.uk

Received: 17 March 2018; Accepted: 17 April 2018; Published: 27 April 2018

Abstract: From the wars of Ancient Greece to the collapsing Islamic State in the present, the same, apparently timeless protagonists appear and their stories told and re-told: the heroes, cowards and other combatants. This article proposes a framework which combines a Foucauldian genealogical approach with his conception of the subject as both constituted in relation to code-oriented moralities, and creatively self-formed in relation to ethics-oriented moralities (Foucault 1992, pp. 5, 25), to understand how it is possible to speak meaningfully of heroes and cowards in the age of the drone and the jihadist. Section one will explore the applicability of Foucauldian genealogy as the methodological basis for understanding present combatants in the context of war. The second section will assess Foucault's 'modes of subjectivation' and 'practices of the self' (Foucault 1992, p. 28), as a means of analyzing the emergence of the subject of war over millennia, with emphasis on the ethical dimension of subjectivity that can be applied to heroes and cowards. Then the third section will use insights from Homer and Augustine to begin to illustrate how Foucault's genealogical approach and his conception of ethical subjectivity combine to enable heroes and cowards to be meaningfully spoken of and better understood in the domain of war today. The purpose of such a study is to set out the basis on which political genealogy after Foucault can provide a nuanced conceptualization of subjectivity in modern war, as those subjects are formed, claimed, valorized and criticized by competing entities in contemporary political discourse.

Keywords: war; genealogy; Foucault; subjectivity; drone; soldier; jihadist

---

1. Introduction

From Afghanistan to Somalia, and from Ukraine to the Philippines, twenty-first century wars are combining new technologies with old practices: terrorism, insurgency, jihad, guerrilla warfare, ethnic conflict, civil war, proxy war, revolution, religious war, and more (Mumford 2013; Hughes 2014; Miller 2013; Cockburn 2015; Coyle 2017). It is common for these different types of warfare to exhibit a number of features, including: first, a desire on the part of political leaders—of governments or groups—to acquire and maintain popular support for the wars they are pursuing; second, for militaries, militias and informal fighting groups to maintain morale and effectiveness; and third, a desire to undermine an enemy's popular support, will to fight, and effectiveness. Just as the gods of Olympus have given way to new gods, and none, old ways of war continually give way to the new. So it is, also, with the stories of war: tales of war that were once captured on papyrus which would last for millennia are now shared on social media in a twenty-four hour news cycle.

At the core of war, however, from Ancient Greece to the collapsing Islamic State in the present, apparently timeless protagonists appear and their stories told and re-told: heroes, cowards and others. Consider some 'cowards' in contemporary political discourse. Journalist George Monbiot has described America's use of drones as 'fighting a coward's war' (Monbiot 2012). Meanwhile, a separate report speaks of 'ISIS cowards' running for shelter in order to escape the same kind of drone that Monbiot criticized as cowardly (Brown 2015). In 2017, the Afghanistan President Ashraf Ghani described the killing by suicide bomber 90 people in Kabul as 'cowardly' (BBC 2017). The common factor here is constituting the Other as 'coward' or 'cowardly' in relation to some act of violence—usually against noncombatants—and against some ethical standard or other.

This article proposes a framework which combines a Foucauldian genealogical approach with his conception of the subject as both constituted in relation to code-oriented moralities, and creatively self-formed in relation to ethics-oriented moralities (Foucault 1992, pp. 5, 25), to understand how it is possible to speak meaningfully of heroes and cowards in the age of the drone and the jihadist. The next section will explore the applicability of Foucauldian genealogy as the methodological basis for understanding a history of present combatants in the context of war[1]. The third section will assess Foucault's 'modes of subjectivation' and 'practices of the self' (Foucault 1992, p. 28), as a method for analyzing the emergence of the subject of war over millennia, with emphasis on the ethical dimension of subjectivity that can be applied to soldiers, jihadists and drone operators today. Then the fourth section will use insights from Homer and Augustine to begin to illustrate how Foucault's genealogical approach and his conception of ethical subjectivity combine to enable heroes and cowards to be meaningfully spoken of and better understood in the domain of war today. Homer and Augustine have been chosen as the starting point for discussion because they each make a distinct, essential contribution to any genealogy of the hero and the coward in modern war. Homer's Achilles has been portrayed as the archetypal military hero throughout the Western history of war, while Augustine—through his just war writings—added an essential ethical dimension to conduct in war that is still present in 'hero' and 'coward' discourses today. The purpose of such a study is to show how political genealogy after Foucault can open up a conceptual space that will provide a more nuanced understanding of subjectivity in modern war, as those subjects are formed, claimed, valorized and criticized by competing entities in contemporary political discourse.

2. Genealogy, Subjectivity and War

War is one of the oldest and most recorded of human activities. Poets, writers and dramatists have made immortals of those who have led and fought in epic battles throughout the ages. From Thucydides' *History of the Peloponnesian War* and Homer's *Iliad* to the *Band of Brothers* made famous in Steven Spielberg's television series, the traits and achievements of heroes and warriors are lauded (Thucydides and Finley 1972; Homer 2017; Ambrose 2017). As much as they are history, these texts and countless others are also concerned with the formation of subjectivity in war as a particular domain of moral experience. Despite the historical, geographic, cultural and linguistic distance between us, the modern reader, and the subjects of those texts, somehow our discursive glimpses of them still hold meaning. Partial meaning, even changing meaning, but meaning all the same. As McWhorter points out, 'Human subjectivity is an historical and always less than complete and stable achievement' (McWhorter 2017, p. 1). This is as true of the subject of war as it is in the emergence of sovereign personhood that McWhorter discusses.

Foucault's genealogical exploration of the ethics of the self in *The Use of Pleasure and The Care of the Self*, offer one means of enabling us to understand how subjectivity has been constituted and re-constituted in war over time (Foucault 1992, 1990). After exploring the relevance of Foucauldian genealogy as the methodological basis of this paper, Foucault's method for engaging with the ethics of the self in the domain of war will be explored in the next section. Such a genealogical approach will demonstrate how the formation of the hero or coward as ethical or unethical subjects of war in the present relies upon—and is continuous with—aspects of subjectivity that emerged in in the past.

---

[1] This paper draws on concepts and material initially developed in my doctoral thesis, 'A Genealogy of the Ethical Subject in the Just War Tradition' (Lee 2010).

In addition, genealogy shows that contemporary constitution and self-constitution of the subject of war *excludes* aspects of ethical subjectivity from the past.

For Foucault, genealogy is 'a matter of analysing, not behaviours or ideas, nor societies and their "ideologies," but the *problematizations* through which being offers itself to be, necessarily, thought—and the *practices* on the basis of which these problematizations are formed' (Foucault 1992, p. 11, *original italics*). The problematizations identified for further discussion in this paper are the 'hero' and 'coward'. Not the apparently consistent characters who bestride history, but subjects who embody distinct ways of being—attitudes of existence—in every age, often as idealized subjects who somehow represent the best and worst of their particular societies. In problematizing heroes and cowards, Foucauldian genealogy is interested in how these subjectivities are formed out of the past. For Foucault, such an approach provides 'a form of history that can account for the constitution of knowledges, discourses, domains of objects, and so on, without having to make reference to a subject that is either transcendental in relation to the field of events or runs its empty sameness throughout the course of history' (Foucault 2002, p. 115). He is not prescriptive about how such a genealogy should be undertaken and leaves open endless possibilities for the researcher. But he also makes clear that a genealogical approach to history is not some quest for a mythic source of a particular idea, theory or knowledge:

> Genealogy does not oppose itself to history as the lofty and profound gaze of the philosopher might compare to the mole-like perspective of the scholar; on the contrary, it rejects the metahistorical deployment of ideal significations and indefinite teleologies. It opposes itself to the search for "origins" (Foucault 1977, p. 140)

Rejection of a 'search for origins' by Foucault appears counterintuitive in genealogical terms. However, it is a specific type of 'origin' that he rejects: the 'apocalyptic objectivity' of the historian who seeks, or claims, to stand 'outside of time' (Foucault 1977, p. 152). Instead, Foucault sees genealogy in subjective terms, viewing and recording the history of humanity: 'the history of morals, ideals, and metaphysical concepts' (Foucault 1977, p. 152). His genealogy seeks '"effective" history [which] differs from traditional history in being without constants' because of the subjective focus of his work (Foucault 1977, p. 153). Edmonds summarises: 'Genealogy is therefore both *effective* and *affective* history; it is an attempt to transform one's habits through the study of history' (Edmonds 2011, p. 48). Note that the subjective element is synonymous with Foucault's genealogy. Carabine's application of a Foucauldian conception of genealogy suggests that it 'is concerned with describing the procedures, practices, apparatuses and institutions involved in the production of discourses and knowledges, and their power effects' (Carabine 2001, p. 275–76). The ethical subject—the individual—is constituted and self-constituting within those discourses, knowledges and power effects. However, there is no originary, exemplar subject to whom the (Foucauldian) genealogist can look for answers. Each is constituted in discourse, emerging in her or his social, cultural and historical context. McWhorter makes the point more elegantly: 'A genealogy casts personhood, on the contrary, as an historically emergent category rather than an ontological fact. By investigating the conditions of its emergence, genealogy exposes personhood's entanglements with networks of power' (McWhorter 2017, p. 3).

Dreyfus and Rabinow describe their own understanding of the functioning of a Foucauldian genealogy as follows: 'Genealogy seeks out discontinuities where others found progress and seriousness. It records the past of mankind to unmask the solemn hymns of progress. Genealogy avoids the search for depth. Instead, it seeks the surfaces of events, small details, minor shifts, and subtle contours' (Dreyfus et al. 1983, p. 106). Certain assumptions are enshrined in such a genealogical approach. The discontinuities mentioned here by Dreyfus and Rabinow indicate Foucault's rejection of natural, or inevitable, development within human experience. Foucault rejects the validity of 'writing a history of the past in terms of the present', seeing relevance instead in 'writing the history of the present' (Foucault 1995, p. 31). He is not looking back through time and asking what happened in the past: he is looking at the present and asking how this particular present became possible.

Where genealogy seeks out the emergence of the ethical subject of war—such as the hero or coward—a number of assumptions apply. The first is that any truth or knowledge claims pertaining to that ethical subject of war are historically situated, constituted in relations of power within multiple social, cultural, institutional and religious discourses. In the West, the dominant discourses have been located in the just war tradition. Second, morality itself—as applied to the subject of war—is contingent upon, and subject to, prevailing, transient ontological and epistemological conditions. Third, subjectivity is similarly contingent and non-essential, with subjectivation and self-subjectivation occurring within relations of power, shaped by code-oriented and ethics-oriented moralities. The emergent ethical subject of war is therefore not a fixed, or even an evolving entity; rather the subject is continually reproduced, located in a line of situated discourses. Having presented a Foucauldian genealogy as the methodological basis for understanding the coward or hero as subjects of war, the next section will propose a practical method to help us understand *how* the ethical subject of war has emerged in different ways throughout history. That discussion will draw upon Foucault's conception of the ethical subject as having both code-oriented and self-forming dimensions.

3. Foucault and Ethical Subjectivity

In 1981, Foucault stated: 'If one wants to analyze the genealogy of the subject in Western civilization, one must take into account not only techniques of domination but also techniques of the self. One must show the interaction between these types of technique' (Foucault 1997b, p. 177). We see here the profound link between genealogy and subjectivity in Foucault's later work. It is in his genealogy that Foucault studies 'the games of truth in the relation of the self with self and the forming of oneself as a subject' (Foucault 1992, p. 6). While individuals may create their own subjectivity through technologies of the self, it is within relations of power that particular subjects—such as the 'hero' or 'coward'—are constituted in discourse. Foucault's technologies of power and technologies of the self-operate along two trajectories that can never operate autonomously: external moral codes to which the subject is expected to conform and ethical self-subjectivication. Foucault says:

> If it is true, in fact that every morality, in the broad sense, comprises . . . codes of behavior and forms of subjectivication . . . then we should not be surprised to find in certain moralities the main emphasis is placed on the code . . . on the other hand it is easy to conceive of moralities in which the strong and dynamic element is to be sought in the forms of subjectivation and the practices of the self. (Foucault 1992, pp. 29–30)

Foucault sought to separate, at least theoretically, technologies of power and technologies of the self to assist in the analysis of their workings relative to moral codes and self-subjectivation. In exploring the emergence of the hero and the coward in war over time, genealogy offers the possibility of identity being formed and self-formed with different degrees of emphasis on codes and self-subjectivation. The next section will highlight how individuals have been incited to conduct themselves as particular kinds of subject of war, by conforming to codified morality. In addition, the extent to which individuals have created their own subjectivity in relation to ethical sources that operate somewhat independently from the moral code. For example, the pursuit of some greater good such as the upkeep of morale on the battlefield, self-sacrifice for a colleague under enemy fire, or the rescue of an innocent.

So, for Foucault, an ethic is associated with creative self-subjectivation on the part of the individual, and to help understand the concept in greater detail it will be helpful to clarify here the difference between his use of the terms 'ethical' and 'moral'. In his understanding of the morality of the classical Greeks, the Hellenic Romans and the early Christians, Foucault saw Greek behaviour as oriented towards individualized ethical practice, while later Romans and Christians employed practices that were designed to meet the obligations of a particular moral code: the moral code being the commonly accepted prohibitions, restrictions and interdictions that shape acceptable behaviour within a given culture. That is, *moral* pertains to accepted codes of behaviour, while *ethical* concerns the individual's choices, conduct and self-subjectivation that may or may not relate to that code. Just war is one example of a codified approach to the conduct of war that has emerged in the West over many centuries (Walzer 2003); a chivalric code would be another (Kaeuper 2016).

The relation to oneself is broken down by Foucault into what he describes as four aspects of subjectivation. In an interview with Rabinow in 1983 Foucault explains these four aspects—the method employed in his subsequently published book The Use of Pleasure—as follows:

> The relationship to oneself has four major aspects. The first aspect answers the question:
> Which is the part of myself or my behavior which is concerned with moral conduct? . . .
> The second aspect is what I call the mode of subjectivication [*mode d'assujettissement*], that
> is, the way in which people are invited or incited to recognize their moral obligations . . .
> The third one is: What are the means by which we can change ourselves in order to become
> ethical subjects? . . . The fourth aspect is: Which is the kind of being to which we aspire
> when we behave in a moral way? (Foucault 1997a, pp. 263–65)

These questions were originally raised in relation to the desiring subject within Classical Greek, Greco-Roman and early Christian cultures. However, Foucault's priority was not on an understanding of sex itself but in the broader issue of the self as subject. In the same interview he comments: 'I am much more interested in problems about techniques of the self and things like that than sex . . . sex is boring' (Foucault 1997a, p. 253). Applying a version of Foucault's four aspects of the techniques of the self can provide greater insight into the ethical subjectivity of the protagonists of war in this paper.

Foucault's describes his four aspects of the relationship to the self as follows. In his first aspect: 'Which is the part of myself or my behavior which is concerned with moral conduct?' (Foucault 1997a, p. 263), Foucault offers examples such as Kant's idealized insistence on right intentions, a contemporary view (from 1983) that feelings guide our moral conduct, while also identifying a Christian view that desire, or perhaps more accurately the struggle against desire, governs moral behaviour. For Foucault, these aspects of the self are a manifestation of the individual's 'ethical substance' (Foucault 1997a, p. 263). This ontological statement assumes that individuals possess a thing called 'ethical substance'. This paper proposes that this concept can be extended further, not settling for a single ethical substance but recognizing that individuals draw upon a range of ethical potentialities within the broad understanding of ethical substance.

For the second aspect Foucault asks how people are 'invited or incited to recognize their moral obligations', in what he calls the 'mode of subjectivation' that acts upon the ethical subject (Foucault 1997a, p. 264). He cites the example of Nicocles, ruler of Cyprus, whose moral obligation stemmed from his desire to maintain a certain position in society, as opposed to his adoption of a certain (in this case Stoic) set of ideological obligations. A Foucauldian genealogy focuses on the specific and situated—as seen in this example of King Nicocles. The difficulty with, or weakness in, this approach is found in the essence of society and social life itself: it is not a vacuum or controlled setting where the subject is acted upon by only one variable or one mode of subjectivation at a time. This leaves the subject in tension when confronted by multiple modes of subjectivation. Further, these competing modes may be promoted by groups or individuals with asymmetric power bases.

It is not possible to isolate aspects of the individual's relationship to herself or himself from the societal power dynamics to which she or he is constantly exposed. At the extreme, if the asymmetric power relation reaches a point of absolute domination, the subject cannot be called heroic—or even ethical—since there is no creative freedom to choose that mode of being. For example, in 2008, two suicide bombers in Iraq were reported to be 'Down's syndrome women', and that their bombs had been set off by remote control (Howard 2008). In this instance, potentially at least, any lack of understanding of the nature or consequences of the actions they were about to undertake, or inability to refuse, would render the women as ethically neutral. They could not be either heroic, cowardly or martyrs: they were used in a relationship of domination for the ends of the individual or group that is morally responsible for the act and its commission. Foucault insists: 'Freedom is the ontological condition of ethics' (Foucault 1997d, p. 284). With no freedom of choice, these particular suicide bombers could act neither ethically nor unethically.

Thirdly, Foucault asks: 'What are the means by which we can change ourselves in order to become ethical subjects (Foucault 1997a, p. 265)? This, for him, is '*asceticism* in a very broad sense' (Foucault 1997a, p. 265). This concerns an individual's choice of actions as she or he constitutes herself or himself as heroic though some form of ethical behaviour. Such an action goes beyond conforming to a certain law and the corresponding moral code of which it is a part; it is a deliberate choice of action intended to produce behaviour that the individual sees as ethical. For example, if a soldier wishes to form herself or himself as an ethical subject in time of war she or he may opt to comply with the Geneva Conventions and the military Rules of Engagement set out for that particular theatre of operations. However, in the course of a particular military engagement that soldier may be presented with a situation where in order to save the life of a wounded colleague or civilian noncombatant, she or he must risk her or his own life—opening the possibility of heroism or cowardice, depending on the actions undertaken. This, in turn, might be prompted by some religious experience, or by a response to the familial bonds that are frequently alluded to in close fighting units, or as a means of demonstrating goodness in a domain of death and destruction.

Finally, the fourth aspect asks: 'Which is the kind of being to which we aspire when we behave in a moral way?' (Foucault 1997a, p. 265). He expands on this question, offering examples such as a desire to 'become pure, or immortal, or free, or masters of ourselves, and so on ... that's what I call the telos [*téléologie*]' (Foucault 1997a, p. 265). Foucault elaborates little on this aspirational aspect of self-constitution as an ethical subject. It may even be a principle that is not accessible to every subject, since some may be constrained by power relations at work, while others may be limited by personal circumstance and actual, or perceived, limitations on choice. To continue the example from the previous paragraph, for the soldier who risks death to save a colleague, the ultimate *telos* of that individual may be to live up to some military code of honour, or to know that when faced with death she or he was able to conquer fear in an act of self-mastery, or with the intention of winning a medal.

Consider the following variations of Foucault's questions as they relate to the four aspects of creative self-forming as an ethical subject of war on the part of the hero or coward. First, which part of myself or my behaviour in the domain of war or political violence is concerned with moral conduct? Personal moral motivations could include: pacifist, non-violent belief; religious piety; a moral upbringing; or self-preservation. Second, how are individuals incited or invited to recognize particular moral obligations in war? For example, what was said to soldiers in a trench on the Western Front in World War One to prompt them to walk forward into near-certain death? What are suicide bombers taught before they self-destruct in the presence of innocent passers-by? The third aspect asks: how should a person behave in order to become ethical? Walking into a hail of bullets; detonating a suicide vest in a market place or a concert hall full of children; confronting a killer? Fourth, what is the ultimate goal of the ethical subject? A peaceful world; a place in heaven or Paradise; a safe society?

To conduct a genealogy of the hero or coward as ethical subject of war, these questions must be asked, repeatedly, about actors at different points in time and across cultures and continents. The answers—such as they might be—lie in the available discourses that have survived: writings, artefacts, pictures, and other fragments from the past. While the parameters of such a genealogy can be specified, and the outline briefly sketched out in this paper, the span of a comprehensive analysis will necessarily be much more extensive than can be achieved here. In order to explore the Foucauldian-based four aspects of subjectivity set out above in relation to the hero or coward, sample relevant texts can be interrogated as follows. First, what are the sources that the various writers draw upon in writing about war and constructing the subject of war in discourse? Why have these sources been chosen in the cultural and social contexts in which the authors are writing? Second, how do the different writers constitute their specific codes around war—especially the moral dimension? Within the moral codes, why would the heroic or cowardly subject choose to act ethically? That is, given the range of behaviours available to the subject, what motivates the individual to make particular moral, heroic or cowardly, choices in relation to war? Third, what are the consequences or rewards for the individual when she or he chooses to act, or not act, heroically in relation to war? Finally, what kind of subject does the individual hope to be in acting in a particular way regarding the conduct of war?

In the section to follow, a brief genealogical sketch of the emergent ethical aspect of the subjectivity of the combatant over time, will illustrate how they can only be meaningfully spoken of as heroes or cowards today by accepting certain continuities and discontinuities with the past. This, however, is only the beginnings of a genealogy, which would take an entire volume—or volumes—to fully explore.

4. Forming and Self-Forming the Subject of War

To better understand the hero as ethical subject of war in the present, Foucauldian genealogy explores the emergence of the hero through multiple histories over time. The 'morals, ideals and metaphysical concepts' (Foucault 1977, p. 152) of the hero are sought out, drawing on Foucault's four aspects of subjectivity—initially in the original context of the historical analysis. Then, the emergence of the hero, as subject, is compared and contrasted over time and different contexts to identify continuities and discontinuities of understanding, of the ontological basis of heroism. Subsequently, continuities and discontinuities between past and present heroes as subjects of war provide greater, more nuanced understandings of what is meant—and not meant—when heroes are spoken of today. Consider, briefly, the emergence of the ethical subject of war in the writings of Homer and Augustine, the genealogical aspects of which include identifying both the basis of their approaches and the relationship between them as they inform the present.

4.1. Honour and Ethical Conduct in Homer's Iliad

Among scholars of Homer's *Iliad*, Adkins is strongly associated with placing 'honour' at the heart of the values that underpin both the poem and the heroic characters and society it constitutes (Adkins 1971, 1982). In his characterization of Achilles' heroism in the *Iliad*, Zanker sees cooperation between warriors as a locus of heroic behaviour. Zanker extends his argument further by introducing a 'justice-based' element of behaviour, 'whereby a hero may feel constrained by a sense of fair play, however defined,' and where 'an emotion like pity feeds into and conditions a degree of altruism' (Zanker 1996, p. 2). So we find that heroism, in the context of the Iliad, can survive a lack of pity, and a lack of altruism. When Achilles hears of the death of his beloved Patroclus at the hand of Hector the Trojan, his sense of vengeance can even be regarded as heroic. Before his final showdown with Achilles, Hector briefly considers approaching Achilles unarmed. However, he does not do so because 'if he approaches Achilles unarmed, Achilles will not pity or respect him but will kill him "like a woman"' (Adkins 1982, p. 314). So Achilles' apparent willingness to kill an unarmed man was still not considered sufficiently ignoble to cost him his hero status.

After killing Hector, 'High o'er the slain [Hector] the great Achilles stands' (Homer 2006, p. 658), again, Achilles does not choose a noble path. Achilles drags Hector's dead body behind a horse, denying him the honour of the glorious dead. Yet the status of 'hero' even survives Achilles degradation of Hector's corpse. The physical bravery and skill at arms somehow outweigh Achilles' character flaw that causes him to mutilate and degrade his vanquished enemy—actions that would be considered both unethical and a violation of the Geneva Conventions (International Committee of the Red Cross 1949) in modern war. The *telos* of the Homeric hero is not simply the acquisition of *honour*; the hero is entitled to booty or gifts from the vanquished. However, as Adkins observes, the promise or expectations of material benefits—gifts—does not motivate Achilles (Adkins 1982, p. 303). There is one other 'divine' consideration: Achilles' conduct towards Hector's corpse is offending the gods. So the gods—most notably, Zeus himself—send Achilles' mother, Thetis, to the great warrior to tell him to ransom Hector's body and allow it to be returned to Priam, Hector's father:

"Lo! Jove [Zeus] himself (for Jove's command I bear)

Forbids to tempt the wrath of heaven too far.

No longer then (his fury if thou dread)

Detain the relics of great Hector dead;

Nor vent on senseless earth thy vengeance vain,

But yield to ransom, and restore the slain." (Homer 2006, p. 714)

Having heard the message sent by the gods, Achilles has a change of heart and agrees to ransom Hector's corpse so that the body can be returned to Priam: with honour preserved on all sides, thereby also maintaining the codes that frame how dead bodies should be treated. Recognizing that these are the merest glimpses into the complexity of the ethical dimension of the hero in Homer's Iliad, consider how the questions based on Foucault's four aspects of creative self-subjectivation can contribute to a genealogical analysis of this 'hero'. To recall, the questions ask: 1. Which part of myself or my behaviour in the domain of war or political violence is concerned with moral conduct? 2. How are individuals incited or invited to recognize particular moral obligations? 3. How should a person behave in order to become ethical? 4. What is the ultimate goal of the ethical subject?

The part of Achilles' character or behavior—the 'ethical substance' (Foucault 1997a, p. 263)—that is concerned with moral conduct, identifies with the code that the warrior should adhere to, as well as a commitment and duty to the gods. While he was prepared to breach the code by violating Hector's corpse, he was incited—instructed—to act ethically and allow the body of his defeated enemy to be returned to the latter's father. In this instance, Achilles' own mother was the messenger of the gods. Achilles, in turn, constitutes himself as ethical in two ways here: first, by obeying the gods and, second, through that obedience he once again conformed to the warrior code. Finally, in this ethical self-forming, the hero can once more be seen in the pursuit of honour and the acceptance of ransom—as is his due.

These brief insights can and should be expanded and critiqued further in an extended genealogy but, for the purposes of this paper, they offer a means of recognizing different aspects of the ethical subjectivity of the 'hero' at that time. They also reveal both continuities and discontinuities with ethical subjectivity found in current 'hero' discourses. For example, the idea of dangerous, close-up, hand-to-hand combat with an enemy is still regarded as heroic. In 2012, Corporal Sean Jones was awarded the Military Cross for leading a 2011 bayonet charge against Taliban fighters in Afghanistan. His medal citation stated that he displayed 'unflinching courage and extraordinary leadership in the face of extreme and tangible danger' (The Telegraph 2012). In contrast, when two US Marines violated the corpses of dead Taliban fighters—by urinating on them—and were subsequently prosecuted for their actions, it is inconceivable that they could maintain any semblance of hero status in the way that Achilles did (Gabbatt 2012).

4.2. Augustine, Ethics and Just War in the Early Christian Era

Over the following centuries in Europe, the Homeric heroism of the warrior in the Classical Greek period gave way to a more structured, and disciplined and collective form of war in the army of the Roman Empire. By the later centuries of the Roman Empire, the Greek gods and Roman gods had been eclipsed by the Christian God, with Christianity recognized as the official religion of the Empire in the fourth century AD. Foucault analyzed practices from both the Hellenistic and Imperial periods whose purpose was to promote the care of the self (Foucault 1997c, pp. 231–32). From the Stoic injunction to 'retire into the self and stay there', to Pliny's advice to a friend to 'set aside a few moments a day ... for a retreat into himself', there are traces of self-forming subjectivity (Foucault 1997c, pp. 231–32). The self was an object to creatively reflect upon, master and take care of: a pattern that 'was well established and deeply rooted when Augustine wrote his *Confessions*' (Foucault 1997c, pp. 231–32; Augustine 2000). Augustine took these self-examining, confessional practices and applied them to

Christian ethics, including the ethical conduct of the soldier in what would become known as the just war tradition. He identified transgressions of purity in thought, word and deed, as needing divine forgiveness and purification (Augustine 2000).

In *The Augustinian Imperative*, Connolly investigates the possibility of a theme of intrinsic moral order that precedes and succeeds Augustine and which, in Augustine, finds its ultimate expression (Connolly 2002, p. 34). Connolly identifies two aspects of moral order or code: order as verb (to order) and order as noun (structure or design) (Connolly 2002, p. 35). For Connolly, Augustine is a carrier of the former, passing on the active order that emanates from God, or some other authority such as the law of nature; it is an ultimate, unquestioned and unchallengeable authority. He does not argue that a singular static, unchanging moral order exists, only that this theme or assumption of moral order can be found at every point in history. Connolly does not seek to endorse or refute this intrinsic moral order but to explore the discursive terrain between that position and its ontological adversary: ethical sensibility. Further, moral and ethical perspectives impact on the 'relational character of identity' when it comes to the subject of war, and subjectivity itself becomes a domain of contestation and analysis (Connolly 2002, pp. 143–44). Separately, Taylor places great emphasis on the role of Augustine in establishing the roots of modern subjectivity, stressing the importance of inwardness and self-reflexivity in the formation of political identity (Taylor 1989, p. 131). Consequently, Augustine's broader Christian ethic informed the means by which a soldier could form himself as ethical.

Augustine set out a key basis for ethical subjectivity when he stated: 'I classify the human race into two branches: the one consists of those who live by human standards, the other of those who live according to God's will' (Augustine 2003, p. 595). 'God's will'—in terms of moral order and direct guidance, in Connolly's reading—is a crucial part of the ethical substance, or basis, of ethical conduct (Connolly 2002, p. 35). Augustine proposed a hierarchy of moral responsibility which extended into the domain of war, within which the ethical subject of war emerged:

> when a soldier kills a man in obedience to the legitimate authority under which he served, he is not chargeable with murder by the laws of his country; in fact he is chargeable with insubordination and mutiny if he refuses. But if he did it of his own accord, on his own authority, he would be liable to a charge of homicide. Thus he is punished if he did it without orders for the same reason that he will be punished if he refuses when ordered . . . .If that is the case when a general gives the order, how much more when the command comes from the Creator! (Augustine 2003, p. 37)

The hierarchy of moral authority created by Augustine with regard to war takes the following form, in increasing order of importance: soldier, general, legitimate [political] authority, the Creator [Augustine's God]. Note, here, that the highest moral authority to which the ethical soldier must conform is divine. Such a compulsory ethical requirement would be alien—offensive even—in many Western, liberal, secular societies today. The authority under which a soldier took life shaped whether or not the actions were classed as 'killing' or 'murder': a difference that was embedded in Western just war reasoning 1600 years ago and still exists. That ethical difference rests on the legitimacy of the authority—within Augustine's moral order—of the one giving the order to kill, not on the status of the soldier or the person being killed.

Moving beyond *City of God*, the 'good' subject of war emerges elsewhere in Augustine's writings as an instrument of divine punishment in the shape of the legitimate ruler who obeys and reinforces God's chastising commands:

> The desire for harming, the cruelty of revenge, the restless and implacable mind, the savageness of revolting, the lust for dominating, and similar things—these are what are justly blamed in wars. Often, so that such things might also be justly punished, certain wars that must be waged against the violence of those resisting are commanded by God or some other legitimate ruler and are undertaken by the good. (Augustine 1994, pp. 221–22)

Augustine describes those who can legitimately be opposed—or rightly punished—in a just war. The subjectivity of those to be punished is formed from unethical conduct such as cruelty, vengefulness and savagery. Such subjects emerge as unethical by opposing Augustine's—and therefore God's—moral code.

More specific to the ethical subjectivity of the individual soldier who fights wars is guidance found in Augustine's *Letter 189 to Boniface*. Boniface was a Roman military commander who 'rebelled against the imperial authorities' in 427AD (Augustine 2001c, p. xxv): 'When you are arming yourself for battle, then, consider this first of all, that your courage, even your physical courage, is a gift from God ... When one makes a promise, one must keep faith, even with an enemy against whom one is waging a war' (Augustine 2001a, p. 217). Augustine is not advising on the tactics of war but on the character of the soldier—on 'keeping faith'. Note that 'courage' comes first for Augustine, though perhaps *moral* courage would be the better expression, because it is considered here to be greater than 'physical courage'. But, even courage in itself is not enough to make someone a 'good' soldier. He is also told that, in relation to both Augustine's words and holy scripture, if there is 'anything you still lack for a life of goodness, then make urgent efforts in prayers and action to acquire it ... God [is] the source of the goodness you have and [ ] every good deed that you do' (Augustine 2001a, p. 218). Consequently, we see here that the ethical substance—to use Foucault's term—of the Christian Roman soldier is rooted primarily in the relationship with the divine. While a full genealogical investigation of the ethical significance of the relationship between the Roman soldier and his Christian God is beyond the scope of this paper, it is already clear that the soldier is required to conduct a work of the self on the self in pursuit of 'goodness'.

4.3. Genealogical Continuities and Discontinuities

A Foucauldian genealogy of the ethical subject of war—hero or coward—seeks out the continuities and discontinuities between not only the past and the present, but also between key moments in the past, the combination of which all contribute to making present ethical understandings of heroism and cowardice possible. Compare one aspect of the ethical subjectivity of the 'hero' of the Classical Greek period and the ethical subjectivity of the fifth-century Christian soldier in the later days of the Roman Empire: the continuities and discontinuities in their respective engagement with the earthly and the divine.

The gods of Olympus communicated their displeasure to Achilles through his demi-god mother, so prompting the warrior to change his behaviour in order to restore his honour and regain favour in their eyes. Later, in Augustine's treatise to Boniface, the Christian military commander is advised to seek a life of goodness through prayer and good actions that extended to the domain of war: keeping faith with enemies. There are apparent similarities of ethical substance between Achilles and Boniface. Each somehow engages with, and responds to, their respective gods. However, the primary motivations and actions of these two individuals show significant discontinuities as well. Achilles *telos*—ultimate aim—was to acquire earthly honour through individual combat which, in turn, would constitute him as a hero and honour the gods. But that honour would remain earthbound: it would never entitle Achilles to join his gods on Mount Olympus in an afterlife. Boniface was later guided by Augustine towards submission and obedience to the commands of the Christian God which would lead to a life of goodness and, ultimately, a place in heaven with his God.

The primary *telos* of the early Christian soldier, therefore, was neither heroism nor honour—though these can be acquired. The *telos* was godliness, which would lead to an eternal place with the Christian God, in heaven, in the next life. And that *telos* was achieved through the soldier recognizing his (it would have been men at that time) need to conduct himself ethically on and off the battlefield, and taking steps to ensure that he did so. Augustine showed several connections between the different aspects of the soldier's ethical subjectivity when he stated: 'Greatness and their own glory belong to warriors who are both very brave and very faithful (that is the source of their *truer praise*), to those who struggle and face danger in order, with the help of God who gives protection and assistance, to bring defeat on an untamed enemy' (Augustine 2001b, pp. 225–26, *italics added*). Faithfulness to God was deemed, here, to be more important than physical bravery, and it was God's help that led to the enemy's defeat.

These very brief historical insights only begin to demonstrate how genealogy can provide an understanding of the emergence of the ethical aspects of the modern subject of war. Homer and Augustine are early contributors to Western thinking on just war ethics and military conduct. A comprehensive genealogy of the modern, Western ethical subject of war would consider multiple contributors to the just war tradition. A genealogy of the jihadist as ethical subject of war would require a similar re-reading of discourses in the Islamic war tradition. Focusing solely on Western just war in the space available here highlights both the potential and vast scope of such a study. Throughout Western history, 'just war' has not been so much a linear, 'homogenous entity in a conceptual march of progress' in ethical thought; instead, it is a tradition characterised by 'continuities, paradigmatic breaks, discontinuities and incommensurabilities' (Lee 2010, p. 12). Between Augustine in the fifth century and today, just a few of the key contributors to just war thinking include: Gratian (twelfth century); Aquinas (thirteenth century); Luther and Vitoria (sixteenth century); Suarez and Grotius (seventeenth century); and de Vattel (eighteenth century) (Reichberg et al. 2006). Over that period, the just war tradition shifted from being rooted in divine will and divine revelation to a basis in human reason and law. Tadashi reinforces this point when he writes of Grotius' seventeenth century contribution to the ontological basis of just war: '[Grotius] does not rely on the just-war doctrine of European medieval theologians, but re-examines the just war doctrine from the viewpoint of natural law based solely on reason' (Tadashi 1993, p. 32).

In attempting to understand the emergence of the subject of war over millennia—and therefore to speak meaningfully of the hero or coward today—the continuities and discontinuities over time are many and significant. For example, it is almost unthinkable in a Western context, for political or military leaders to constitute the subjectivity or actions of a modern-day soldier or other combatant in terms of God's will or divine judgement. The secularizing of the just war tradition over recent centuries has ensured as much. Elshtain observes that American soldiers are trained—like the training of allied soldiers from the UK and across NATO—to avoid both intentional and unintentional killing of the innocent: 'No one is encouraged, or even allowed, to call the killing of civilians "God's will" or, even worse, an act carried out in God's name' (Elshtain 2004, p. 21). She then contrasts that secular Western approach with appeals to divine authority in the training materials of 'Islamist radicals', quoting: 'You have to kill in the name of Allah until you are killed ... Our enemies are fighting in the name of Satan. You are fighting in the name of God' (Elshtain 2004, pp. 21–22). The terrorist fighting today in the name of Allah is thereby constituted as the radical, violent Other, opposed by Elshtain's ethical subject who creatively self-constitutes by exercising restraint in seeking to protect civilians in war.

In Foucauldian genealogical terms, the discontinuity between the different divinely-mandated actions of Homer's Achilles or Augustine's Boniface, and the Western secular combatant of today is clear. In contrast, while the gods of Achilles and Augustine are not the same as the god of the Al-Qaeda fighter or the Islamic State jihadist, there is at least some continuity in the notion of military activity being commanded by a divine being. A comprehensive genealogy would have to consider how the jihadist has emerged over time and contexts in different non-Western, non-Christian, Islamic discourses. The Introduction referred to the Afghanistan President Ashraf Ghani in 2017, when he spoke of the 'cowardly' suicide bomber who killed 90 people in Kabul (BBC 2017). The simple—perhaps simplistic—interpretation is to point to the killing of civilian noncombatants as a violation of the ethics of war, and it is certainly a violation, and constituting the perpetrator as cowardly.

A richer, more provocative re-reading—from a Western perspective and perhaps from a more conventional Islamic perspective—is to try and understand if or how the suicide-bomber jihadist seeks to form himself or herself as ethical. Atran asks an uncomfortable question after observing a '[m]oral commitment to sacrifice for their group without regard for their own material reward. As long as jihadis show such moral commitment, as martyrdom missions attest to, then even overwhelming material efforts to destroy the jihadi movement may not be enough. But what gets group commitment going in the first place' (Atran 2010, p. 298)? Genealogy offers the possibility of a much more nuanced understanding of the ethical subjectivity of fighters, like jihadists, in unconventional modern wars: the moral basis of their actions; their justifications for killing noncombatants; and the relationship between violence, religion and a divine *telos* which is alien to much of Western society.

In similar physical domains of political violence like Afghanistan, Syria and Iraq, genealogy offers the prospect of a deeper understanding of the subjectivity of the drone operator who conducts lethal operations. While Monbiot sees America's use of drones as cowardly (Monbiot 2012), Pittman goes further in constituting the subjectivity of the drone operator: 'He is a drone "pilot". He and his kind have redefined the words "coward", "terrorist", and "sociopath". He is the new face of American warfare' (Pittman 2013). Rejecting such characterisations, drone operators have described the importance of discriminating between combatants and noncombatants when using lethal force, and the ways in which advanced technology improve upon previous air power practices (Lee 2014, pp. 42–43). The criticism of drone operators by Monbiot and Pittman is partially based on physical separation from the modern battlefield as they remotely fly their Predator and Reaper aircraft from several thousand miles away. No physical courage is required. Yet in terms of ethical subjectivity, they still exhibit some continuity with the (moral) 'courage' of Augustine's ethical subject of war identified above. Despite Pittman's accusation of sociopathy and enthusiasm for killing among drone operators, Grossman's study, *On Killing*, tells of the difficulty many combatants have in overcoming 'their innate resistance to killing their fellow human beings' (Grossman 2009, p. 13). The ethical subjectivity of the drone operator, like other modern combatants, is much richer and subtle than crude stereotyping will permit, though it remains difficult to see how they can be considered 'heroic' in the classical sense.

5. Conclusions

This paper has only just begun to scratch the surface of the insights that can be gleaned from a Foucauldian genealogy of the ethical subject in the domain of war. It is beyond the scope of this paper to conduct such a genealogy here, but a potential framework has been proposed and the workings of such a genealogy have been explored. For Foucault, genealogy is 'a form of history that can account for the constitution of knowledges, discourses, domains of objects, and so on, without having to make reference to a subject that is either transcendental in relation to the field of events or runs its empty sameness throughout the course of history' (Foucault 2002, p. 115). The ethical subject of war—the hero, the coward, and many more—is not transcendental but culturally, socially, politically and historically situated. Foucault distinguished between code-oriented moralities and subjective, ethics-oriented moralities in his own genealogy of the ethical desiring subject (Foucault 1992, p. 28ff.). Such a distinction can never be absolute; code-oriented and ethics-oriented moralities are mutually constituting and do not operate independently upon the subject. However, despite the limitations involved, when applied genealogically these concepts offer an effective (though admittedly imperfect) means of untangling the layers of meaning that are inscribed onto those subjects who occupy the domain of war in these opening decades of the twenty-first century.

Conflicts of Interest: The author declares no conflict of interest.

References

Adkins, Arthur W. H. 1971. Homeric Values and Homeric Society. *The Journal of Hellenic Studies* 91: 1–14. [CrossRef]

Adkins, Arthur W. H. 1982. Values, Goals and Emotions in the Iliad. *Classical Philology* 77: 292–326. [CrossRef]

Ambrose, Stephen E. 2017. *Band of Brothers: E Company, 506th Regiment, 101st Airborne from Normandy to Hitler's Eagle's Nest*, 25th ed. New York: Simon & Schuster Paperbacks.

Atran, Scott. 2010. *Talking to the Enemy: Faith, Brotherhood, and the (Un)making of Terrorists*. New York: Ecco Press. New York: Ecco Press.

Augustine, Saint. 1994. Against Faustas the Manichean. In *Augustine: Political Writings*. Edited by Ernest Fortin and Douglas Kries. Translated by Douglas Kries, and Michael W. Tkacz. Indianapolis: Hackett, pp. 221–22.

Augustine, Saint. 2000. *Confessions and Enchiridion*. Translated by Albert C. Outler. Grand Rapids: Christian Classics Ethereal Library.

Augustine. 2001a. Letter 189 to Boniface. In *Political Writings*. Edited by Margaret Atkins and Robert Dodaro. Cambridge Texts in the History of Political Thought. Cambridge and New York: Cambridge University Press, pp. 214–18.

Augustine. 2001b. Letter 229: Augustine to Darius (429/430). In *Political Writings*. Edited by Margaret Atkins and Robert Dodaro. Cambridge Texts in the History of Political Thought. Cambridge and New York: Cambridge University Press, pp. 225–26.

Augustine. 2001c. *Political Writings*. Edited by Margaret Atkins and Robert Dodaro. Cambridge Texts in the History of Political Thought; Cambridge and New York: Cambridge University Press.

Augustine, Saint. 2003. *City of God*. Translated by Henry Bettenson. London: Penguin Books.

BBC. 2017. Kabul Bomb: Afghan Leader Condemns 'Cowardly' Attack. Available online: http://www.bbc.co.uk/news/world-asia-40109568 (accessed on 1 June 2017).

Brown, Larisa. 2015. Incredible Footage Shows ISIS Cowards Running for Cover after Trying to Hide Armoured Vehicle under Palm Tree before It Is Destroyed by RAF Drone's Hellfire Missile. *Daily Mail*. July 9. Available online: http://www.dailymail.co.uk/news/article-3155202/Incredible-footage-shows-ISIS-cowards-running-cover-trying-hide-armoured-vehicle-palm-tree-destroyed-RAF-drone-s-Hellfire-missile.html (accessed on 4 March 2018).

Carabine, Jean. 2001. Unmarried Motherhood 1830–1990: A Genealogical Analysis. In *Discourse as Data*. Edited by Margaret Wetherell, Stephanie Taylor and Simeon Yates. London: Sage Publications Ltd., pp. 267–310.

Cockburn, Patrick. 2015. *The Rise of Islamic State: ISIS and the New Sunni Revolution*. London and New York: Verso.

Connolly, William E. 2002. *The Augustinian Imperative: A Reflection on the Politics of Morality*. London: Rowman & Littlefield Publ.

Coyle, James. 2017. *Russia's Border Wars and Frozen Conflicts*. New York and Berlin/Heidelberg: Springer.

Dreyfus, Hubert L., Paul Rabinow, and Michel Foucault. 1983. *Michel Foucault, beyond Structuralism and Hermeneutics*, 2nd ed. Chicago: University of Chicago Press.

Edmonds, James S. 2011. Criticism without Critique: Power and Experience in Foucault and James. *Foucault Studies* 11: 41–53. [CrossRef]

Elshtain, Jean. 2004. *Just War against Terror*. New York: BasicBooks.

Foucault, Michel. 1977. Nietzsche, Genealogy, History. In *Language, Counter-Memory, Practice: Selected Essays and Interviews*. Edited by Donald Bouchard. Ithaca: Cornell University Press.

Foucault, Michel. 1990. *The History of Sexuality. Vol. 3: The Care of the Self*. Reprinted. London: Penguin Books.

Foucault, Michel. 1992. *The History of Sexuality. Vol. 2: The Use of Pleasure*. Reprinted. London: Penguin Books.

Foucault, Michel. 1995. *Discipline and Punish: The Birth of the Prison*, 2nd Vintage Books ed. New York: Vintage Books.

Foucault, Michel. 1997a. On the Genealogy of Ethics. In *The Essential Works of Michel Foucault 1954–1984 Volume 1: Ethics*. Edited by Paul Rabinow. New York: The New Press, pp. 253–80.

Foucault, Michel. 1997b. Sexuality and Solitude. In *The Essential Works of Michel Foucault 1954–1984 Volume 1: Ethics*. Edited by Paul Rabinow. New York: The New Press, pp. 175–84.

Foucault, Michel. 1997c. Technologies of the Self. In *The Essential Works of Michel Foucault 1954–1984 Volume 1: Ethics*. Edited by Paul Rabinow. New York: The New Press, pp. 223–51.

Foucault, Michel. 1997d. The Ethics of the Concern for Self as a Practice of Freedom. In *The Essential Works of Michel Foucault 1954–1984 Volume 1: Ethics*. Edited by Paul Rabinow. New York: The New Press, pp. 281–301.

Foucault, Michel. 2002. Truth and Power. In *The Essential Works of Michel Foucault 1954–1984 Volume 3: Power*. London: Penguin.

Gabbatt, Adam. 2012. US marines charged over urinating on bodies of dead Taliban in Afghanistan. *The Guardian*, September 24. Available online: https://www.theguardian.com/world/2012/sep/24/us-marines-charged-dead-taliban (accessed on 12 February 2018).

Grossman, Dave. 2009. *On Killing: The Psychological Cost of Learning to Kill in War and Society*, rev. ed. New York: Little, Brown and Co.

Homer. 2006. *The Iliad of Homer*, 1899 ed. Ebook 6130. Translated by Alexander Pope. Project Guttenberg. Available online: http://www.gutenberg.org/files/6130/6130-pdf.pdf (accessed on 20 February 2018).

Homer. 2017. *Iliad*. London: Vintage Classics.

Howard, Michael. 2008. Bombs Strapped to Down's Syndrome Women Kill Scores in Baghdad Markets. *The Guardian*, February 2. Available online: https://www.theguardian.com/world/2008/feb/02/iraq.international1 (accessed on 20 February 2018).

Hughes, Geraint. 2014. *My Enemy's Enemy: Proxy Warfare in International Politics*. Brighton, Portland: Sussex Academic Press.

International Committee of the Red Cross. 1949. The Geneva Conventions of 1949 and Their Additional Protocols. Available online: https://www.icrc.org/en/war-and-law/treaties-customary-law/geneva-conventions (accessed on 25 February 2018).

Kaeuper, Richard W. 2016. *Medieval Chivalry*. Cambridge Medieval Textbooks; Cambridge and New York: Cambridge University Press.

Lee, Peter. 2010. *A Genealogy of the Ethical Subject in the Just War Tradition*. London: King's College London.

Lee, Peter. 2014. Rights, Wrongs and Drones: Remote Warfare, Ethics and the Challenge of Just War Reasoning. *Air Power Review* 16: 30–49.

McWhorter, Ladelle. 2017. Persons and Sovereigns in Ethical Thought. *Genealogy* 1: 16. [CrossRef]

Miller, Martin A. 2013. *The Foundations of Modern Terrorism*. Cambridge: Cambridge University Press.

Monbiot, George. 2012. With Its Deadly Drones, the US Is Fighting a Coward's War. *The Guardian*, January 30. Available online: https://www.theguardian.com/commentisfree/2012/jan/30/deadly-drones-us-cowards-war (accessed on 3 March 2018).

Mumford, Andrew. 2013. *Proxy Warfare*. War and Conflict in the Modern World; Cambridge: Polity Press.

Pittman, Vic. 2013. Cowardice Redefined, The New Face of American Serial Killers. *Salem-News.com*, April 18. Available online: http://www.salem-news.com/articles/april182013/american-killers-vp.php (accessed on 25 February 2018).

Reichberg, Gregory M., Henrik Syse, and Endre Begby, eds. 2006. *The Ethics of War: Classic and Contemporary Readings*. Malden and Oxford: Blackwell Pub.

Tadashi, Tanaka. 1993. Occupying Armies and Civil Populations in Nineteenth-Century Europe. In *A Normative Approach to War: Peace, War and Justice in Hugo Grotius*. Edited by Onuma Yasuaki. Oxford: Clarendon Press, pp. 19–65.

Taylor, Charles. 1989. *Sources of the Self*. Cambridge: Cambridge University Press.

The Telegraph. 2012. Soldier Who Led Afghanistan Bayonet Charge into Hail of Bullets Honoure. *The Telegraph*, September 28. Available online: https://www.telegraph.co.uk/news/worldnews/asia/afghanistan/9571522/Soldier-who-led-Afghanistan-bayonet-charge-into-hail-of-bullets-honoured.html (accessed on 25 February 2018).

Thucydides, Rex Warner, and Moses I. Finley. 1972. *History of the Peloponnesian War*, rev. ed. The Penguin Classics; Harmondsworth, Eng. Baltimore: Penguin Books.

Walzer, Michael. 2003. *Just and Unjust Wars: A Moral Argument with Historical Illustrations*, 3rd ed. New York: BasicBooks.

Zanker, Graham. 1996. *The Heart of Achilles: Characterization of Personal Ethics in the Iliad*. Ann Arbor: University of Michigan Press.

genealogy

MDPI

Article

A Political Genealogy of Dance: The Choreographing of Life and Images

Julian Reid

Faculty of Social Sciences; University of Lapland; 96300 Rovaniemi, Finland; reidjulian@gmail.com

Received: 3 May 2018; Accepted: 25 June 2018; Published: 28 June 2018

Abstract: This article provides a genealogical critique of the history and modernity of dance. In doing so it establishes the political importance of dance as an art not principally of the body and its biopolitical capacities for movement, but of images and imagination. It traces the development of dance as an art of imagination, lost and buried in the works of Domenico da Piacenza, Jean-Georges Noverre, and Loïe Fuller, as well as its counter-movement expressed in the work of Rudolf Laban. It also locates contemporary dance within this political conflict by exploring new works, especially those of Ivana Müller, which call upon beholders to use their imaginations through the evocation of histories and memories. Such works can be understood to be deeply political, it will argue, because they work to transform society by creating time for a belief in the impossible. At its best, dance does not simply incite bodies to move but suspends movement, transforming the very image of what a body is capable of. These aims and practices of dance speak to contemporary concerns within political practice, theory, and philosophy for a reawakening of political imagination in times of crisis and neoliberal hegemony.

Keywords: dance; choreography; life; image; imagination; movement; power; genealogy; biopolitics

1. Introduction

This article concerns the political genealogy of dance. In what sense, if any, can we call dance an art of the political? How have power relations shaped the historical development of dance and how has its development functioned to alter arrangements of political power? What kind of politics does dance enable us to imagine or does it simply serve to reinforce dominant images of power? How does dance connect up with other practices and theories concerned with the choreographing of power in political philosophy?

Every genealogy of dance, as of every other object, is inevitably partial and singular. In addressing dance this article will be dealing simply with western aristocratic and theatrical dance, without taking into account non-aristocratic and non-western dance, or popular dance of the modern period. To create a genealogy of the whole of dance history would require much more extensive study than is possible here. This article will also be singular in its aims, in terms of the nature of what it searches for within dance history. In contrast with previous attempts to genealogize dance (Jarvinen 2014; Burt 2004), I seek to theorize the concept which dance contains within itself, of itself, as a political art of image-making, and connect that with the image of dance in political philosophy, showing how important this image has been to trends within contemporary political philosophy concerned with the problem of what various political philosophers have theorized as 'the life of images'. Dance and philosophy support each other, I will argue, in the endeavor of operating upon the present, and transforming the real by acting upon it, impregnating it with images drawn from the past, which might now take on the future, in a movement which it is the task of political genealogy itself to create—one which dispels nostalgia, conquers melancholy, and is neither happy nor sad, but affective.

Of course, throughout the modern era dance has served to reinforce dominating images of power, including those of 'monarchy, national identity, gendered identity, racialized identity, and ritualized identity' while also demonstrating 'the ability to stand apart, acting as a critical theory of society' (Franko 2006, p. 4). 'The body in motion' has been choreographed in projection of virtually every national identity of the modern era while the questioning and exposure of the function of the body and its movements in the choreographing of political power has been the task which dance has set itself wherever it has sought to be subversive and critical (Franko 2006, p. 6). In essence, these are the stakes in which dance has been understood to be political by those concerned with its politics—as an art which partakes in a wider struggle over and for the significance and meaning of the body and its capacities for movement. Is there any sense, however, in which dance can be found to problematize the centrality of the body to politics, both in its conservative and oppressive forms, and in its subversions of those very regimes? In what ways, if any, does dance problematize movement as a property of bodies and their politics? Is dance an expression, in other words, of what Michel Foucault has enabled us to see as biopolitical modernity, or is it a source of opposition to biopolitics?

2. An Art of Images

This article traces the ways in which amid the historical development of dance there emerged an attempt to construe dance not as an art of the body and its movement, either in support of or in contestation of political power, but as an art which pitches itself against the body and which seeks to free the image of movement from its ties to the body. Of all the arts, dance is arguably the most fundamentally engaged in the problem of the biopolitical. Much of dance has of course involved attempts to foreground and materialize the body. It is represented as existing in overlap with the field of somatics, and practices dedicated to reifying the body, the potency of bodies, and the 'love of movement and curiosity about the physical body' (Eddy 2009, p. 6). However, its history and present development also entails important attempts, I will argue, to struggle *against* the body. The history of dance is a history of both these impulses; to foreground and materialize the movements of which bodies are capable, as well as to free the image of movement from its ties to the body.

Because so much of the scholarship and literature around dance have represented it as an art of and for the body, this article addresses the latter impulse and the other strand within dance history, whereby exponents of dance have attempted to free the image of movement from its prison of bodies and their capabilities. This was evident explicitly in the 19th century in the art of Loïe Fuller and especially her 'Serpentine Dance'; heralded by the art critic Paul Adam in 1893 as a 'new art' itself emergent 'from a new body, relieved of the weight of its flesh, reduced to a play of lines and tones, whirling in space' (Ranciere 2013, p. 94). The poet Mallarmé was, as we will see, to make similar claims for Fuller's novelty. Contemporary theorists of dance, such as Tom Gunning, and the philosopher Jacques Rancière have made convincing reiterations of this thesis (Gunning 2003; Ranciere 2013). Dance is, in essence, neither simply an art of the body or simply of movement as is commonly supposed, nor is it an art simply of time as it has otherwise sometimes been argued (Agamben 2013, p. 10). It is an art principally of images and their choreography. The history, however, of how dance became an art of images, pitched against the body, has yet to be recovered or explicated. It did not simply begin, in the late 19th century, with Fuller and the wider phenomenon of serpentine dancing, as is sometimes supposed. At the very least we have to contextualize the development of Fuller in a deeper history, one which makes sense of the relations of her art not only to the 18th century works of the French choreographer, Noverre, but to the very first treatise on dance, written in the 15th century, by Domenico da Piacenza, who taught dance at the court of the Sforza in Milan (Thesiger 1973, p. 283). While Rancière will help us piece together relationships of Fuller to Noverre, we will also draw from recent work by Agamben to situate both Fuller and Noverre in genealogical relationships to Domenico. All of this indicates the importance of the image of dance in philosophy itself for the development of the function of imagination in dance.

3. Domenico da Piacenza and Dance as Art of Phantasmata

Giorgio Agamben's relatively recent tract, *Nymphs*, addresses the origins of the modernity of dance, and in doing so, focuses on a much neglected text which is nevertheless of fundamental importance for the genealogy of dance as a political art of image making, *On the Art of Dancing and Choreography*, by Domenico da Piacenza (Agamben 2013, pp. 6–10). Writing in the 15th century, Domenico detailed six fundamental aspects of the art of dance: measure, memory, agility, manner, measure of the ground, and phantasmata (Agamben 2013, p. 7). To date, it is the aspect of measure which scholars have focused on to define Domenico's theory of dance (Thesiger 1973, pp. 282–84). Yet phantasmata were just as important Domenico maintained. Phantasmata are the products of what the Greeks called phantasia; the function of the spirit which we now name imagination (Braga 2010, p. 2). They were of key importance, Domenico held, for the art of dance. "Note that whoever wants to learn the art, needs to dance according to phantasmata" he wrote (Smith 1995, p. 13).

Phantasmata do not, for Domenico, however, refer simply to images. Phantasmata is a 'physical quickness' the control of which necessitates that 'at each tempo one appears to have seen Medusa's head ... and be of stone in one instant, then, in another instant, take to flight' (Smith 1995, p. 13). Such a definition of phantasmata as 'physical quickness' might seem odd, or at least at variance from traditional understandings as being simply products of imagination. However, when we consider the observations of the function of phantasmata in the behavior of the possessed, such as those said to have been afflicted with phantasmata in the convent of Loudon, we discover how their function was said to induce 'an astonishing quickness ... such quickness and violence, that no one in the world, however agile the person might be, could do anything approaching to it' (Madden 1857, p. 291). Phantasmata, in other words, are to be understood as a particular kind of image, inductive of a speed of bodily movement, but which unlike in their function within the possessed, can in turn, be controlled and measured, such that the body alternates between a stone-like stillness and bird-like flight. 'The true locus of the dancer is not the body and its movement but the image as a "Medusa's head, as a pause that is not immobile but simultaneously charged with memory and dynamic energy" (Agamben 2013, p. 10).

4. Noverre and Dance as a Living Image of the Passions

Writing in the 18th century, the French choreographer, Jean Georges Noverre, in his letters, which, as an exposition on the theories and laws governing dance, are said to have no equal (Beaumont 2004, p. xi), also embellished the relation between dance and imagination. Writing on ballet, he described how 'a ballet is an image, or rather a series of images connected one with the other by the plot which provides the theme of the ballet' (Noverre 2004, p. 9). However, Noverre's mission was to revolutionize such a conception of dance as a mere provider of images for plots, declaring himself charged with the task of 'devising ballets with action' in order to 're-unite action with dancing' (Noverre 2004, p. 10). A *scene d'action*, according to Noverre, should be 'full of fire ... where the dance should speak with fire and energy; where symmetrical and formal figures cannot be employed without transgressing truth, without enfeebling the action and chilling the interest' (Noverre 2004, p. 13). A well-composed dance, in Noverre's terms, was one that does not merely provide images with which to tell preconceived stories, but which is 'a living image of the passions' (Noverre 2004, p. 16). An image which 'lives', in Noverre's view, is one that contains within it many different gradations, many different oppositions, variations of light, and shades to observe' (Noverre 2004, p. 13). In this context he argued against the conventions of 18th century dance which held that any one dance should depict just two images only, and that these two images should be symmetrically opposed and unvarying in their nature. An example which Noverre gave was that of where a band of nymphs which:

> ... at the unexpected sight of a troupe of young fauns, takes flight hurriedly in fear; the
> fauns, on their side, pursue the nymphs with eagerness, which generally suggests delight:
> presently, they stop to examine the impression they have made on the nymphs; at the same

time the latter suspend their course; they regard the fauns with fear, seek to discover their designs, and to attain by flight a refuge which would secure them against the danger which threatens; the two troupes approach; the nymphs resist, defend themselves and escape with a skill equal to their agility (Noverre 2004, pp. 12–13).

Such a choreography of two images only, where one expresses the desire of the fauns, and the other that of the fear of the nymphs, makes, Noverre argued, for a 'cold and formal performance' (Noverre 2004, p. 13). In contrast, and against this tradition of symmetry and contrived opposition, Noverre pitched his principle of action; so that from any two passions, be they fear and desire say, there results 'a multitude of images, each more animated than the other' (Noverre 2004, p. 13). Only then could we speak, he argued, of an art of dance in which images 'live' a life of truth through the affirmation of their multiplicity, their inventiveness, and capacities for endless variation.

The role of the concept of image has been largely missed in the critical reception of Noverre's work, right up until the present day. For historians such as Jocelyn Powell, Noverre was simply a naturalist, working in alliance with other naturalists of the period throughout the dramatic arts, to enable art to approximate to nature better (Powell 1988). Rancière, in his *Aisthesis*, describes well the ways in which Noverre's theory offered a 'revolution in representative logic ... opposing the organic model of action as body, ideal proportion, and the entire system of conventions linking subjects to genres and modes of expression' by seeking a more 'direct expression of emotions and thoughts' (Noverre 2004, pp. 6–7). Nevertheless, like Powell, he fails to identify in Noverre's revolutionary manifesto for dance the centrality of the role of images. In contrast to the traditional story-telling function of the images created by dance, Noverre opposed, as Rancière well describes, 'an art in which every bodily gesture and every grouping of bodies tells a story and expresses a thought' (Noverre 2004, p. 7). At stake in this opposition of Noverre to the traditional story-telling function of dance was what would develop historically into a 'new idea of fiction' (Noverre 2004, p. 100). One that substitutes plot 'with the construction of a play of aspects, elementary forms that offer an analogy to the play of the world' (Noverre 2004, p. 100). The point, however, is that this revolution was testimony also to an emancipation of the life of images in dance; an emancipation of the image from its status in subordination to narrative, giving privilege to the life of the image as the object of dance as such.

5. Fuller and Dance as the Pure Play of Images

It was in the 19th century choreography of the American, Loïe Fuller that Rancière saw the development of such a new idea of fiction coming to a greater fruition. Fuller was famous for her Serpentine Dance in which her body remained static while the long dress she wore was swirled in creation of a play of lines which, in turn, 'draw the shape of a butterfly, a lily, a basket of flowers, a swelling wave, or a wilting rose' in a 'pure spinning, spirals and swirls centered and guided by her body (Ranciere 2013, p. 95). The Serpentine entailed the rejection of the kind of classical model of beauty, based on symmetry and proportion, which Noverre's choreographic manifesto had also encouraged. The Serpentine represented, as Rancière describes, 'the destruction of the organic as the natural model of beauty' by opposing a 'perpetual variation of the line whose accidents endlessly merge' against the 'order of geometric proportion' (Ranciere 2013, p. 95). The static nature of Fuller's body, suborned to the spinning and swirling activities of her dress veiling it, also represented, following Rancière, 'the potential of a body by hiding it' (Ranciere 2013, p. 96). Her dress was 'the supplement that the body gives itself to change its form and function (Ranciere 2013, p. 96).

Fuller's art entailed 'the invention of a new body' whereby the body becomes a 'dead center in the midst of movement', engendering new forms through its staticity. Such forms, be they that of a butterfly, a lily, a basket of flowers, a wave or a rose, are not characters in a story that Fuller's dance helps tell. Their movements do not enjoin in an operation of plot making. Instead, they represent a new idea of fiction as a 'pure display of a play of forms', abstract, in so much as it tells no story, but instead tell only the event of their apparition (Ranciere 2013, p. 100). However, for Fuller's Serpentine Dance to be understood, and for its importance in the historical development of the art of dance to be appreciated, the role of images has to be addressed. For what her dance did was to turn the body into a site for the creation of a pure play of images, engendering new imaginary forms in ways that spoke directly to Noverre's demand that dance become an art for the creation of a 'multiplicity of images' (Noverre 2004, p. 13). In fact, Fuller's dance went, at the very least, one step further than that incited by Noverre, for what is masterly in the Serpentine Dance is that she not only makes images dance, but that she creates one particular image, that of a veil. Rancière supposes that her dress functions *as* a veil (Ranciere 2013, p. 96). In fact it is only an image of a veil. We know of course that her body is within the dress. However, a veil, for it be veiling, must function to hide something that incites us to ask what is behind it. Fuller's dress does not hide her body, or incite us to ask that question. For we already know the answer to the question of what is veiled by it; her veil is purely an image that dances.

Long before Rancière, Fuller inspired the poet Mallarmé, who described likewise the ways in which her practice, 'an invention without utility', caused a fading away of the 'imbecility' of the traditional placing of permanent sets in opposition, by dint of her 'choreographic mobility' (Mallarmé 2001a, pp. 114–15). Rancière's account of how Fuller's art worked to destroy the tyranny of such rules of symmetrical proportion within dance and choreography is in many ways only a supplement to Mallarmé's much earlier account. Indeed, in Mallarmé's wider writings on dance we can find an account of dance as an art of images in ways very much in accordance with what I am arguing here. 'The sole imaginary training consists', he wrote, 'during these ordinary hours frequenting the world of dance, of wondering before each of these strange steps, each of these strange attitudes, these points and taquetes: "what can this mean?' Dance transports us to a world in which we 'function in full daydream', where 'the poetic instinct' reigns, providing 'revelation in its true light of thousands of latent imaginations' (Mallarmé 2001b, pp. 112–13)".

This is not to argue that the body is not nevertheless present in Fuller's art. As Ann Cooper Albright has convincingly argued, 'Fuller's body is undeniably present' (Albright 2007, p. 5). Addressed in its entirety Fuller's art encapsulates the great paradox of dance as I see and explore it here, in so far as it deploys the body in order to vaporize the body, suborning it to the image. Others, Cooper Albright included, may well interpret her art as a different kind of attempt to foreground the body in dance. Fuller's legacy was expressed historically in the development of dance through path-breaking works of the 20th century, including, notably, those of Isadore Duncan and Mary Wigman. She is often described as having 'modernized' dance through her execution of new ideas concerning stagecraft, music, and scene design (Sommer 1980, p. 389). However, as Rancière argues, Fuller's work remains, in spite of that, in actuality, outside of the modernity of dance. It cannot be reconciled with the expressionism of Duncan and Wigman, both of whom sought, in their practices and performances, to manifest a total expression of every movement of which a body is capable (Ranciere 2013, pp. 104–5). Fuller, in contrast with those who followed in her wake, was not concerned with mapping the body, revealing each of its different potentials, but with subordinating the body to the life of images. For Fuller the body was not the subject of dance. Nor movement. In contrast, the body operates within her work as a mere instrument for the creation of endless imaginary forms. It is in that sense that she subordinated the body within dance to a life of images—a point missed in Rancière's otherwise illuminating analysis. She was, in this sense, more true to Noverre's 18th century ambitions for the modernity of dance; that it should become an art given over to the life of images. The body itself, we might say, was transformed in her work, into a font for a multiplicity of images, irreducible to bodily movement or even the body itself. Her body expressed nothing of its inner movements. Instead her body created purely imaginary forms that existed outside of it. The movement of those images, while in some sense depending on her body, nevertheless did not belong to her body.

6. Laban and Dance as the Disciplining of Images

Fuller's legacy might well be seen in the development of the work of artists such as Alwin Nikolais whose *Tensile Involvement*, which premiered in 1953, for example, freed dance in a similar way as that of Fuller, from the body, moving the gaze away, to abstract shapes (Thompson 2004, pp. 159–60). On the whole, however, Fuller's influence would become weaker, with the onset of the modernity of dance as it has been known and established. In the middle of the 20th century, Rudolf Laban, in his celebrated work, *The Mastery of Movement*, wrote of the need for dancers to use their imaginations but not with a view to dancing in creation of images. Indeed Laban wrote of the need for dancers not simply to use their imaginations but to train them (Laban 2011, pp. 22–24). Laban is often regarded within dance theory and the history of choreography as having contributed to the increasing experimentalization of the art and especially to a privileging of improvisation as a method (Carter 2000, p. 184). The truth is more ambiguous. A disciplining of imagination is what Laban inaugurated within the late 20th century development of dance; in ways that overturned Noverre and Fuller's wishes for it. The body remained, in the work of Laban, an instrument for the expression of 'mood and inner attitude' (Laban 2011, p. 22). Imagination in this context, following Laban, was also to be utilized as a means towards the expression of the body's inner movements. The movement and energy of images, that which concerned Domenico as much as it did Noverre and Fuller, was altogether lost in the standardization of the concept of human movement which Laban achieved whereby human movement was always to be understood as bodily movement. Understanding what I propose to call *choreographic life* requires, in contrast, following the lost modernity of dance still latent within the forgotten genealogy of dance buried in the works of Domenico, Noverre, and Fuller. Their idea, of images themselves, as 'charged' with autonomous powers to render still, to fix movement, as well as to mobilize and dynamize, is crucial for an understanding of the life of images. It does not merely concern the role of the image in dance, or the disposition of dancers towards images, but the life of images as such. Nevertheless, the art of dance and choreography is a powerful source of thinking and performativity for the development of a theory of the life of images.

7. The Contemporary Return to Dance as an Art of Images

One can see the concern of dance with images expressed, once more today, in a contemporary turn within dance itself towards the development and performance of works that, as Ramsay Burt has argued, call upon beholders to use their imagination through the evocation of histories and memories. Such works, Burt argues, are deeply political, because they 'have the potential to transform society by creating time for a belief in the impossible' (Burt 2009, p. 442). Perhaps nowhere is this more strongly expressed than in Ivana Müller's recent performance piece, *While We Were Holding It Together* (Müller 2012). As Maaike Bleeker has argued convincingly, the piece transforms movement itself, rendering it an element of perception, rather than being something 'out there' which we perceive (Bleeker 2012, p. 67). In Deleuzian terms, the piece performs the mobility of images, showing us not simply images of movement, but inducing the movement of which images alone are capable (Deleuze 1986, 1989). It entails bodies. Indeed, bodies are indispensible to the performance, but they are deliberately and consistently immobilized into statuesque forms. For the duration of the performance, five bodies stand or sit motionless on stage, apparently frozen in poses of different kinds, while verbally articulating what they each imagine their particular pose to signify. Each pose adopted generates a multitude of different imaginaries or imaginative acts. The pose of the body is subordinated to the articulated imaginary. Thus what the audience witnesses in the performance is the operation through which images transform bodies, in spite of their apparent stasis, choreographing them in time, moving them according to the powers of the image each time created. It is in other words a celebration of the superior power of the image over the body, the life of the imagination, and the choreography of images, in ways that speak back historically to the lost legacies of Noverre and Fuller. Müller's performance forces us to understand and grasp the contemporary politicization of dance and choreography, as an art of the image; celebrating its emancipation from its traditional subordination to corporeal movement. The images in *While We Were Holding It Together* do not simply incite movement in the manner understood as fundamental in Domenico's treatise, they transform the very image of bodies.

8. The Image of Dance in Philosophy

However, it is not enough simply to address dance as an art of the image. Instead we have to address the image of dance in philosophy. For dance itself is an image. Numerous philosophers before us have attempted to enlist the image of dance to enhance their own concepts of life and of movement. As Claire Colebrook has already detailed, in many traditional modes of philosophy dance figures as a meaningful movement only so far as it occurs within an already imagined form of life (Colebrook 2005, pp. 5–8). For this reason, Colebrook has tried to reimagine dance as a movement without ends, such that it precludes any appropriation by philosophy (Colebrook 2005, p. 5). I believe, on the other hand, while recognizing this conflict over the image of dance, that we can nevertheless make a particular image of dance; the image of the movement of images. We know, if we follow Gaston Bachelard, that there is an image of flight, and that this image, involving ascent from the earth, is integral to the psychic life of the human (2002). More integral than flight is this image of dance, which is to say this image of the movement of images. Because dance is the movement through which images themselves are choreographed by humans in time, dance must be construed as the image of the movement of the image. It is not one movement among other movements. It is the primary form of movement to which all images are beholden. It is literally how images move and are moved. The task of dance, as an art form, is to evoke this. More fundamental still is the fact that in our choreographing of images we are all called upon to dance all the time. Flight, following Bachelard, is a superior image. It is the highest image. It is the image which gives rise to human elevation. Nevertheless it is only an image among images. The image of flight, in particular, cannot be distinguished other than in its relation with the image of the fall (Bachelard 2002, pp. 91–109). Dance is different. It is neither an image of elevation or of gravity, but of the choreography of time through which the distinction between movements of fall and flight are erased. If we think the image in this way, then, we are no longer faced with the question of how to make rise that which has fallen, but how to dance such that our falling itself becomes reconciled with the choreography of moves through which we transform our bodies.

9. Badiou and Dance as Aerial Earth

In a beautifully written chapter of his book, *Handbook of Inaesthetics* (Badiou 2005), Alain Badiou describes something of this paradox of dance. He does not engage Bachelard, but instead, Nietzsche's concept of dance. Nevertheless much of what he has to say about dance could as well be accredited to Bachelard. 'Dance', following Nietzsche, Badiou argues, 'is a body that forgets its fetters, its weight' and in being so 'dance is what allows the earth to name itself "aerial"' (Badiou 2005, p. 57). The fundamental question of dance, he argues, is that 'of the relation between verticality and attraction' (Badiou 2005, p. 58). The place of these two forces in the body which dances, we are to suppose, if we follow Badiou's reading of Nietzsche, allows it 'to manifest a paradoxical possibility: that the earth and the air may exchange their positions, the one passing into the other' (Badiou 2005, p. 58).

Badiou recognizes that this is not simply a definition of dance, as if dance existed outside of history, but merely an 'image of dance' (Badiou 2005, p. 59). One can as easily conceive dance, as Laban and many others within the history of modern dance have done, as an 'external constraint imposed upon' an otherwise supple body . . . 'a regime of the body in which the body is exerted for the sake of its subjection to choreography' (Badiou 2005, p. 59). There is a risk also in privileging the aerial and the vertical, in dance and other terms, of glorifying a specifically western aesthetic at expense of others, especially the more ground-based aesthetics of Africanist dance practices, for example (Welsh 2004, p. 34). Nevertheless, as Badiou makes clear, Nietzsche, as much as we might suppose Bachelard, participates in the struggle between these different and opposed images of dance, which are as much a part of western dance history as is the history of the image of dance within western philosophical thought. Any image of dance that entails a submission of the body to a preconceived choreography, *a la* Laban, is not, as far as Nietzsche was concerned, dance at all. It is more akin to the militarized body of the western way of war (Badiou 2005, p. 59). Dance, in contrast, is the aerial body, the vertical body (Badiou 2005, p. 59) otherwise celebrated in Bachelard's work.

The power of the image of flight can also be literal of course. In 1987, the West German teenager, Mathias Rust, flew his one-engine Cessna aircraft out of Helsinki and into Soviet air space, landing eventually, in Moscow's Red Square. "I wanted to build an imaginary bridge between East and West", he said later, in explanation of his actions. Rust would spend over a year in a Soviet labor camp, but his literal flight of imagination led to the firing of two of Gorbachev's main opponents of his Perestroika reforms, the Defense Minister, and Air General, and it could well be argued that this made a significant contribution to the end of the Cold War, culminating as it did not long after, in the fall of the Berlin Wall, and collapse of the Soviet Union.

Rust's flight is celebrated in a homage performance, Uberflieger, by the dance artist Katja Dreyer (2011) who also appears in Müller's *While We Were Holding It Together*. The piece aestheticizes the political work which the image of his flight performed, detailing as it does, also, the artist's attempt to make contact with Rust and involve him in the performance; an invitation he declined. The piece conveys the disconnection between spaces in which images of flight circulate, in art, in politics, in the psyche, and in the air, while nevertheless expressing the fundamentality of connections between these spaces. It matters little that Rust does not appear in conversation within the piece, or maybe it matters more that he does not. The strongest of solidarities between spaces is often not only imagined but silent.

Something similar might be observed in the relations between dance and philosophy itself. Bojana Cvejić has argued that Badiou theorizes dance as if 'dance doesn't exist empirically' (Cvejić 2015, p. 13). It is true that his text on dance contains no reference to actual works of dance, only engaging with what Nietzsche and Mallarmé have had to say about dance within the debate over the image of dance in philosophy itself. The same observations could be made of Nietzsche and Bachelard, although neither of them were involved in any dispute over the image of dance, and simply employed their own images of it, as flight. Likewise, of course, much of the art within dance that has been working to produce dance as an art of the image, as well as to produce particular images of dance, has done so without resort to explicit support from philosophy either. Do these apparent disconnections not nevertheless contain within them the quietest of solidarities? Do they not testify to the imaginal qualities of a bond?

10. Agamben and the Life of Images

To reground dance as an art of images, an art of movement, but not of the body, instead of the movement of images, and as an art which struggles against the body, is nevertheless to reground dance as an art of life; the life of images, or imaginal life. Images themselves however are ambiguous when it comes to our own lives. As much as an image may give us life, so may it as well take our life. How, as Agamben asks, do we turn an image that arrests our life into an image that charges us with life, such that time itself is reset, and put back into motion? 'There is a life of images that is our task to understand', as he expresses it, in *Nymphs* (Agamben 2013, pp. 4–5).

Domenico da Piacenza, the great choreographer of the 15th century, understood this task to be fundamental to the art of dance. Domenico described images not only as that which the dancer must learn to control and measure in order to master the art, but as entities equipped with a particular power; the power of arrest (Agamben 2013, p. 8). What determines the relative mastery of the dancer is her ability to confront and subsume images while surviving this power which images would otherwise subject her to, such that she is able to keep moving. Every dancer, in order to learn and master the true art of dance, we can suppose, is at risk of falling, if she does not survive this power of arrest.

In the relatively mundane space of the theatre this drama of the risk of the dancer's fall is decided by what goes on in the mental confrontation with images. Carolina Bergonzoni has described it well. To suffer the suspension of one's movement and nevertheless keep moving is precisely the task of the dancer, and one which testifies to the contemporaneity of Domenico, she maintains (Bergonzoni 2016, p. 24). However, beyond the theatre this drama of the risk of the fall manifests itself in terms of the threats which madness poses to the subject, and of dreams which turn into nightmares (Agamben 2013, p. 14). For all images are as dangerous as they are potentially emancipative.

Fundamentally there are two types of image, but common to both kinds of image is the power of arrest. Arrest us is what images do. They force us to look. In looking we know not what form of arrest we will be subject to. For the power of arrest is also of two kinds. There are those images that in arresting us serve to take our time. They seize our gaze and yet give nothing in return. Instead they drain us, hold us, transfix us, deplete us, make us less than we are, and in some cases simply kill us; images that do not return our gaze; images that proffer no real reciprocity to our gaze. The name I give to this class of image is the abyssal image.

Then, there is a second class of image that does quite the opposite. It too is an arresting form of image, but it is an image that transforms us through its operation of arrest. In arresting us it gives us life; an image that startles and shocks, which causes us to desire, to feel, and be affected, as well as any other of a range of potential affects. An image which fascinates us, and which gives back more than we are ever able to give it. So the problem of the life of the image may well be posed in terms of the question of where to look. Indeed, not simply where to look but how to look. For one and the same image may very well contain both powers of arrest at the same time. Whether we live a life of encounter with abyssal or aerial images will in any case determine the nature of the life so lived.

To grasp the life of images we also have to address the power of the gaze, which in its seizure of movement, transforms that which moves, into an image. The gaze, in its operation, terminates the movement of that which is in motion (Lacan 2004, p. 117). The rendering of that which lives, and which in life moves, into an image, is itself a terminal operation. Lacan, long before Agamben bore witness to this 'time of arrest' in dance, described it as 'the fascinatory effect' (Lacan 2004, pp. 117–18). The fascinatory effect is that which 'has the effect of arresting movement and literally, of killing life. At the moment the subject stops, suspending his gesture, he is mortified' (Lacan 2004, p. 118). The gaze, that operation by which we produce images out of life, is essentially an 'anti-life' and 'anti-movement' function (Lacan 2004, p. 118). There is, in other words, a fascism to the gaze, which subtracts life from images. Images in themselves cannot become fascist, until they fascinate, and that power of fascination is only ever latent, without their meeting with a gaze. Dance thus exists at a nexus of relations not only between imagination, movement, life, and madness, but also of fascism.

11. 'Another Political Imagination'

The navigation of this paradox of the life of the image is fundamental to the task of the construction of what the arch-genealogist Foucault called 'another political imagination' (Foucault 2005, p. 185). For it is only in doing so that we will understand the ways in which imagination can function both as the source of subjection as well as the source of action. It is not a question of choosing imagination over reason, as the romantics would have us choose. Nor is it obviously a question of seeing in imagination the source of human subjection as so many of the modernist traditions in philosophical and especially political thought would have us see. Instead it is a question of negotiating the relation between the two classes of image I can only schematically sketch the nature of here; the abyssal and the aerial. Moreover, it is a question of understanding how these two classes of image function always within the same image at any one time. In other words it is a question of addressing the inherent dangerousness of images with a view to comprehending how the life of the image functions in a consistently vertical movement between abyssal and aerial spaces. Without images, without an understanding of the movement that occurs between these two classes of image especially, we cannot hope to comprehend the ways by which we move between these two forms of space. Images are not, as Henri Lefebvre would have us believe, simply 'fragments of space' empowered with the abilities to fragment space itself (Lefebvre 1991, p. 97). It is not 'the image' that 'kills' (Lefebvre 1991, p. 97), for there is no unitary thing such as 'the image'. Our reception of and movement within spaces themselves are dependent upon images, the ways in which they meet our gaze. The eye is not averse to tactile experience. The problem is to parse the differences between images that kill space and images that create space. In dance this is the problem the dancer herself faces at each moment in which her dance potentially develops. With gesture and the performance of presence she may change the nuance of the space in which she acts (Bergonzoni 2016, p. 22). Should she fail the space in which she acts risks collapsing and her performance falls into its abyss. Lefebvre himself noted the importance of dance as a practice endowed with the power to produce space, but was ignorant of how dance deploys images and not simply bodies to do so (Lefebvre 1991, p. 205; see also McCormack 2008).

12. *Fascinance* and *Fascinum*

Bracha Ettinger approaches an account of this problematic in her development of a concept of what she calls *fascinance* (2006). *Fascinance* is what happens to the gaze when it encounters an image that gives life rather than taking it. It is in that sense the opposite effect of what Lacan described in terms of the *fascinum*. It is the transformational aesthetic effect that occurs in the subject when his or her gaze is returned by the image that fascinates (Ettinger 2006, p. 61). In the *fascinum* that Lacan described, the gaze is not returned, for whatever reason, and the subject is determined, stopped in its movement, by this event of non-reciprocity of the image; another way of conceiving the aestheticization by which, as Walter Benjamin argued, fascism itself is established (Caygill 1998, pp. 116–17).

In the case of *fascinance* the image puts the subject into movement, and optimally, transforms it. To explicate her case, Ettinger gives a reading of Marguerite Duras's novel *The Ravishing of Lol Stein* (1966), the narration of which centers on a dance ball in which the main character, Lol Stein undergoes an encounter with an image which would seem to possess precisely such a potential. *The Ravishing of Lol Stein* is, as Kimberley Philpot Van Noort has observed, a novel in which 'everyone is dancing' (Van Noort 1997, p. 195). Lol is very definitely there to dance but she is also there to see and bear witness to the performance of another dance, that of Tatiana Karl with her fiancé Michael Richardson. This image, that of Karl and Richardson dancing, contains both powers of fascinum and fascinance, possessing the power to transform Lol from girl to woman as well as to withhold that transformation. As it happens Lol's movement from girl to woman is arrested and the rest of the novel tells the story of her attempts to recreate the same or a similar encounter with an image by which she might complete her passage, by turning *fascinum* into *fascinance*, so to speak (Ettinger 2006, pp. 62–63). An encounter with an image whose transformative potential has failed, and the attempts to recreate a comparably endowed image, in order to escape from *fascinum* into *fascinance*, is, Ettinger argues, the story of the ravishing of Lol Stein.

How can an image affect such a transformation? How can an image deny its own potential to transform? In the case of Lol, her potential transformation from girl to woman is located in an image of two lovers dancing, a man and a woman. It is for Lol, 'a fascinating image she wants to see again and again' (Ettinger 2006, p. 73). An image not just of a man, but a man who 'in front of the desiring and fascinated gaze of Lol', the girl, is desiring another female figure, a woman, a mother figure, who likewise is fascinated and desiring the man, in representation of the image of Lol as the woman she actually desires to become (Ettinger 2006, pp. 73–74). Lol is, Ettinger argues, not yet ready, as a girl, to love the man in question, and desires only to gaze at the dance-image and become a part of it, 'by the transgressive force of fascination that will include her' (Ettinger 2006, p. 64). But how could such an image possibly perform such a transformation? What is the nature of this 'transgressive force' that Duras portrays and Ettinger identifies in the image in question?

What quality differentiates it from the image that performs the opposite effect? For Ettinger, it is a question of difference not of the image as such, but of affect. This power and difference in affect infiltrates the field of perception and shapes the image such that it becomes, either the purveyor of *fascinance* or *fascinum* (Ettinger 2006, p. 67). Either the image welcomes her into it, making its space 'shareable', Ettinger maintains, or it will shut her out, closing its space, fragmenting the potential by which a space in which she, Lol, is implicated, might have become shared. The image here is merely a shutter, which either opens or closes, upon a space, depending on the operation of an affect. The image itself is dead matter, neither animate nor inanimate, immobile, until it is moved, by the power of affect. The gaze of *fascinance* is, if we follow Ettinger, 'an affective vibration' (Ettinger 2006, p. 85). It allows a 'glimpse at the forever out-of-time-and-space' by which 'the forever-future and the archaic past join in the now of the co-eventing in the Real' and 'transform the old scar or mark' (Ettinger 2006, p. 85).

13. The Image of Time

What is the 'forever out-of-time-and-space' if not the time-image which we encounter in the philosophy of Deleuze? The image, that is to say, of Time itself? Is it not, also the small non-time-space in the very heart of time that we also encounter in the work of Arendt (1993, p. 13)? The potential of dance is to render 'time visible and its forms and continuity sensible' (Burt 2009, p. 447). Ramsay Burt has detailed a number of different contemporary dance performances which function this way including those by Ivana Müller, Xavier Le Roy, and others. Works which not only create time for a belief in the impossible, but which do the seemingly impossible, by giving us an image of time itself (Burt 2009, pp. 445–52). This is a power which theorists, notably Susanne Langer, have credited to other arts, particularly music, in ignorance of the power of dance (Langer 1953, pp. 109–19). Deleuze identified it especially with cinema (Deleuze 1989, 1986). However, in Deleuze's analysis the encounter with this image does not enable movement; instead, it disables. The disablement is only superficial. For the encounter with time-images deepens us, taking us down, from the surfaces of movement on which we are otherwise positioned, in our sensory-motored lives. In doing so it makes us a subject. For subjectivity itself emerges, not in movement as such, but in the gap between a received and an executed movement (Deleuze 1989, p. 47). It is not, as Deleuze argues, 'motor or material, but temporal and spiritual' (Deleuze 1989, p. 47). What is crucial in Deleuze's treatment is that it is the image that generates affect. Affect does not simply enter, infiltrating a field of perception, shaping an image; it is instead the encounter with an image, which produces the affect, and the image of time especially. Affect, according to Deleuze, belongs to the gap, between stimulation and response. In this sense affect inhabits an image, because it is an image that fills that gap. This is what Deleuze called the recollection image (Deleuze 1989, p. 47).

In terms of its movement within time the aerial image is also more complicated than Ettinger's analysis allows us to understand. It is not simply initiatory of a movement from girl to woman in the manner she argues it to be, for it is the cause of a forward backwardness which deepens our relation with the past every bit as much as it renders the future more shallow. The Japanese novelist, Yukio Mishima, understood and conveyed this in his *Runaway Horses* (2000). There we encounter the character Honda, whose mnemic images of his childhood friend, Kiyoaki, produce a movement that is not from boy to man, but man-boy. When he was young there was but one reality for Honda, while the image of the future was multiple, 'swelling with immense possibilities' (Mishima 2000, p. 7). Now he is old reality takes many forms, and it is the past which seems 'refracted into innumerable possibilities (Mishima 2000, p. 7). Each of his images of his childhood friend, Kiyoaki, contains its own reality, and effectively annuls the real with its weight of presence. Inside of it he moves backwards, in time, opening the past, fragmenting it into its innumerable possibilities, transforming from man to boy. Images of what had occurred became constitutive of what could have occurred, and what could have occurred takes on the form of the more vivid than real. Is this the recollection image that Bergson spoke of and which Deleuze also theorized (Deleuze 1989, p. 47)? No, this is not simply an image that recalls some scene that happened in the past; for this is an image which operates as a function of the future by giving the past all the multiplicity and possibility which futuricity entails. It is not simply that the future becomes impoverished, narrow, on account of the potency of the image of Kiyoaki for Honda. Instead the future gives what it has, in terms of its multiplicity and possibility to the past, such that the past becomes future-full. Honda's future retains the images of Kiyoaki, apparently drawn from the past, such that they make them into 'objects to come' (Deleuze 1989, p. 52).

14. Choreographing Images and Their Movements

This is the paradox of the aerial image, and its relationship to movement. It enables an ascent to subjectivity, but it is an ascent that proceeds downwards. This is not to be confused with the movement of descent that Bachelard described when he addresses 'the imaginary fall' (Bachelard 2002, pp. 91–109). Indeed, the somewhat simplistic differentiation between ascending and descending movement upon the vertical axis of imagination that Bachelard proposes has to be revised accordingly. It is not simply that there is an upward axis of imagination that is true and a downward axis of imagination that is false (Bachelard 2002, p. 92). Bachelard proposes that up is the only true direction that the imagination is geared toward, while down is a direction we take when present in the order of the real. In contrast one falls high every bit as much as one ascends down. The upward fall is what characterizes the encounter with the aerial image every bit as much as the downward climb characterizes the abyssal image. An upward climb would qualify only the most banal of images, as much as the downward fall.

This movement of the aerial image is not to be confused with choreographies of 'aerial dance'. Aerial dance, as it is known and regarded in performance studies and research emerged sometime around 1960s, and with its roots in land art, is concerned with expressing the deep imbrications of human subjectivity with weather and atmospheres (Rogers 2012, p. 63). Instead the aerial image as I am theorizing it here is concerned with choreographing human defiance of atmospheric limits. Nor however is this movement initiated by the aerial image merely temporal or spiritual in the manner that Deleuze argues it can be understood, once we do away with a motorized or material understanding of movement. It is also political. It is a movement that goes back as much as it goes forwards with a view to operating upon the present, and transforming the real by acting upon it, impregnating it with images drawn from the past, which now take on the future, in a movement which dispels nostalgia, conquers melancholy, is neither happy nor sad, but affective. 'So it is that time reenacts the most curious yet earnest spectacles within the human heart. The past makes its appearance again, with all its mingled dreams and aspirations' (Mishima 2000, p. 29). This spectacle, of the genealogical past made present, future-full with all its dreams and aspirations, ready, now to be realized, is that of the image of a movement by which the subject climbs downward, falling upward, forward back, through time, and into new spaces. Hence, it is that images which appeared dead come back to life and charge us with a life which brings past and future into a relay in the present. The name for this form of life, constituted by a genealogical movement through time and choreographed in and by dance, is imaginal life.

15. Conclusions

This paper has outlined a political genealogy of dance. It has traced the way in which dance emerged and became conceptualized as an art, not simply of the body and its movement, as commonly supposed, but an art of struggle with and against the body, and as an art of images and their choreography. This paper has demonstrated this by tracing the consistency of the image of dance itself from one of the earliest works on dance, that of Domenico da Piacenza in the 15th century, through to the 18th century and the work of Noverre, into the 19th century and the work of Fuller. This was then followed by an account of the ways in which the roles of images in dance were subject to discipline in the 20th century, and then more recently by a return of the idea of dance as an art of images in the contemporary era. Inevitably, much more work is needed to flesh out this genealogy in greater detail and with more historical nuance, but nevertheless a foundation is provided here. The paper has also sought to link up the notion of dance as a political art of images with the image of dance in political philosophy, showing how important this image has been to trends within contemporary political philosophy concerned with the problem of what Agamben, Bachelard, Foucault, Badiou, Deleuze, and others have contributed to in terms of what I have called the life of images. Dance and philosophy support each other in the endeavor of operating upon the present and transforming the real by acting upon it, impregnating it with images drawn from the past, which might now take on the future, in a movement which it is the task of political genealogy itself to create—one which dispels nostalgia, conquers melancholy, and is neither happy nor sad, but affective.

Funding: This research received no external funding.

Conflicts of Interest: The author declares no conflicts of interest.

References

Agamben, Giorgio. 2013. *Nymphs*. London: Verso.

Albright, Ann Cooper. 2007. *Traces of Light: Absence and Presence in the Work of Loïe Fuller*. Middletown: Wesleyan University Press.

Arendt, Hannah. 1993. *Between Past and Future*. London and New York: Penguin.

Bachelard, Gaston. 2002. *Air and Dreams: An Essay on the Imagination of Movement*. Dallas: Dallas Institute Publications.

Badiou, Alain. 2005. *Handbook of Inaesthetics*. Stanford: Stanford University Press.

Beaumont, Cyril W. 2004. 'Introduction' in Jean-Georges Noverre. In *Letters on Dancing and Ballets*. Alton: Dance Books.

Bergonzoni, Carolina. 2016. *Fantasmata* and Presence: A Comparison between Domenico da Piacenza (1455) and Simona Bertozzi. *Congress on Research in Dance Conference Proceedings* 26: 21–26. [CrossRef]

Bleeker, Maaike. 2012. Media Dramaturgies of the Mind: Ivana Müller's Cinematic Choreographies. *Performance Research* 17: 61–70. [CrossRef]

Braga, Corin. 2010. "Imagination", "imaginaire", "imaginal" Three concepts for defining creative fantasy. *Journal for the Study of Religions and Ideologies* 6: 16.

Burt, Ramsay. 2004. Genealogy and Dance History: Foucault, Rainer, Bausch and de Keersmaeker. In *Of the Presence of the Body: Essays on Dance and Performance Theory*. Edited by André Lepecki. Middletown: Wesleyan University Press, pp. 29–45.

Burt, Ramsay. 2009. History, Memory and the Virtual in Current European Dance Practice. *Dance Chronicle* 32: 442–67. [CrossRef]

Carter, Curtis L. 2000. Improvisation in Dance. *The Journal of Aesthetics and Art Criticism* 58: 181–90. [CrossRef]

Caygill, Howard. 1998. *Walter Benjamin: The Colour of Experience*. London and New York: Routledge.

Colebrook, Claire. 2005. How can we tell the Dancer from the Dance? The Subject of Dance and the Subject of Philosophy. *Topoi* 24: 5–14. [CrossRef]

Cvejić, Bojana. 2015. From Odd Encounters to a Prospective Confluence: Dance-Philosophy. *Performance Philosophy* 1: 7–23. [CrossRef]

Deleuze, Gilles. 1986. *Cinema 1: The Movement Image*. London: Continuum.

Deleuze, Gilles. 1989. *Cinema 2: The Time-Image*. London: Athlone Press.

Dreyer, Katja. 2011. *Uberflieger*. Available online: http://vimeo.com/19484229 (accessed on 27 June 2018).

Eddy, Martha. 2009. A Brief History of Somatic Practices and Dance: *Historical Development of the Field of Somatic Education and its Relationship to Dance*. *Journal of Dance and Somatic Practices* 1: 5–27. [CrossRef]

Ettinger, Bracha L. 2006. Fascinance and the Girl-to-m/Other Matrixial Feminine Difference. In *Psychoanalysis and the Image*. Edited by Griselda Pollock. Oxford: Blackwell.

Foucault, Michel. 2005. Dialogue between Michel Foucault and Baqir Parham. In *Foucault and the Iranian Revolution*. Edited by Janet Afary and Kevin B. Anderson. Chicago and London: Chicago University Press, pp. 183–89.

Franko, Mark. 2006. Dance and the Political; States of Exception. *Dance Research Journal* 38: 3–18. [CrossRef]

Gunning, Tom. 2003. Loïe Fuller and the Art of Motion Body, Light, Electricity, and the Origins of Cinema. In *Camera Obscura, Camera Lucida: Essays in Honor of Annette Michelson*. Edited by Richard Allen and Malcolm Turvey. Amsterdam: Amsterdam University Press, pp. 75–90.

Jarvinen, Hanna. 2014. *Dancing Genius: The Stardom of Vaslav Nijinsky*. Basingstoke: Palgrave Macmillan.

Laban, Rudolf. 2011. *The Mastery of Movement*. Alton: Dance Books.

Lacan, Jacques. 2004. *The Four Fundamental Concepts of Psycho-Analysis*. London and New York: Karnac.

Langer, Susanne. 1953. *Feeling and Form*. New York: Charles Scribner's Sons.

Lefebvre, Henri. 1991. *The Production of Space*. Oxford: Blackwell.

Madden, Richard Robert. 1857. *Phantasmata or Illusions or Fanaticism*. London: Newby.

Mallarmé, Stéphane. 2001a. Another Dance Study: Settings and the Ballet. In *Mallarme in Prose*. Edited by Mary Ann Caws. New York: New Directions.

Mallarmé, Stéphane. 2001b. Ballets. In *Mallarmé in Prose*. Edited by Mary Ann Caws. New York: New Directions.

McCormack, Derek P. 2008. Geographies for Moving Bodies: Thinking, Dancing, Spaces. *Geography Compass* 2: 1822–36. [CrossRef]

Mishima, Yukio. 2000. *Runaway Horses*. London: Vintage.

Müller, Ivana. 2012. While We Were Holding It Together. Available online: https://vimeo.com/23973875 (accessed on 27 June 2018).

Noverre, Jean-Georges. 2004. *Letters on Dancing and Ballets*. Alton: Dance Books.

Powell, Jocelyn. 1988. Dance and drama in the eighteenth century: David Garrick and Jean Georges Noverre. *Word & Image: A Journal of Verbal/Visual Enquiry* 4: 678–91.

Ranciere, Jacques. 2013. *Aisthesis*. London and New York: Verso.

Rogers, Amanda. 2012. Geographies of the Performing Arts: Landscapes, Places and Cities. *Geography Compass* 6: 60–75. [CrossRef]

Smith, A. William. 1995. *Fifteenth Century Dance and Music: Treatises on Music*. Hillsdale: Pendragon.

Sommer, Sally R. 1980. Loie Fuller's Art of Music and Light. *Dance Chronicle* 4: 389–401. [CrossRef]

Thesiger, Sarah. 1973. The Orchestra of Sir John Davies and the Image of Dance. *Journal of the Warburg and Courtauld Institutes* 36: 277–304. [CrossRef]

Thompson, M. J. 2004. Doing your thing? Trisha Brown's object lesson. *Women & Performance: A Journal of Feminist Theory* 14: 153–63.

Van Noort, Kimberly Philpot. 1997. The Dance of the Signifier: Jacques Lacan and Marguerite Duras's Le Ravissement De Lol V. Stein. *Symposium: A Quarterly Journal in Modern Literatures* 51: 186–201. [CrossRef]

Welsh, Kariamu. 2004. *African Dance*. Philadelphia: Chelsea House.

genealogy

MDPI

Article

On the Genealogy of Kitsch and the Critique of Ideology: A Reflection on Method

Andrius Bielskis

Centre for Aristotelian Studies and Critical Theory, Mykolas Romeris University, LT-08303 Vilnius, Lithuania; andrius.bielskis@mruni.eu

Received: 17 January 2018; Accepted: 11 February 2018; Published: 17 February 2018

Abstract: This paper examines similarities and differences between the genealogical approach to social critique and the Marxist critique of ideology. Given the key methodological aspects of Michel Foucault's genealogy—the fusion of power and discourse and the Nietzschean notion of the aesthetization of life—the paper argues that Hollywood kitsch maybe interpreted as a new *dispositif*. A key task of the genealogy of kitsch is to analyze the effects of fake Hollywood narratives: how they form and normalize us, what kind of subjectivities they produce, and what type of social relations they create. *La La Land*, a 2016 American musical, is discussed as a way of illustration. Theorists of the Frankfurt School also advanced their critiques of the popular culture and its forms of kitsch; yet they followed Marx and his conception of ideology. The paper concludes that the differences between genealogy and the critique of ideology are philosophical. Foucault rejected the Marxist conception of history and the notion of ideology as false consciousness. Kitsch, for a genealogist, is formative rather than repressive; it makes people pursue banal dreams. For a Marxist critic, popular culture as a form of ideology dulls our critical capacities and, therefore, leaves the status quo of alienation intact.

Keywords: Foucault; genealogy; kitsch; critique of ideology; Marx; power; discourse; Hollywood

1. Introduction

Philosophical discussions on the nature of social critique have oscillated between two intellectual camps over recent decades. Risking a great simplification, I am tempted to call these two camps postmodernist, on the one hand, and Marxist and neo-Marxist, on the other hand. By postmodernism, in a somewhat old-fashioned manner, I mean the social critique inspired by Friedrich Nietzsche, Michel Foucault, and other French poststructuralists. The philosophical impact of Nietzsche's and Foucault's genealogical projects to social theory has been recently overshadowed by the reemergence of neo-Marxist critical theory. Given the bankruptcy of the legitimacy of neoliberal capitalism today, the skepticism towards the Marxist concept of ideology inspired by Nietzsche and Foucault needs to be reexamined. In particular, we need to understand the philosophical reasons why Foucault rejected the notion of ideology and how this rejection allowed him to advance his genealogical critique of power and its discourses, the critique which was different from the then dominant Marxist critique of power and ideology. Postmodern theorizing was at its peak during the rise of neoliberalism in the 1990s when capitalist growth was stable while the welfare state institutions were still intact. To advance a Foucauldian critique of discursive power regimes, as opposed to a Marxist critique of ideology, was then a novelty: the concept of ideology, as Foucault argued, presupposed a necessary opposition to the existence of truth, which, following Nietzsche, he chose to disregard. The rejection of the notion of ideology seems to be less convincing today.

Thus, in this paper I want to re-examine the points of convergence and divergence between the genealogical approach to social critique and the Marxist critique of ideology. I examined elsewhere how Nietzsche's and Foucault's genealogies might be extended and used to critique different forms of kitsch and how they shape society and our individual identities (Bielskis 2005). The key methodological aspects of Michel Foucault's genealogy are the fusion of power and discourse and the Nietzschean notion of the aesthetization of life. Given these philosophical premises, the paper argues that Hollywood kitsch maybe interpreted as a new discursive regime. A key task of the genealogy of kitsch then is to analyze the effects of fake Hollywood narratives. Theorists of the Frankfurt School, on the other hand, also advanced their critiques of popular culture and its forms of kitsch, but they followed Marx, rather than Nietzsche, in their critiques of popular culture as ideology. However, despite these philosophical differences, there are significant similarities and convergence between Foucault's genealogy and the Marxist critique of ideology. Furthermore, to understand Foucault's work adequately is impossible without reference to Marx and to the Marxist debates of the time. A key task of this paper will focus on articulating them as well as explaining how the genealogy of kitsch and the critique of ideology can supplement one another in the attempts to analyze and resist dominant power relations.

2. On Genealogy and Its Key Methodological Aspects

Foucault's remarks on Wilhelm Dilthey's distinction between understanding and explanation are a good place to start in order to understand the key methodological principles of Foucault's genealogy. Foucault's ironic tone towards Dilthey's insistence that human sciences should not follow the logic of explanation in natural sciences and his claim that "understanding is the mythical figure of a human science restored to its radical meaning as exegesis" (Foucault 2000b, p. 258) are instructive. Foucault was skeptical towards, to put it in Paul Ricoeur's words, "the hermeneutics of faith". He did not consider it important to uncover the original meaning of texts through their careful exegesis. Similarly, Foucault was not interested in continuing the flow of meanings of historical texts by applying them to the present as Gadamer proposed. Rather he followed Nietzsche in thinking that the main task of his critical analysis was to establish what function discourses serve in normalizing and forming us as subjects of existing institutional power relations. Furthermore, Foucault followed Nietzsche's claim that the essential features of interpretation are "shortening, omitting, filling-out, inventing, falsifying" (Nietzsche 2006, p. 112). He argued that

> There is never, if you like, an *interpretandum* that is not already *interpretans,* so that it is as much a relationship of violence as of elucidation that is established in interpretation. Indeed, interpretation does not clarify a matter to be interpreted, which offers itself passively; it can only seize, and violently, an already-present interpretation, which it must overthrow, upset, shatter with the blows of a hammer. (Foucault 2000b, p. 275)

Furthermore, we should not understand Foucault's genealogy as a heavy-handed theoretical methodology with deductively established first principles, which are then applied to the analysis of existing power relations and social institutions. In an interview, Foucault described his way of working as an experimentation whose aim is the transformation the self:

> I am an experimenter and not a theorist. I call a theorist someone who constructs a general system, either deductive or analytical, and applies it to different fields in a uniform way. That isn't my case. I am an experimenter in the sense that I write in order to change myself and in order not to think the same things as before. (Foucault 2002, p. 240)

Given that Foucault saw one of the key aims of genealogy "to be otherwise", to transform oneself against the odds of normalization and existing discursive power structures, the notion of writing as a transformative activity is instructive here. He saw writing, among other things, as a means of changing oneself. Writing as a way of being otherwise thus becomes the key genealogical activity. Yet change here has no teleological structure. Foucault refused to conceptualized "being otherwise" and the transformation of the self through the notion of an ethical *telos*—a universal moral standard to measure our lives with (as in Kant) or a eudaimonious life possible only by practicing virtues (as in

Aristotle). Equally, Foucault also refused to conceptualize transformation in the simplified Marxist terms of universal collective liberation. Rather he understood change employing such concepts as the techniques of the self, experimentations with pleasure, and the aesthetization of one's life. Commenting on the second volume of the *History of Sexuality* Foucault argued that the main aim of the Stoic ethics was an aesthetic one: it was based on "the will to live a beautiful life, and to leave to others memories of a beautiful existence", something which was not "an attempt to normalize the population" (Foucault 2000a, p. 254).

The theme of aesthetization of one's life is essential for us to understand Foucault's project of genealogy. It is akin to Nietzsche's dictum of giving style to one's character spelled out in the famous paragraph 290 of *The Gay Science*. There Nietzsche urges us to give style to our individual characters by incorporating both our weaknesses and strengths in such a way that the whole—an individual character and the way it is lived through on the daily basis—would embody "the force of a single taste" (Nietzsche 2001, p. 164). It requires "long practice and daily work", but also strength and power to submit to the constraints of a single style. Interestingly, Nietzsche adds that it is of secondary importance whether the style is good or bad; what matters is that it is "one taste". Thus, although the stylization of one's life has the function similar to that of ethics (i.e., its aim is to have power over oneself; to cultivate one's nature by imposing stylistic constraints on it; to follow one's own law), it is entirely an aesthetic endeavor: when the work is completed it should delight our eyes. Beauty, writes Nietzsche, promises happiness while ugliness "makes one bad and gloomy" (Nietzsche 2006, p. 75; Nietzsche 2001, p. 164).

Foucault elaborates this insight in *The History of Sexuality*. He argued that one of the pillars of Greek ethical discourse was focused on the theme of constituting "a kind of ethics which was an aesthetics of existence" (Foucault 2000a, p. 255). Juxtaposing genealogy and the aesthetization of life to Jean-Paul Sartre's notion of authentic life, Foucault argued that, instead of aiming to be "true to our true self", we "have to create ourselves as the work of art" (ibid., p. 262). On the basis of the aesthetics of self-creation he then invoked the notions of the *ars erotica*, *scientia sexualis*, and *enkrateia*. In the historical analysis of sexuality, Foucault showed a sharp contrast between the ancient art of sexual enjoyment (*ars erotica* as he called the discourse on sex in diverse cultures of Japan, China, India, and Rome; in *ars erotica* "truth is drawn from pleasure itself") *and* scientific discourse on sexuality where truth telling becomes an obsessive imperative. The Christian practice of confession stands between the ancient practices of *ars erotica* and the modern fixation on the pseudo-scientific truth telling of *scientia sexualis* which medicalizes and pathologizes sexual behavior. In short, Foucault, whether rightly or wrongly, saw sexuality in modern Europe as being normalized and structured through (pseudo)scientific discourses rather than through creative attempts to imagine and invent the new forms of sexual experience. Thus, Foucault (when discussing the issue of gay culture) could say that what is needed is not liberation based on discovering the truth about one's homosexuality but the invention of new forms of pleasure and creativity.

Yet the most important methodological aspect of Foucault's genealogy is his novel approach to power and discourse as intimately linked to one another. His dictum that in political philosophy the kind's head should still be cut off is a good starting point for us to enquire into the complexity of Foucault's approach. Indeed, it is precisely this claim—political philosophy and the focus on power as its key concept should not be erected around the problem of law, prohibition and sovereignty—that distinguishes Foucault's genealogy from the Marxist critique of ideology. Étienne Balibar once remarked that Foucault's theoretical productivity may be understood "in terms of a genuine struggle with Marx" (Balibar 1992, p. 39). Indeed, part of this struggle was Foucault's philosophical rejection of the Marxist conception of power. Although for Marx the issue of power could not be conceived outside the forces and relations of production, his understanding of social power still presupposed and relied on the existence and the functioning of the state. That is, even if "true" power always lies beyond the centralized institution of the state, the state is essential in enforcing the dominant social form through the solidification of capitalist property relations. In Marxist view, power is always the power of the dominant class whose dominance is possible due to the fact that it *legally* owes and actually controls the means of production. For Foucault, such approach still depends too much on the juridical-repressive hypothesis which, oddly enough, Marxism shares with the liberal tradition of political philosophy. Although in different ways, both Marxism and liberalism see power as repressive and as linked to the state. For liberals, as long as the state power is exercised to protect individual rights, its repressive coercion is right and just, while for Marxism political power functions, on the one hand, by reinforcing and protecting the social power of the bourgeoisie and, on the other hand, through the repression of dissent of the working class.

By theoretically fussing power and discourse Foucault rejected the Marxist conception of political power as merely repressive. He also rejected the simplified version of Marxist historical materialism according to which the economic base of society determined its ideological superstructure. Although Foucault never explicitly disputed Marx's claim that the base of power lies in the capitalists' ownership of the means of production and in their actual control of the economy, he nonetheless rejected the simplistic hierarchy between the base and the superstructure. Foucault also rejected the notion, so prevalent in the nineteen century, that the key functioning of power in modernity was to produce and enforce a hierarchically structured and centralized social whole. He decoupled discourse and truth from the economic base and in *The Order of Things* argued that Marx, far from producing the paradigmatic shift in sciences, continued and elaborated a "Ricardian type of economic theory" (Foucault 1970, 2000b, p. 270).

More importantly, by rejecting Marx's Hegelian philosophy of history, its humanism and the subordination of the domain of ideology to the economic base, Foucault elaborated his decentered and pluralistic conception of power. Power thus understood presupposes that the struggles for emancipation cannot have a utopian finality which, once achieved, will bring about a society freed from repression and alienation. It also meant that power should be analyzed in the Nietzschean terms of subjectivity production and normalization. Foucault's pluralistic account of power as intimately linked to discourse and the multiplicities of its meanings effected in his highly original analysis of different power institutions supported by and supporting discursive regimes. It spanned *from* the enquiry of prisons and the transformations of punitive disciplinary practices aimed at the "soul" rather at the body; the history of sexuality and how normalizing discursive regimes produced new sexual identities and new experiences of pleasure *to* his study of governmentality and new forms of biopolitical power.

Power rarely functions without the mediation of language, thus discourse is always part of power games, its strategies and tactics. As a professor of the history of systems of thought, Foucault was always interested in the effects language and discourses have in shaping us. Yet, as a number of commentators made it clear (Kelly 2014), although he took on board aspects of Marx's materialism, his materialism was of a certain kind. Foucault's Nietzschean turn made him acutely aware of how discourse and language shape and produce our material and bodily existence. Thus, Foucault's genealogical inquiry into the workings of power is not that of a traditional political realist *à la* Hobbes or Thucydides: what matters are not real wars and battles with swords, guns and bloodshed. Rather the battleground becomes language itself. The discourses and their meanings power produces are to be studies by a genealogist not for the sake of themselves. The question of truth of their propositions is not the primary object of a genealogical inquiry and hermeneutics is not its method. The meaning of a discourse is studied from outside: its effects, rather than truth value, are what matter. Yet genealogy is a historical inquiry (thus history for Foucault is of paramount importance), because it is history rather than "human nature" that creates us and "bears us". Humanity is a historical project and precisely because it is so, genealogy as a historical enquiry is so important. As Foucault put it himself:

> Here I believe one's point of reference should not be the great model of language and signs, but that of war and battle. The history which bears and determines us has the form of war rather than that of language: relations of power, not relations of meaning. History has no 'meaning', though this is not to say, that it is absurd or incoherent. On the contrary, it is

> intelligible and should be susceptible of analysis of down to the smallest detail—but this is
> in accordance with the intelligibility of struggles, of strategies and tactics. (Foucault 1980,
> p. 114)

3. The Genealogy of Kitsch

I have argued that kitsch should be understood as a *dispositif* which, together with its key network of institutions, shapes our identities and bodily experiences (Bielskis 2005, p. 65–85). *Dispositif* is a regime of intelligibility consisting of "strategies of relations of forces supporting, and supported by, types of knowledge' (Foucault 1980, p. 196). A regime of intelligibility or discursive regime then is a set of institutions and power structures enabling certain types of knowledge to be both intelligible and authoritative. A text or a narrative is not necessarily a *dispositif*. It has to have a network of institutions due to which the text becomes important: institutions and institutional power gives authority and effectiveness to the text. Without the institutions of power, a text would have no impact, no material importance, no effects and bearing on us. Foucault's genealogy, and the notion of *dispositif* in particular, focusses on the link between knowledge and power. It focuses on the politics of truth. The question then is on what basis can we say that kitsch is a new *dispositif*? Furthermore, why kitsch?

The aesthetic aspect of genealogy briefly discussed above allows us to see the genealogical significance of art, bad art, taste, and bad taste. If the key aim of genealogy is to aid the disruption of existing discursive regimes and power structures and open the space of freedom for us to be otherwise, to create ourselves as artists create their works of art, then the institutionalized forms of ugliness, their dissemination and their *effects* become of great importance. A simple definition of kitsch is that it is an exemplification of bad taste and bad art. Following Kant's discussion on taste and art, we can assert that signifying something as kitsch necessarily implies a judgement of taste. Both art and kitsch therefore are honorific terms (Barrett 1973). Yet kitsch, as a concept and cultural phenomenon, has a number of characteristics. It is banal; its portrayal of life lacks reality and truthfulness; it simplifies and sentimentalizes the objects it depicts; it does not have stylistic integrity; it is devoid of necessary reflectivity so essential to art; it flatters and seduces its consumers; it serves and fosters escapism; and, finally, it aims at popularity and commercial success through its fake imagery, narrative and form. One of the most popular and often consumed genres of kitsch is low-quality Hollywood films.

Hollywood kitsch is a *dispositif* because of its pervasive narratives and because of the complex network of powerful institutions which both transmits these narratives and reinforces them. Hollywood production and distribution companies, film studios, cinematography schools, promotion and advertising firms, TV, newspapers, cinemas and other media channels are some of the institutions in the service of the daily production and consumption of Hollywood kitsch. Hollywood film industry is a multibillion-dollar business which creates powerful myths and dreams and in so doing shapes our identities, our material existence, the way we imagine ourselves, and interact with others. Its influence and power can also be illustrated by the simple fact that Hollywood production, rather than European cinema, dominates in major European cinema theaters. Given its pervasive influence, the genealogy of kitsch thus understood becomes an important task for a genealogist.

To advance the genealogical critique, of course, does not mean to assert that all Hollywood films are kitsch. Thus, as stated above, the genealogy of kitsch requires an initial judgement of taste: the choice is to analyze only those cinematographic examples that do not meet the aesthetic criteria of good films. Yet good films are rare. Thus, given the sheer volume of Hollywood production, it will not be a mistake to assume that the majority of films ordinary people watch in cinemas or at home meet at least some of the characteristics of kitsch mentioned above. The key to the genealogy of kitsch, however, is not the judgement of taste *per se*, but how these fake narratives form us, how they normalize us, what kind of subjectivities they produce, and what type of social relations they create. That is to say, although the examination of the lack of aesthetic qualities of kitsch is a constitutive part of the genealogy of Hollywood kitsch, the far more important and indeed difficult task is to analyze the possible *effects* of these discourses of kitsch.

I have argued that one of the key narratives of Hollywood kitsch is the inverted ascetic ideal of romantic love (Bielskis 2005, p. 68–76). In *On the Genealogy of Morality* Nietzsche introduced the concept of ascetic ideals. The traditional ascetic ideal of Christian Europe was God. Belief in God meant living a life subordinated to God, that is to say, to nothingness according to Nietzsche. Yet the nihilism of the traditional ascetic ideal had *effects* which produced a specific kind of human being and life, the life of *ascesis*. The ascetic existence meant living a life of suspended bodily functions—no sex, no bodily pleasures, fasting, in short the life of mortification of body in order to please God and in so doing purify the soul. What mattered for Nietzsche as a genealogist was to analyze both the historical transformations of the traditional ascetic ideal once God was out of the picture *and* the effects these transformations and embodiments of the ascetic ideal had produced on us. By spelling out the historical transformations of the ideal which now fill the empty space of God—Truth in the case of sciences; neutrality, objectivity, and Facts in historiography (i.e., the belief that history can recover objective truth about the past); the avoidance of life, fame and marriage in and for the sake of philosophy; in arts Christian God *à la* Wagner or the disinterestedness of the judgement of taste (as in Kant)—Nietzsche shows how these ideals shape us. In short, Nietzsche's ascetic ideals—the bastards of the dead God—are in a way similar to John Searle's status functions: they are the symbolic places of authority, the signifiers, which, no matter what their content is, dispense power and in doing so shape and structure our lives.

The ideal of romantic love as portrayed in Hollywood kitsch is a further transformation and inversion of the traditional ascetic ideal. It provides meaning to our consumer lives in our secular capitalist societies. The value form penetrates the social body: nearly all our social relations have become commodified. It is a dystopia turned into a grim reality. In the neoliberal dystopia everything should be a commodity and everything should be bought and owned. In addition, since fully commodified social life (it is indeed an impossibility) is meaningless because everything (and everyone) can be exchanged due to its exchange value (and because there is and cannot be a thing that has absolute value), there ought to be an ideal which transcends the meaninglessness of consumer economy. Romantic love is this ideal. Love is outside of the economy (it cannot be bought), yet because it so, it gives meaning in the midst of the meaninglessness of the commodification of social relations. The inverted ascetic ideal subordinates our lives to the search of love in the similar way lives were subordinated to God, the traditional ascetic ideal. Yet it is an inversion of the ascetic ideal because kitsch, contrary to the Christian ideal, promises happiness here and now: "a painless existence surrounded by commodities" and, of course, by happy and conflict free love which transcend the value form. Thus, the

> ideal of happy love within contemporary cinematographic Hollywood kitsch functions through the denial of (...) any element of tragedy. The structure of the portrayal of innocent romantic love within Hollywood kitsch is almost always the same. The short intrigue caused by obstacles or unfavourable circumstances are always overcome at the end—the passionate love between two lovers overcoming all obstacles always triumphs. The narrative structure of these films finishes at the point where the major challenge looms, namely, to portray how this beautiful love, being able to overcome all 'dramas' and obstacles, survives and is lived through in daily mundane life. It is precisely this lack of reflectivity, the lack of 'realistic' reflection about the dynamics of love and life in general, that makes this type of cinematographic production kitsch.

> (Bielskis 2005, p. 69 & 73)

What I want to argue now is that today the ideal of romantic love and the idea of the American dream, as the paradigmatic narrative structure against which happy ending Hollywood films are recognized as authoritative and persuasive, have been transformed due to the bankruptcy of neoliberalism. The American dream is dead in Hollywood today, that is, post-2008 economic crisis. This is not say, of course, that there are no banal American dream movies produced after 2008 or that they will not be produced in the future. There are and they will be. Yet there is a shift in mood and this shift is best exemplified, in my mind, in *La La Land*, a 2016 musical romantic comedy-drama, the film which, far from being an example of Hollywood kitsch, is nonetheless significant for the genealogy of kitsch. However, before I discuss it, it is important to say something briefly about the American dream.

Noam Chomsky in his recent book *The Requiem for the American Dream* argues that the American dream has always had large elements of myth. Yet to a certain extent, it was true during the Golden Age of 1890s, in 1920s and then in 1960s. It was an optimistic belief that no matter how poor people were, provided their determination to work hard, they would achieve a level of prosperity, freedom, and equality: they could buy a house, a car, and their children could go to schools and universities (Chomsky 2017). According to Chomsky, given the unprecedented levels of inequality, wealth concentration, lack of social mobility, and the rocketing high college and university fees, this dream, despite its continued appropriations by the propaganda of the ruling elite, is over today. In a similarly way, although less pessimistically, Cullen (2004) argues that the American dream has had a number of historical transformations and that ambiguity was at its very core. According to Cullen, from the early ideals of English religious dissenters dreaming to worship God as they pleased and Abraham Lincoln's idea of economic advancement and upward social mobility to the failed ideal of social equality of 1960s, and the personal fulfilment, fortune and fame in its portrayals by Hollywood, the American dream signified the ideal of opportunity, happiness and freedom for everyone.

As far as Hollywood is concerned, the American dream, roughly put, is the idea that no matter who one is or what kind of social background she or he comes from, provided the protagonist is a decent individual who fights for justice and has determination to pursue one's dreams, such a person will always win and will achieve happiness. The idea is that anyone who is good can achieve happiness. The crown jewels of this happiness is romantic love. The rewards the hero receives are victory, the triumph of good over the evil, recognition, financial reward, but the most important of them is love: the courageous hero or heroine is embraced by a beautiful woman or a handsome man. The American dream then consists of all the good things together: the victory over evil, public recognition, fame and the love of one's perfect match. The dream is the togetherness of professional recognition, success and perfect love. There is no place for tragedy in Hollywood kitsch.

La La Land (written and directed by Damien Chazelle) breaks with this tradition by introducing a tragic element into, otherwise, mainstream Hollywood narrative. "Not bad is great" is the punchline of the story, expressed by Sebastian towards the end of the movie. Two young beautiful individuals—Mia Dolan (Emma Stone), an aspiring actress, and Sebastian Wilder (Ryan Gosling), a jazz pianist—are struggling to succeed in their professional careers. Sebastian dreams of playing authentic, non-popularized jazz. Unable to make ends meet Sebastian is forced to do gigs he hates, while Mia struggles through unsuccessful auditions. Their aspiration and hope to achieve the American dream puts them together, but the failure to realize them also sets the couple apart. Valuing his love for her, he takes up a job with a mediocre jazz band which castrates him as a musician, while she is fed up with rejection and decides to quit. They split, yet Sebastian still encourages Mia to go to an audition which changes her fortune. Five years later Mia is a movie star married to another man, while Sebastian has his jazz club and now plays the music he loves, yet they are no longer together. Mia stumbles into Sebastian's club, he plays their love song, they imagine what their lives would have been had their careers and love been celebrated and fulfilled. Now the American dream is just in their imaginations. So she stands up and leaves with her husband.

It is an enjoyable film, yet there is a point of criticism to be made. The film is genealogically important, because good films capture a new mood and tend to influence other, less sophisticated, productions. The novelty of the film, especially given that it is a musical, lies in the tragic element, in its "not bad is great" motto. Hollywood is the mirror of American society and its dreams, it is never stupid; it has to adjust by capturing the failing aspirations and unfulfilled hopes. Neoliberalism is failing on its own terms. Not only has it produced grotesque levels of inequality, it has failed to generate sustainable economic growth and investment.[1] The financialization of the economy allowed wage compression to go unnoticed and, due to the fraud and gross criminality of banks, produced the biggest economic crisis since the 1930s (Harvey 2005, 2010; Piketty 2014; Mason 2015). The American dream is dead indeed. Hence the victory of Donald Trump: by openly proclaiming that the dream is dead, he promised to make America great again and won the simple souls and minds of America.

A lie in the film is this: in a similar manner to cinematographic kitsch (e.g., Richard Curtis film *Notting Hill*, 1999) *La La Land* portrays Hollywood stars as if they were ordinary people, people who are constrained by their social circumstances, class, and modest means. A Hollywood celebrity is not an ordinary soul constrained either by the petit-bourgeois mores of marital fidelity (*à la* once married always married) or by their modest financial means. Hollywood celebrities marry, divorce and marry again as often as they please. So the fact that Mia is happily married (?) and has a child does not necessary justify her decision to stick with her reality of "not bad is great" and forget the dream of her true love unfulfilled. For if, as the narrative suggests, Sebastian is the love of her life (Mia to Sebastian: "I'm always gonna love you" and he replies: "I'm always gonna love you too"), and the only person who always believed in her talent as well as helped her to become a star, why wouldn't she pursue her dream of true love now that she (and he) achieved her professional dream? Leaving this question unanswered, the film lacks truthful reflectivity, thus its tragic element is excessively seductive and therefore suspect.

As far as genealogy is concerned, the problem with kitsch is that it leaves things as they are. It encourages escapism and never challenges existing power structures. It certainly does not question class power. The myth of the American dream and its numerous portrayals by Hollywood kitsch creates and legitimizes the illusion that any decent individual without structural resistance and collective struggles can achieve their constitutional rights: freedom and happiness. Now that this dream is dead, it remains to be seen what kind of new forms of kitsch will take its place.

4. The Critique of Ideology and the Genealogy of Kitsch

For the remainder of this paper I want to address the relationship between the genealogy of kitsch thus understood and the Marxist critique of ideology. A Marxist critic of ideology may object: the genealogy of kitsch is all fine, but how is it different from the critique of popular culture as a form of ideology advanced by the Frankfurt school? Furthermore, why the genealogy of kitsch rather than the critique of ideology? Since it is impossible to answer these questions in detail in the rest of the paper, my task will be to raise questions and make several suggestions rather than provide fully articulated philosophical arguments.

Although the content and analysis of the concrete examples of kitsch and popular culture may be indeed similar, the difference between the genealogy of kitsch and the critique of ideology lie in their different philosophical premises. Simplifying considerably, it boils down to the philosophical differences between Marx and Nietzsche. That is, Foucault took his philosophical inspiration predominantly from Nietzsche, while the critics of ideology follow Marx. Ever since Marx's (and Engels') formulations of ideology and his materialist conception of history spelled out in *The German Ideology* (1846/Marx and Engels 1998) and in *A Contribution to the Critique of Political Economy* (1859/Marx 1999) the notion of ideology has had several essential characteristics.

First, ideology, as Marx conceived it, is the dominant ideas of the ruling class. The control of material forces of society allows the ruling class to be its intellectual force. Therefore, ideology organically stems from and mirrors the existing material forces and power relations of a given society. Second, the main function of ideology is to justify and legitimize existing power relations in such

---

[1] Harvey (2005, pp. 154–57) argues that neoliberalism, despite its aspiration to create wealth, has failed to produce economic growth: from the 1970s to the present the average global growth has been a bit more than 1% as compared to 3.5% during the 1960s, while the enormous growth of financial sector has produced a great amount of fictitious wealth in the hands of the very few.

a way that the dominant ideas are accepted as "natural". Ideology, so Antonio Gramsci argued, is successful when its ideas and values become the common sense of the whole society rather than just of the ruling elite. Third, since ideology is a distorted view of the world, its critique presupposes the distinction between science and truth, on the one hand, and ideology as false consciousness, on the other hand. Fourth, ideology conceals alienation and exploitation making individuals passive and docile. It fosters banal popular culture and consumerism which, as Herbert Marcuse argued, create one-dimensional human existence. Finally, ideology relies on the notion of the subject either in the positive or in its negative sense. Positively, the subject is implied in the early Marx's conception of species being, but also in the humanism of the British school of ethical Marxism. Louis Althusser's theory of ideology is the most obvious example of the negative conception of the subject: ideology constitutes individuals into subjects of the repressive state apparatus and enables the reproduction of labor power and, therefore, capitalism.

Not all critics of ideology would agree on all of these points. For example, Althusser, who from the company of the critics of ideology is philosophically closest to Foucault, got rid of alienation and humanism from his critique of ideology. Now, Foucault, following Nietzsche, went further and rejected the notion of ideology altogether. He argued that

> The notion of ideology appears to me to be difficult to make use of, for three reasons. The first is that, like it or not, it always stands in virtual opposition to something else which is supposed to count as truth. Now, I believe that the problem does not consist in drawing the line between that which, in a discourse, falls under the category of scientificity or truth, and that which comes under some other category; rather, it consists in seeing historically how *effects of truth are produced within discourses that, in themselves, are neither true nor false.* The second drawback is that the concept of ideology refers, I think necessarily, to something of the order of a subject. Thirdly, ideology stands in a secondary position relative to something which functions as its infrastructure, as its material, economic determinant ... (Foucault 2002, p. 119, emphasis added)

The critique of ideology does indeed presuppose either the Hegelian-Marxian notion of history or, at least, the notion of human liberation beyond the exploitation of the capitalist relations of production. So even in Althusser's structuralist Marxism, the theory of ideology implies and points to a possibility of emancipation from the repression and exploitation in capitalism. However, leaving Althusser aside (after all, he was not the keenest critic of ideology at work), the aim of the critique of ideology is to uncover alienation and exploitation in the hope of collective liberation. A part of such critique is the critique of popular culture which, following the Frankfurt school's analyses, takes the shape of a popular ideology. Through the different forms of kitsch and entertainment generated by the culture industry, ideology deprives the working men and women from their revolutionary potential.

The culture industry and its different forms of kitsch dull our critical capacities and, therefore, leave the status quo of alienation intact. Therefore, for example, Max Horkheimer and Theodor Adorno argued that films "no longer need to present themselves as art. The truth that they are nothing but business is used as an ideology to legitimize the trash they intentionally produce" (Horkheimer and Adorno 2002, p. 95). Adorno defined kitsch as the beautiful without the ugly which becomes "taboo in the name of that very beauty that it once was and that contradicts in the absence of its own opposite" and argued that kitsch, in its embodiments of trash art and popular culture, was the parody of catharsis (Adorno 2002, pp. 47–48, 239). Marcuse followed their suit and, also, argued (yet less convincingly than Adorno) that popular culture functions as an ideology. According to him, it fosters fake needs produced and satisfied by capitalism, manipulates and oppresses people by making them superficially happy, yet dulled and passive.

Although Foucault acknowledged his admiration for the Frankfurt school in the late 1970s (Foucault 2002, pp. 273–74), he, as we saw, rejected the Hegelian-Marxist philosophy of history, the concept of ideology, and the sharp contrast between truth and power. On the subject of history, Foucault's position was uncompromising: "humanity does not gradually progress from combat to combat until it arrives at universal reciprocity, where the rule of law finally replaces warfare; humanity installs each of its violences in a system of rules and thus proceeds from domination to domination" (Foucault 2000b, p. 378). Nonetheless, he incorporated Marx's thought into his theorizing, arguing that it is impossible to write critical history without "using a whole range of concepts directly or indirectly linked to Marx's thought and situating oneself within a horizon of thought which has been defined and described by Marx" (Foucault 1980, p. 53).

By rejecting Marxism (especially dialectical materialism and the so-called repressive hypothesis) without however rejecting Marx, Foucault was bound to conceptualize political struggles in terms of localized attempts to resist power structures (rather than "the power structure", as Marcuse used to call it). His philosophical materialism, which he learned from Marx and his teacher Althusser, meant his realism in politics. Rather than hoping for the utopia of global revolution (as many pseudo-idealist Marxists did), he conceptualized genealogy in terms of micro resistance. If discourse is fused with power, then discourse and truth do become the key political question. If there is no outside of power and power is formative rather than just repressive, then, indeed, genealogical critiques are our attempts to disrupt the existing discursive regimes which, hopefully, allow us to offer our own, alternative, discursive regimes and power relations. Genealogy then, as opposed to the Marxist critique of ideology, has no linear direction: power relations provoke other power relations. Thus, if indeed we follow Foucault, we should understand the genealogy of kitsch in these terms as well: it is an attempt to disrupt the *dispositif* of kitsch we find ridiculous yet effective in making others stupid.

5. Conclusions: Ideology or Kitsch? Marx and Foucault

So what shall we make of all this? Which is better: the Foucauldian genealogy of kitsch or the Neo-Marxist critique of ideology?

Foucault, of course, was right that we should resist both the vulgar and romanticized teleology of history. The grand narrative of history is gone for good, so is the nineteenth century proletariat as the homogeneous and self-conscious political subject. Foucault is also right that even in an emancipated society there will be power relations, thus genealogical analysis has something important to teach us. It teaches us to engage in the analysis of localized power relations and, once cracks in them are identified, advance strategic resistance. Yet, Foucault, seduced by Nietzsche and the *Weltanschauung* of the day, pushed his philosophical conclusions too far: even if there is no outside of power, there are structural differences as far as different power relations are concerned. Marx's historical materialism, especially his analysis of the relations of production, is essential today for theorists to advance their critiques of the structural power of those who control capital and command production.

It is not necessary to draw a sharp dividing line between power and truth, on the one hand, and subscribe to the philosophy of history together with its belief in the utopian future, on the other hand, in order to retain the utopian aspect rooted *not* in the utopian future but in normative rationality. We should reject the Nietzschean idea of power against power, of our will to power against their will to power. Foucault's politics of truth should also be avoided, if it does, indeed, presuppose the outside of truth (after all, how else should we understand his "effects of truth produced within discourses which, in themselves, are neither true nor false"?). For us to engage in localized struggles of resistance successfully, we need to provide good reasons not only for those who are engaged in the struggles, but also for others. As such, these reasons and arguments supporting them maybe good or bad, better or worse, but their goodness is never to be judged *only* on the basis of the effects they produce.

Nietzschean-Foucauldian genealogy is right: kitsch is not repressive. Kitsch does not oppress, as Marcuse wrongly argued in his critique of popular culture. It forms and makes people pursue illusions and banal dreams. Hollywood certainly has no sinister intention to control and repress. It reflects the dreams, hopes and aspirations of people but also shapes them. Furthermore, it encourages us to believe in "human, all too human" banality. Yet the critics of ideology are also right to argue that kitsch makes people docile and passive, the fact so convenient for the rich and powerful.

Finally, without collapsing the irreconcilable, we need Foucault's and Marxist analyses together. Contrary to Foucault's hardcore Nietzscheanism, it does not make sense today to reject ideology as an outmoded concept. Ideology does serve the interest of the powerful and thus the critique of ideology has an important role to play in social sciences. In particular, critical analyses ought to show what kind of discursive regimes and ideological utterances have produced the effects they have enabling us to tolerate the grotesque levels of inequalities existing today. As Alasdair MacIntyre convincingly put it, "money generated a new kind of hierarchy, a hierarchy of patent absurdities—for you have to be a fool to believe that you should be paid that amount of money—yet absurdities that are treated with great solemnity. We are not supposed to laugh at the foolishness of the rich" (MacIntyre 2015, p. 14). To understand and expose this ideology is indeed an urgent task for both Foucauldian and Marxist critics.

Acknowledgments: I am very grateful to Eleni Leontsini for her critical remarks (especially her comments on the American dream) and editorial suggestions on the first draft of this paper.

Conflicts of Interest: The author declares no conflicts of interest.

References

Adorno, Theodor. 2002. *Aesthetic Theory*. London and New York: Continuum.

Balibar, Etienne. 1992. Foucault and Marx: The Question of Nominalism. In *Michel Foucault: Philosopher*. Edited by Armstrong, Timothy J. Hemel Hempstead: Harvester Wheatsheaf.

Barrett, Cyril. 1973. Are bad works of art "works of art"? In *Philosophy and the Arts*. Edited by Vesey, G. London: Macmillan, pp. 183–93.

Bielskis, Andrius. 2005. *Towards a Postmodern Understanding of the Political: from Genealogy to Hermeneutics*. Basingstoke and New York: Palgrave-Macmillan.

Chomsky, Noam. 2017. *The Requiem for the American Dream: the Principles of Concentrated Wealth and Power*. New York: Seven Stories Press.

Cullen, Jim. 2004. *The American Dream: A Short History of an Idea that Shaped a Nation*. Oxford: Oxford University Press.

Foucault, Michel. 1970. *The Order of Things*. London: Tavistock.

Foucault, Michel. 1980. *Power/Knowledge. Selected Interviews and Other Writings 1972–1977*. New York: Pantheon Books.

Foucault, Michel. 2000a. *Ethics: Essential Works of Michel Foucault*. Vol. I; Edited by Rabinow, Paul. London: Penguin Books.

Foucault, Michel. 2000b. *Aesthetics: Essential Works of Michel Foucault*. Edited by Faubion, James D. London: Penguin Books, vol. II.

Foucault, Michel. 2002. *Power: Essential Works of Michel Foucault*. Edited by Faubion, James D. London: Penguin Books, vol. III.

Harvey, David. 2005. *A Brief History of Neoliberalism*. Oxford: Oxford University Press.

Harvey, David. 2010. *The Enigma of Capital and the Crises of Capitalism*. Oxford: Oxford University Press.

Horkheimer, Max, and Theodor Adorno. 2002. *Dialectic of Enlightenment*. Stanford: Stanford University Press.

Kelly, Mark G. E. 2014. Foucault against Marxism: Althusser beyond Althusser. In *(Mis)readings of Marx in Continental Philosophy*. Edited by Habjan, Jernej and Jessica Whyte. Basingstoke and New York: Palgrave-Macmillan, pp. 83–98.

MacIntyre, Alasdair. 2015. The Irrelevance of Ethics. In *Virtue and Economy*. Edited by Bielskis, Andrius and Kelvin Knight. Farnham and Burlington: Ashgate.

Marx, Karl, and Friedrich Engels. 1998. *The German Ideology*. New York: Prometheus Books.

Marx, Karl. 1999. *A Contribution to the Critique of Political Economy*. Moscow: Progress Publishers.

Mason, Paul. 2015. *Postcapitalism: A Guide to Our Future*. London: Penguin.

Nietzsche, Friedrich. 2001. *The Gay Science*. Cambridge: Cambridge University Press.

Nietzsche, Friedrich. 2006. *On the Genealogy of Morality*. Cambridge: Cambridge University Press.
Piketty, Thomas. 2014. *Capital in the Twenty-First Century*. Cambridge and London: Harvard University Press.

genealogy

MDPI

Article

Foucault and Foucault: Following in Pierre Menard's Footsteps

Riccardo Baldissone

The Westminster Law & Theory Centre, University of Westminster, London W1W 6XH, UK;
r.baldissone@westminster.ac.uk

Received: 16 April 2018; Accepted: 14 May 2018; Published: 23 May 2018

Abstract: In his short story *Pierre Menard, autor del Quijote*, Borges describes the extraordinary and paradoxical feat of an imaginary 20th century French writer who recomposes, as it were, part of Cervantes' early modern masterpiece. Borges' duplication of the text of the *Quijote* is meant to give narrative shape to the acknowledgement that a text acquires different meanings in different epochs. This essay first sets Borges' approach to the construction of the past within a lineage of authors, which harks back to Nietzsche and points to Foucauldian genealogies. It then renews the endeavour of Borges' character Menard, as it reproduces significant portions of Foucault's 1971 paper *Nietzsche, la généalogie, l'histoire*. Whilst the selections of the Foucauldian text are not simply rewritten, as they are given a new English translation, they are also recombined and reconsidered in the light of our contemporary cultural and political context, which underwent significant changes during the apparently short span of time that separates us from the composition of Foucault's seminal work.

Keywords: Foucault; Borges; Nietzsche; Pierre Menard; genealogy; repetition; history; narrations

---

In his short piece *Pierre Menard, autor del Quijote*[1] (Borges 1974), Jorge Luis Borges recalls the feat of an imaginary 20th century French writer who endeavours to write the *Don Quijote*. Of course, Borges does not need to explain to his Argentinian readers that the *Don Quijote* is a novel written by Cervantes in 17th century Spain. However, Borges specifies that Menard "did not want to compose another *Quijote*—which would have been easy—but *the Quijote*" (Borges 1974, p. 446).

Menard himself defines his task as *asombroso*[2] (Borges 1974, p. 447), that is, inspiring awe and commanding respect—and astonishing indeed is the comparison that Menard suggests between his object of interest (the *Quijote*) and the objects of interest of theologians and metaphysicians. Each of these objects, "the objective world, God, causality, universal forms—Menard explains—is no less previous and common than my famed novel"[3] (Borges 1974, p. 447). *Anterior*, previous and *común*, common, are the two unassuming adjectives with which Borges understatedly depicts the shared condition of metaphysical *and* historical objects, namely, their alleged objectivity.

This shared condition allows Borges to extend his devastating treatment of metaphysical notions also to a historical product, which is nothing less than the masterpiece of Spanish literature. However, this extension requires a change of method.

Narrations allow Borges to put metaphysical ideas such as immortality, infinity, absolute memory, and unlimited knowledge to the test of practices: once actualized in the fictional world of a story, metaphysical ideas produce consequences that are at odds with any possible expectation grounded

---

1 Where not otherwise specified, translations are mine.
2 "*Mi propósito es meramente asombroso.*"
3 "*El término final de una demostración teológica o metafísica—el mundo externo, Dios, la casualidad, las formas universales—no es menos anterior y común que mi divulgada novela.*"

on experience. In other words, the narrative actualization of metaphysical ideas exposes their practical untenability.

In dealing with the already fictional text of the *Quijote*, Borges relies instead on the methods of literary criticism. In particular, he analyzes the text in the light of the historical context of its author. Yet, he deploys this analytical tool from within a fiction,[4] which leaves the text of the *Quijote* unchanged, but which moves its date of composition up to the early 20th century. This temporal shift, which would be indefensible in the actual chronology of Spanish literature, allows Borges' differential reading of the same text of the *Quijote* as another text.

Borges quotes twice the same sentence, first from Cervantes' text and then from Menard's: " ... truth, whose mother is history, emulous of time, depository of deeds, witness of the past, example and adviser to the present, warning for the future"[5] (Borges 1974, p. 449). Though this sentence reads the same in both quotations, Borges understands it in two fairly different ways.

"Written in the seventeenth century, written by the 'lay genius' Cervantes, this enumeration is a mere rhetorical praise of history"[6] (Borges 1974, p. 449). On the contrary, Borges argues, in Menard's text, the very idea of history as the mother of truth is astounding: "Menard, as a contemporary of William James, does not define history as an inquiry into reality but as its origin. Historical truth, for him, is not what has happened; it is what we judge to have happened"[7] (Borges 1974, p. 449).

By highlighting Menard's technique of deliberate anachronism, Borges makes fiction deliver, so to speak, a powerful illustration of the impermanence of texts, which are constantly subjected to our projective reconstruction. Unfortunately, this acknowledgement is still far from commonsensical: however, it was not completely new in 1939, when Borges' story appeared in print.

A retrospective chain links Borges' fictionalized reflections on textual transformations with a series of texts and authors. Borges is well aware of Eliot's considerations on the reciprocal influence of past and present literature: Eliot contends that "the past should be altered by the present as much as the present is directed by the past" (Eliot 1920, p. 50). Borges captures this contention in a lapidary sentence: *"cada escritor crea a sus precursores"* (Borges 1952, p. 90), each writer creates her predecessors.

In turn, young Eliot in Paris is fascinated by Charles Péguy, and he is familiar with Péguy's reversal of historical sequences. In Péguy's account, the very muse of history, namely Clio, claims that the first water-lily painted by Monet repeats the subsequent ones (Péguy 1932). Similarly, in 1915 Benedetto Croce boldly declares that because historical judgment is cast in the present, all history is contemporary history (Croce 1915): this claim is then to reach the English-speaking readership through the work of Collingwood.

As to Péguy, he is strongly influenced by Bergson, but he dies on the Western front in 1914, six years before Bergson's Oxford lecture on possibility as a retroactive projection.[8] I would quote here the core assumption of this presentation, which is not often mentioned in English: *"le possible est l'effet combiné de la réalité une fois apparue et d'un dispositif qui la rejette en arrière"* (Bergson 1934, p. 129), the possible is the combined effect of a reality once it has appeared, and an apparatus that projects it backward.

---

[4] We may say that Borges put to the test of narrations the theoretical insight of the principle of *als ob*, as put forth by Vaihinger (1924).

[5] " ... *la verdad, cuya madre es la historia, émula del tiempo, depósito de las acciones, testigo de lo pasado, ejemplo y aviso de lo presente, advertencia de lo por venir.*"

[6] "*Redactada en el siglo diecisiete, redactada por el 'ingenio lego' Cervantes, esa enumeración es un mero elogio retórico de la historia.*"

[7] "*Menard, contemporáneo de William James, no define la historia como una indagación de la realidad sino como su origen. La verdad histórica, para él, no es lo que sucedió; es lo que juzgamos que sucedió.*"

[8] Bergson writes in the introductory note to the essay *Le Possible et le Réel* (Bergson 1934, p. 115) that the latter is "the development of certain views presented at the opening of the 'philosophical meeting' at Oxford, September 24, 1920." The essay first appears in a Swedish version on the journal *Nordisk Tidskrift*, as a testimony of Bergson's regret at being unable to deliver in person a speech in Stockholm on the occasion of his reception of the Nobel Prize for literature.

However, if I may abuse the mathematical language of calculus,[9] the limit of this series of theoretical contentions seems to be Nietzsche's chaotic construction of reality, which includes the historical past. Nietzsche maintains that our engagement with reality would be better construed as the operation of temporarily ordering chaos.[10] Accordingly, we may construct the past as series of ordering activities.

Moreover, we may also consider the previous reflections upon the past as a series of historiographic ordering activities, and if we extend this series in the direction of the future, it would for sure include another text, namely the Foucauldian essay *Nietzsche, la généalogie, l'histoire* (Foucault 1971).

Foucault's paper appears in a 1971 collection of writings in honor of Jean Hyppolite. Forty-seven years after its publication, this Foucauldian text may perhaps appear less surprising to its readers, but it has surely gained a reference status: the essay is not only generally invoked as an introduction to Nietzsche's genealogical approach, but it is also often construed as the Foucauldian endorsement of *the* genealogical method. Yet, this alleged genealogical method is not even mentioned by Foucault, who stages instead history and genealogy as two veritable characters of a virtual drama.

In Foucault's construction, history and genealogy are the two antagonistic mediators with our past. Though they are not personified entities such as Péguy's Clio, the muse of history, they are nonetheless endowed with features and agency, as it were: in the Foucauldian text, genealogy retrieves, genealogy requires, genealogy demands, genealogy does not oppose itself, genealogy does not pretend, genealogy does not resemble, genealogy is situated, genealogy seeks, genealogy is, genealogy gives rise, and, in the end, genealogy returns.

As we all know, the deployment of abstract notions as sentence subjects is a powerful stylistic tool: it imparts agency and identity on these notions, by making them perform as grammatical subjects. However, in the case of genealogy, this rhetorical strategy may prove counterproductive, as it may suggest that the very notion of genealogy precedes, at least logically, actual genealogical endeavours.

Such a priority would not be too surprising, as it would appear as a particular instance of the still widely accepted priority of theories over practices. This general priority is well established in Western thought: it is first formalized by Aristotle in regard to both biological cycles and human activities. We have to wait for the Young Hegelians to have the priority of theory first questioned, albeit in the name of the rather equivocal notion of praxis.

However, Stirner's bold rejection of concepts (Stirner 2000) opens the way for the Nietzschean emancipation of practices. As already recalled, Nietzsche's construction of a chaotic reality undermines the objectivity of reality's orders. As a consequence, it also undermines the rationale of theory's priority over practice, namely, the supposed ability of theory to represent the order of things.

After Nietzsche, we can no longer naively appeal to the order of things. On the contrary, the appeal to how things stand would be better acknowledged as a theological legacy, as Wittgenstein too realizes in a moment of Spinozian enlightenment, whilst he is fighting on the Russian front: "*Wie sich alles verhält, ist Gott. Gott ist, wie sich alles verhält*" (Wittgenstein 1961, p. 79), how things stand, is God. God is how things stand.

Wittgenstein is notoriously not interested in history, but we may easily extend his equation into the past, and say: "how things happened, god was and still is." Considering that the historiographic endeavour is famously defined by Ranke as the display of the past "*wie es eigentlich gewesen*"[11]

---

9   I put forth this disclaimer just in case I had Bricmont, Sokal, or one of their epigones among my readers.

10   "[N]*icht 'erkennen', sondern schematisiren, dem Chaos so viel Regularität und Formen auferlegen, als es unserem praktischen Bedürfniß genug thut*" (Nietzsche 1888, 14[152]), not "knowing" but schematizing—to impose upon chaos as much regularity and form as our practical needs require.

11   Ranke's *dictum* somewhat restates Thucydides (Thucydides 1942)'definition of the task of the historian in *Historiae* 1.22.4: τῶν τέ γενομένων τό σαφέσ σκοπεῖν [*tōn te genomenōn to saphes skopein*], to investigate the certainty of the events. It echoes even more precisely Lucian of Samosata: τοῦ δὴ συγγραφέωσ ἔργον ἕν—ὡσ ἐπράχθη εἰπεῖν [*tou dē syngrapheōs ergon hen—hōs eprakhthē eipein*] (Lucian of Samosata 1959, p. 54), the historian's sole work is to tell how things happened.

(Ranke 1956, p. 57), how it really was, a surprising link between historical positivism and theology would emerge.

This link perhaps does not escape the attention of Benjamin, who, possibly hinting at Marx's definition of religion as the opium of the people, rates Ranke's history as "the strongest narcotic of the [19th] century" (Benjamin 1999, p. 463). In particular, if we focus on legal history, we would recognize Ranke's principles at work in the writings of Maitland. And yet, if we were to apply a pharmacological definition to Maitland's work too, we should take into account his specific role as legal historian.

Whilst modern historians can claim a tradition that goes back to Herodotus, legal history is literally an early 19th century German invention. Hugo and Savigny distance themselves from both the mere collation of legal texts and the teleological subsumption of legal material under the transhistorical principle of natural law. Their new historical approach to law has a decisive impact also on English legal history, especially through the influence exerted by Gierke on Maitland.

We may say that legal history as such puts into motion, so to speak, the static horizon of legal studies. Of course, nowadays this role is taken up by legal genealogies—or at least, I like to think so. However, legal histories, unlike positivist history, never have a narcotic effect. Rather, legal historians at the same time let emerge and domesticate the legal past. They make available in the legal field the enormous energies of history, which, according to Benjamin, "are bound up in the 'once upon a time' of classical historiography" (Benjamin 1999, p. 463).

For sure, Maitland's legal history is not soporific. Its cultural functioning may instead be compared, mutatis mutandis, to the cultural dynamic of Freud's invention of the unconscious, as construed by Deleuze and Guattari. In *L'Anti-Œdipe*, our authors contend that Freud lets emerge sexual repression, but only in the shape of its Oedipalized recasting (Deleuze and Guattari 1972). In other words, Freud acknowledges desire, but only within the boundaries of the family novel and its three characters: father, mother, and Oedipus.

In a similar way, Maitland (and most legal historians) acknowledges legal history, but only in the shape of safely distanced historical objectivity. Maitland famously urges to rescue all shreds of legal evidence from the oblivion (Maitland 1888), but only—as Benjamin would say—at the price of "their 'enshrinement as heritage'" (Benjamin 1999, p. 473). We may recognize in this result the immobilizing power of representation, which, even in its critical version, inevitably reifies its objects.

We may well liken the freezing effect of representation on its objects to a deep narcosis. On the contrary, the effect of the representation of the past *on readers* may even be galvanizing, as it offers them the excitement of dealing with historical facts and events from the safe position of observers. In the case of potential collaborators to the historical enquiry, it even lures them into the interactive game of a safe archival quest, which displays the vestiges of the past at no risk whatsoever.

This engagement with an attenuated version of the past may be compared, within the pharmacological domain, to an immunization. More than 50 years ago, Roland Barthes puts to use this comparison to expose the homeopathic recovery of institutions such as the Army and the Church in cinematographic and theatrical representations[12] (Barthes 1957). It may well be possible to understand this limited exposure which prevents a wider one as a more general trope of the theatre of representation.

Biological immunization can be induced by inoculating a weakened or dead pathogen, its toxins, or one of its surface proteins. If we continue the analogy, we may similarly understand the effect of representation on its historical objects as a paralysis, a permanent blockage, a desiccation, or a reduction to surface or epiphenomenal occurrences. To counter this effect, we would need to pursue at once the reintegration and the dynamization of historical evidence.

An available tool for both integrating and fluidifying historical notions is modern dialectics. As reconfigured by Hegel, dialectics claims the contradictory nature of each and every entity,

---

[12] Barthes considers Fred Zinnemann's movie *From Here to Eternity*, and the plays *Les Cyclones* and *The Living Room* by Jules Roy and Graham Greene respectively.

by internalizing the oppositional structure of the logic of identity.[13] According to Hegel, a necessary inner strife precedes, at least logically, the external ones. However, both inner and outer fissures are the result of the simple partitive operation of negation, which posits an already common logical space.

I already recalled Deleuze and Guattari's construction of Freudian repression. In particular, they insert between Freud's repressor and repressed a third element, which is the Oedipalized subject on whom repression can be exerted. Deleuze and Guattari define this Oedipalized subject as the disfigured or displaced repressed.[14] Such a displacement is needed because of the incommensurability of the repressor and the repressed: in order to be subjected to repression, the repressed has first to be recast according to the perspective of the repressor.[15]

If we try to translate Deleuze and Guattari's threefold dynamic of repression in Hegelian terms, the Oedipalized subject as a displaced repressed may play the role of a nonvanishing mediator between the repressor and the repressed. Unlike the Hegelian mediator, which temporarily engages with its opposite before vanishing (as such) as the effect of sublation, the mediating intervention of the displaced repressed will not cease.

It is then not by chance that the two extremes of the possible negations of human otherness, namely genocide and assimilation, seem to require the previous covering of the other with its substitute image—which is, generally, a dehumanized one. Even a successful reduction of the other, either to nil (genocide) or to self (assimilation), can never completely erase the other if only because of the previous duplication of this very other: and of course, it is up to the genealogist to produce to the court of readership this other's rest, residue, and reminder.[16]

We may even attempt a generalization of the threefold dynamic of repression, and we may extend this dynamic to the wider field of representation. In this case, representation would appear as a unilateral and thus violently reductive intervention of the representing subject upon the object to be represented. This intervention would result in a disfigured or displaced representation of the object: in turn, such representation would substitute the object itself by covering it up, as it were.[17]

This disfiguring effect would not reach its apex in its self-declaring instances, such as, for example, Francis Bacon's paintings. On the contrary, the covering power of representation would be better exerted through the mimetic ability of images. The peak of disfiguration would then be reached when the disfigured representations become indistinguishable from the supposedly represented objects.

We do not need to invoke Baudrillard to recall the terrifying effect of film and television hyperreality: in the regime of actually existing democracies, media better cover up by covering, so to speak. If I may follow Lucian of Samosata in staging another dialogue of the dead, I would have Guy Debord asking Isaiah Berlin why our current human rights legislation does not contemplate the existence, let alone the defence, of a freedom *from* information.

Apparently, these considerations would imply the indictment of repetition as the most vicious tool for manipulating both reality and history. As a consequence, they would also throw a disturbing light upon Kierkegaard's proposal of repetition as an alternative to both Platonic recollection and

---

[13] More precisely, in the *Science of Logic* Hegel (2010) constructs conceptual entities (including mathematical ones, p. 99) as beginnings, that is, a combination of their determinate being with a likewise determinate negation that produces a higher and richer concept (p. 33). The Hegelian *Science of Logic* is at the same time the exposition of a technique of construction of reality and its application: from a Nietzschean perspective, it works as an ordering machine that cannot be detached from its objects, as they only *become* objects in the very process of being ordered.

[14] "[L]'*image défigurée du refoulé, ce sont les pulsions incestueuses*" (Deleuze and Guattari 1972, p. 142).

[15] "*C'est dans un même mouvement que la production sociale répressive se fait remplacer par la famille refoulante, et que celle-ci donne de la production désirante une image déplacée qui représente le refoulé comme pulsions familiales incestueuses*" (Deleuze and Guattari 1972, p. 142).

[16] I am particularly fond of English legal doublets and triplets, which are themselves a reminder of their role of interface between Law French and its Anglophone milieu.

[17] "[L]*e désir réprimé est comme recouvert par l'image déplacée et truquée qu'en suscite le refoulement*" (Deleuze and Guattari 1972, p. 142).

Hegelian mediation (Kierkegaard 2009). Yet, our good Danish Lutheran would surely agree with his Swabian co-religionist Hölderlin on the close association of danger and salvation.[18]

In the course of modernities, and especially their lower stage, the complaint about the numbing danger of repetition is played as a contrapuntal accompaniment to the praising of innovation. Viktor Sklovskij (1991) even constructs repetition as the ground from which the figure of остранение [*otstranenie*], estrangement, emerges by contrast.[19] In turn, the notion of estrangement, in its German version of *Verfremdungseffekt*, is deployed by Bertolt Brecht in his struggle with the mimetic power of theatre.[20]

Just like Plato, Brecht warns his audience against theatrical duplication because he himself is under the fascination of representation: and unlike Plato, Brecht can build upon a tradition of self-policing Lutheran consciousness. On the other side of the political spectrum, Schmitt hails the power of real life breaking through "the crust of a mechanism that has become torpid by repetition" (Schmitt 1985, p. 15). Freud instead does not target repetition as resistance to change: he rather casts it as an active expression of death drive (Freud 1920), which is, arguably, his defensive rationalization of the otherwise unjustifiable horrors of the First World War.

Of course, we may also detect in the modern despising of repetition more than an echo of the Platonic loathing for φαντάσματα[21] [*phantasmata*], the copies that are bad because they are not directly modelled on the ideas. On the contrary, Deleuze openly claims the reversal of the priority of Platonic ideas over their copies (Deleuze 1966): in their Latin version of *simulacra*, Deleuzean bad copies are no longer subordinated to their Platonic models, but they refer to each other in an infinite chain of differing and deferring, which Derrida previously defines as *différance* (Derrida 1963).

In the understanding of both Deleuze and Derrida, repetition alters. However, whilst both authors forcefully *argue* about the altering power of repetition, we may follow Borges' example and *play* repetition as an alternative to both representation and its supposed models. Such a practiced alternative to representation and objectivity would be pursued, in the words of Nietzsche, "not in order to refute them—what business is it of mine to refute!—but, as befits a positive mind, to replace the improbable with the more probable and in some circumstances to replace one error with another"[22] (Nietzsche 2006, p. 6). In other words, the practice of repetition may reveal itself as a more productive error than representation and its previous metaphysical avatars.

The borrowing of literary techniques may perhaps appear questionable. Yet, most turning points in Western thought profit from importing, so to speak, tools and equipment from theatrical and literary practice. Whilst Parmenides writes in poetry, Plato invents philosophical dialogue as a transposition of dramatic writing. The narrative form of the gospels then shapes Christian discourse, and the Latin novel of Apuleius prompts Augustine's autobiographical account. Descartes constructs the modern philosophical subject on the model of Augustine's *Confessiones*, possibly through the mediation of Abelard's epistolary persona: for sure, Rousseau endows this modern subject with emotions under the influence of Abelard's lover and correspondent Héloïse.

As to historical accounts, since Herodotus, they share narrative devices with fiction. Despite Thucydides' early truth claim, documentary evidence is only explicitly appealed to by Cusanus and

---

18 Hölderlin (1966, p. 463) famously writes in his poem *Patmos* (lines 3–4): "*Wo aber Gefahr ist, wächst / Das Rettende auch.*" But where danger is, there grows / the saving power too.

19 Sklovskij writes of метод[ом] остранения [*metod(om) otstraneniya*], technique of estrangement, in his 1917 essay Искусство как Приём [*Iskusstvo kak Priyem*], Art as Device.

20 "*Einen Vorgang oder einen Charakter verfremden heißt zunächst einfach, dem Vorgang oder dem Charakter das Selbstverständliche, Bekannte, Einleuchtende zu nehmen und über ihn Staunen und Neugierde zu erzeugen*" (Brecht 1967, p. 301). To defamiliarize [*verfremden*] an event or a character is simply to take what to the event or character is obvious, known, evident and produce surprise and curiosity out of it.

21 Plato (Plato 1900–1907), *Republic* 599a.

22 "[N]*icht indem sie widerlegte—was habe ich mit Widerlegungen zu schaffen!—sondern, wie es einem positiven Geiste zukommt, an Stelle des Unwahrscheinlichen das Wahrscheinlichere setzend, unter Umständen an Stelle eines Irrthums einen andern*" (Nietzsche 1887, *Vorrede* 4). Available online: http://www.nietzschesource.org/?#eKGWB/GM-Vorrede-4.

Valla in the 15th century[23] (Valla 1517), on the model of religious textual disputes. However, to say it with Foucault, whilst traditional history strives to transform the monuments of the past into documents, "in our time, history is that which transforms documents into monuments" (Foucault 1972, p. 8). Though not all contemporary historians would be happy to define their work as the production of historical narrations, most of them would describe their activities as less a deciphering than an ordering of the past.

In this perspective, "the problem is now—again quoting Foucault—to constitute series: to define the elements proper to each series, to fix its boundaries, to reveal its own specific type of relations, to formulate its laws, and, beyond this, to describe the relations between different series" (1972, p. 8).

I have already stretched the notion of series in order to include textual objects that are, at the same time, historical objects and attempts at ordering historical objects. I would add to this series, which goes from Nietzsche's *Zur Genealogie der Moral* to Foucault's *Nietzsche, la généalogie, l'histoire*, a further element. More precisely, following the example of Borges' fictional character Pierre Menard, I will produce this other element as the repetition of Foucault's essay.

My task is definitively less difficult than Menard's. Not only a much shorter chronological gap severs me from the previous author of my text: I am also happy to endorse many of the text's statements, which thus seem to be already mine,[24] so to speak. Moreover, whilst as a reader I will deal with the original text in French, as a writer I will produce its *doppelgänger* in English: and because English is my working language, this will relieve me from the effort required to the Francophone Menard of learning Spanish. I have no doubt that no one would object to this language transfer, considering that the use of quotations in English translation meets universal approval.[25]

I recalled that in Borges' text, both the (identical) quotations from Cervantes and Menard are followed by their respective interpretation. In my text, I will only include my version,[26] and the interpretation of its 2018 re-composition. Moreover, I will not even attempt to draft the whole text of *Nietzsche, la généalogie, l'histoire*. Such an undertaking would exceed the limits of my essay, just like the recollection of all the events of a whole day by Funes—another Borgesian character—requires another whole day.[27] However, considering that Menard's exertion does not go beyond the ninth and thirty-eighth chapters of the first part of *Don Quixote*, together with a fragment of chapter twenty-two, I will be contented with the partiality of my effort: and following Lucian's advice on writing history, I will try to order my fragments εἰσ καλὸν[28] [*eis kalon*] (Lucian of Samosata 1959, p. 64), that is, as pleasantly as possible. Then let the play begin.

"Why does the genealogist Nietzsche refuse, at least in certain cases, the quest for origin (*Ursprung*)? First, because this quest strives to recover the exact essence of the thing, its purest possibility, its identity as carefully folded on itself, its form as unmoving and preceding everything external, accidental and successive. The quest for such an origin is the attempt to find 'that which was already there,' the 'precisely that' of the image which is exactly identical to its object."[29]

---

23 Following the argument put forth at the council of Basel (1431 on) by Nicholas of Cusa, for whom he works as a secretary, Lorenzo Valla shows in his 1440 *De Falso Credita et Ementita Constantini Donatione Declamatio* (printed in 1517) that the document of the alleged donation of Constantine is a late forgery, by conducting a philological comparison of this text with surviving documents from the time of Constantine.

24 This appropriation will reveal soon its projective limits.

25 Considering at least my own opinion in regard, I should probably rather write "nearly universal approval."

26 I will let Foucault speak in the notes.

27 In *Funes el memorioso*, Borges recalls his character's feat: "*Dos o tres veces había reconstruido un día entero; no había dudado nunca, pero cada reconstrucción había requerido un día entero*" (Borges 1974, p. 488). Two or three times he reconstructed a whole day: he never had doubts, but each reconstruction required a whole day.

28 Lucian of Samosata (1959, p. 64) argues that τὸ τοῦ συγγραφέωσ ἔργον [*to tou syngrapheōs ergon*], the work of the historian, is similar to that of the sculptor, inasmuch as the historian's task is εἰσ καλὸν διαθέσθαι τὰ πεπραγμένα [*eis kalon diathesthai ta pepragmena*], to arrange the events in a beautiful way.

29 "*Pourquoi Nietzsche généalogiste récuse-t-il, au moins en certaines occasions, la recherche de l'origine (Ursprung)? Parce que d'abord on s'efforce d'y recueillir l'essence exacte de la chose, sa possibilité la plus pure, son identité soigneusement repliée sur elle-même, sa forme immobile et antérieure à tout ce qui est externe, accidentel et successif. Rechercher une telle origine, c'est essayer de retrouver 'ce qui était déjà', le 'cela même' d'une image exactement adéquate à soi*" (Foucault 1971, p. 148).

Written in 2018, after the spreading of Science and Technology Studies, and especially after Latour's contention that the "out-there-ness" or, in more ordinary terms, the objectivity of scientific facts is the consequence of the scientific work rather than its cause (Latour and Woolgar 1979), these sentences bundle together historical, philosophical, and also *scientific* objectivity.

"And freedom, wouldn't freedom lay at the root of the human being, wouldn't freedom link her to being and truth? Actually, freedom is but 'an invention of the ruling classes'."[30]

After forty years of neoliberal revolution, the Foucauldian reference to Nietzsche's reminder that freedom is a tool of social discrimination would assume a sinister prophetical tone. However, because in my text this quotation appears *post festum*, it rather conveys a double indictment of freedom. On the one side, it underlines the inextricable association between the notions of free market and free individual, and their joint responsibility in our contemporary disasters.[31] On the other side, the modern specificity of this association does not contradict the historical path of freedom as a mark of privilege: and we know that privileges cannot be overcome simply by virtue of their hypothetical (and unlikely) universal redistribution, which would still perpetuate authoritarian constructions of realities.

No doubt, the notion of freedom demands a genealogical approach, which would rescue it from its alleged immutability, but I dealt with it elsewhere.[32] Here, I will give a similar treatment to other concepts. Let's start with truth.

"Truth is a kind of error that cannot be confuted, undoubtedly because it was so hardened by history's long-lasting cooking that it became inalterable. And anyway, the very question of truth, the right, which truth bequeaths to itself, to refuse error and to oppose itself to appearance, the way in which truth was alternately available to wise men, and then it was reserved only to men of piety, and, after that, it was withdrawn to an unattainable world where it played at once the role of consolation and imperative, and at last it was rejected as a useless notion, superfluous and contradicted on all sides, —is it not all this a history, the history of the error called truth?"[33]

Foucault sketches his four-stage history of truth five years after the Derridean depiction of the history of Western thought as a series of substitutions of centre for centre (Derrida 1967): however, I am writing this text also after Lyotard's proposal of a narrative paradigm (Lyotard 1979). Despite his unhappy choice of the prefix "post" before the word "modern," Lyotard's suggestion helps us to make room for rethinking the first three stages of the history of truth without having to substitute them with a fourth one. We may well read the ontology of Greek wise men, the theology of the men of piety, and the naturalism of modern scientists, as steps in the path of onto-theo-physio-logy.[34]

Nowadays, we can construct Western thought as an ontotheophysiological path, insofar as we no longer sever theoretical objects from their processes of production. This severance can instead at last appear as an operation shared by classical philosophers, theologians, and modern scientists alike. We may define this appearance, in Nietzschean terms, as an *Enstehung*, that is, an emergence.

---

[30] *"Et la liberté, serait-elle, à la racine de l'homme, ce qui le lie à l'être et à la vérité? En fait, elle n'est qu'une 'invention des classes dirigeantes'"* (Foucault 1971, p. 148). Actually, Nietzsche writes that "the theory of the freedom *of the will* is an invention of the ruling classes" (Nietzsche 1996, p. 305), my italics. *"Die Lehre von der Freiheit des Willens ist eine Erfindung herrschender Stände."* (Nietzsche 1878, p. 29). Available online: http://www.nietzschesource.org/#eKGWB/WS-9.

[31] Of course, we all know that both the freedom of the market and the freedom of the individual are fictions. Yet, they do act as powerful regulative ideas and measuring sticks for actual practices.

[32] See my monograph *Farewell to Freedom*, which is in print for University of Westminster Press.

[33] *"La vérité, sorte d'erreur qui a pour elle de ne pouvoir être réfutée, sans doute parce que la longue cuisson de l'histoire l'a rendue inaltérable. Et d'ailleurs la question même de la vérité, le droit qu'elle se donne de réfuter l'erreur ou de s'opposer à l'apparence, la manière dont tour à tour elle fut accessible aux sages, puis réservée aux seuls hommes de piété, ensuite retirée dans un monde hors d'atteinte où elle joua à la fois le rôle de la consolation et de l'impératif, rejetée enfin comme idée inutile, superflue, partout contredite, —tout cela n'est-ce pas une histoire, l'histoire d'une erreur qui a nom vérité?"* (Foucault 1971, p. 149–50).

[34] The term "ontotheology" is probably a Kantian coin: Heidegger turns it into a description of the metaphysical double concern with *theos*, god or ultimate reality, and *onta*, beings. I rather read it as a genealogical recapitulation of the two first major stages of Western philosophy, namely the ontological stage, which is centred on being, and the theological one, which is centred on the Christian god. Yet, this definition misses to quote the third and current stage, which is centred on the scientific notion of nature: my suggested term "onto-theo-physio-logy" thus accounts also for *physis*, that is, nature in Greek.

"Emergence is always produced within a specific state of forces. (. . .) Whilst descent designates the quality of an instinct, its degree or its failure, and the mark it leaves on a body, emergence designates a place of confrontation; we should still refrain from imagining it as a closed battleground where a struggle takes place, a field where the opponents would be equal; it rather is—the example of good and bad ones proves it—a 'non-place,' a pure distance, the fact that the opponents do not belong to the same space."[35]

I write after Marc Augé's deployment of the term "non-places" as the definition of spaces of transience, such as motorways, airports, and concentration camps (Augé 1997). Yet, this is neither Foucault's use of the expression "non-place," nor mine. On the model of Foucault's neologism *hétérotopie* (Foucault 1984), heterotopy, I would rather call such interstitial non-place a diatopy, that is, a place in-between.

I also write after Donna Haraway's agglutination of the categories of "nature" and "culture" into the term "naturecultures,"[36] which names the multiplicity of ontological realities that includes, but also exceeds, modern nature as defined by Western sciences (Haraway 2003). For example, colonial (and postcolonial) confrontations would be better construed as multiversal clashes of naturecultures, whose opposing parties neither belong to the same space nor to the same universe.

A less visible lack of common ground is hinted to by Lyotard with his recovery of the French legal term *différénd* (Lyotard 1983). A *différénd* is a case of conflict that cannot be equitably resolved for lack of an encompassing rule of judgement. Lyotard argues for the generalization of the notion of *différénd*, to which he intends to bear witness. The mention of the non-place bears witness at once of incommensurability and disproportion within confrontations: it is a reminder of the double character of domination.

"The relation of domination is a 'relation' no more than the place where it is exerted is a place. And that's precisely why in each moment of history domination fixes itself in a ritual; it imposes obligations and rights; it constitutes careful procedures. It establishes marks, it engraves memories on things and even on bodies; it accounts for debt. It is a universe of rules that is not intended to soften, but instead to satisfy violence."[37]

Similarly to the considerations on freedom, these spine-chilling depictions of debt, as written in 2018, are more a picture of the present than the memory of a barbaric past. They evoke the neoliberal hegemonic idiom of accountancy as codified violence, which engraves its memories and expectations on human bodies. Nevertheless, this is not yet enough. Neither rituals nor mathematical procedures could work as systems of rules without interpretations.[38]

"But if interpreting means appropriating, by violence or subreption, a system of rules that by itself has no essential meaning, and imposing upon it a direction, bending it under a new will, making it enter another game and submitting it to explanatory rules, then the becoming of humanity is a series of interpretations. And genealogy should be its history: a history of morals, of ideals, of metaphysical

---

[35] "*L'émergence se produit toujours dans un certain état des forces. (. . .) Alors que la provenance désigne la qualité d'un instinct, son degré ou sa défaillance, et la marque qu'il laisse dans un corps, l'émergence désigne un lieu d'affrontement; encore faut-il se garder de l'imaginer comme un champ clos où se déroulerait une lutte, un plan où les adversaires seraient à égalité; c'est plutôt—l'exemple des bons et des mauvais le prouve—un 'non-lieu', une pure distance, le fait que les adversaires n'appartiennent pas au même espace*" (Foucault 1971, p. 155–56).

[36] Haraway's notion of natureculture also transcends the boundaries of species: "A dog and handler discover happiness together in the labor of training. That is an example of emergent naturecultures" (Haraway 2003, p. 52).

[37] "*Le rapport de domination n'est pas plus un 'rapport' que le lieu où elle s'exerce n'est un lieu. Et c'est pour cela précisément qu'en chaque moment de l'histoire elle se fixe dans un rituel; elle impose des obligations et des droits; elle constitue de soigneuses procédures. Elle établit des marques, grave des souvenirs dans les choses et jusque dans les corps; elle se fait comptable des dettes. Univers de règles qui n'est point destiné à adoucir, mais au contraire à satisfaire la violence*" (Foucault 1971, p. 157).

[38] The same Galileo, who inaugurates the modern world by endowing the traditional book of nature with an original mathematical language, does not forget to pay respect to the necessary interpreting mediation of the alphabetical language.

Genealogy **2018**, 2, 19

concepts, a history of the concept of freedom or of the ascetic life as emergences of different interpretations. It's a matter of making these emergences appear as events in the theatre of procedures."[39]

These considerations on the violent or malicious nature of interpretation also apply to the operations of which they are the result. In other words, they aptly describe my own operation of translating the Foucauldian text, as well as the operation of producing it anew, as I am claiming here. In both cases, I cannot deny that I am imposing upon Foucault's text a direction, that I am bending it under a new will, and that I am making it enter another game. Nevertheless, more in general, similar admissions should also be made whenever we *quote* a text: in this case, though we simply "produce the evidence," as the legal expression goes, at the same time we also somewhat fabricate the proof. It is then not surprising that these admissions make historians feel very uneasy.

"Historians seek as much as possible to erase that which can betray, in their knowledge, the place from which they watch, the moment in which they are, the position that they take, and that which is inevitable in their passion."[40]

I am aware that by authoring this sentence in 2018, I am running the risk of tarring all historians with the same brush. During the last nearly fifty years—I may be reminded—many a historian made more than a step towards embracing a perspectival view.[41] Nevertheless, the multiple erasures of place, time, and desire simply cannot be addressed as an epistemological issue. Epistemology, if any, is an outcome of the reduction of the processes of production of knowledge to standard knowing procedures. This transition is witnessed by the semantic shift of the Greek word μέθοδοσ [*methodos*], from the path of the enquiry to its modus operandi.[42] More in general, the construction of the objectivity of the various objects of knowledge involves the erasure of the traces of their production.

Platonic forms, Aristotelian essences, the various versions of the Christian god, and modern nature all profit from this erasure, which allow them to be always already there.[43] Though the "already-there-ness" of the historical past may appear as a mere truism, it is inextricably intertwined with the "already-there-ness" of these metaphysical objects. To put it bluntly, objectivity is the articulation of history and metaphysics.

"In appearance, or rather according to the mask it wears, historical consciousness is neutral, stripped of all passion, and committed solely to truth. But if it asks itself and, more generally, if it interrogates all scientific consciousness in its history, it discovers the forms and transformations of the will to know which is instinct, passion, inquisitorial relentlessness, cruel refinement, malice; it discovers the violence of bias: bias against ignorant happiness, against the vigorous illusions by which humankind protects itself, bias against all that which is dangerous in the enquiry and disquieting in the discovery. The historical analysis of this great will to know that runs through humankind thus shows both that there is no knowledge that is not based on injustice (that within knowledge itself, there is no right to truth or a foundation for truth), and that the instinct of knowing is wicked (that there is something murderous in it, and that it neither can, nor wants to do anything for the happiness of humans)."[44]

---

[39] *"Mais si interpréter, c'est s'emparer, par violence ou subreption, d'un système de règles qui n'a pas en soi de signification essentielle, et lui imposer une direction, le ployer à une volonté nouvelle, le faire entrer dans un autre jeu et le soumettre à des règles secondes, alors le devenir de l'humanité est une série d'interprétations. Et la généalogie doit en être l'histoire: histoire des morales, des idéaux, des concepts métaphysiques, histoire du concept de liberté ou de la vie ascétique, comme émergences d'interprétations différentes. Il s'agit de les faire apparaître comme des événements au théâtre des procédures"* (Foucault 1971, p. 158).

[40] *"Les historiens cherchent dans toute la mesure du possible à effacer ce qui peut trahir, dans leur savoir, le lieu d'où ils regardent, le moment où ils sont, le parti qu'ils prennent,—l'incontournable de leur passion"* (Foucault 1971, p. 163).

[41] For example, we may consider the likes of Jenkins, Munslow, Southgate, Bunzl and McCullagh.

[42] This shift happens in Plato's dialogues, between the *Phaedo* and the *Sophist*.

[43] We may say that classical philosophers, Christian theologians and modern scientists all play similar games: they produce their objects—forms, being, god, nature—and they erase this production, so that each of these objects becomes, in the words of Borges, *anterior y común*, previous and common. Classical philosophers, Christian theologians and modern scientists then appeal to the alleged objectivity of their products in order to legitimate themselves as interpreters.

[44] *"En apparence, ou plutôt selon le masque qu'elle porte, la conscience historique est neutre, dépouillée de toute passion, acharnée seulement à la vérité. Mais, si elle s'interroge elle-même et si d'une façon plus générale elle interroge toute conscience scientifique*

Though this unsparing attack on the will to know may seem excessively pessimistic, it just shows the dark side of knowledge as a self-standing endeavour. This ambivalence is first detected in a specific technique of knowledge, namely writing, by Plato himself. Plato borrows the Homeric term φάρμακα [*pharmaka*], which defines both poisonous and healing herbal drugs,[45] in order to bestow these contradictory effects upon writing.[46] Derrida (Derrida 1967–1968), and after him Stiegler (2010), generalize this ambivalence to cultural techniques at large. The resulting pharmacology of cultural practices knows no antidote, but of healing paths that work by giving back users the role of producers. A similar shift may be seen at work in Nietzsche's writing trajectory.

"The Untimely spoke of the critical use of history: it was a matter of dragging the past to court, of cutting its roots with the knife, of wiping off the traditional veneration, of freeing man and not leaving him with no other origin than the one he wants to acknowledge. Nietzsche reproached such critical history for detaching us from our real sources and for sacrificing the very movement of life to the exclusive concern for truth. (...) In a way, genealogy comes back to the three modalities of history that Nietzsche recognized in 1874. Genealogy returns to these modalities beyond the objections that Nietzsche was then raising against them in the name of life, of its power to affirm and create. But genealogy is back to these modalities by transforming them: the veneration of monuments becomes parody; the respect for old continuities becomes systematic dissociation; the criticism of past injustices in the name of the truth that we hold now, becomes the destruction of the subject of knowledge at the hands of the injustice of the will to know."[47]

Writing in 2018, Nietzsche's trajectory, which escapes the blind alley of critique through the openings of production, becomes more easily recognizable in its recent further developments. Let's briefly recapitulate this path. Nietzsche's early rejection of critical rejection, as it were, gives way to a more productive engagement with his objects. And whilst the destructivity of the unbridled will to know is still at work—albeit against itself and its very subject—parody and dissociation bypass the confrontational impasse of the critical approach, and they instead multiply the intervention options. In 1980, this multiplication takes off again in a renewed shape. Following Serres (1977), Deleuze and Guattari (1980) advocate the addition of a minor science: this non-canonical history of knowledge lays close to the core of the Western canon, of which nonetheless it would escape the apparatus of capture. A further step in this path, heralded by Feyerabend's scathing treatment of the so-called scientific method (Feyerabend 1975), is Latour's joint construction of past and present health science, together with his proposal of a Nietzsche-inspired theory of ontologically productive relations (Latour 1984): and even more relevant to this trajectory is Latour's evocation of a parliament with things (Latour 1991).

Humans and nonhumans would seat side by side in this metaphorical deliberative organ, which allows Latour to redesign at once knowledge and politics. The constitutive enmeshment of humans

---

dans son histoire, elle découvre alors les formes et les transformations de la volonté de savoir qui est instinct, passion, acharnement inquisiteur, raffinement cruel, méchanceté; elle découvre la violence des partis pris: parti pris contre le bonheur ignorant, contre les illusions vigoureuses par lesquelles l'humanité se protège, parti pris pour tout ce qu'il y a de périlleux dans la recherche et d'inquiétant dans la découverte. L'analyse historique de ce grand vouloir-savoir qui parcourt l'humanité fait donc apparaître à la fois qu'il n'y a pas de connaissance qui ne repose sur l'injustice (qu'il n'y a donc pas, dans la connaissance même, un droit à la vérité ou un fondement du vrai) et que l'instinct de connaissance est mauvais (qu'il y a en lui quelque chose de meurtrier, et qu'il ne peut, qu'il ne veut rien pour le bonheur des hommes)" (Foucault 1971, p. 170).

45 φάρμακα, πολλὰ μὲν ἐσθλὰ μεμιγμένα πολλὰ δὲ λυγρά [*pharmaka, polla men esthla memigmena polla de lygra*], drugs, many that are healing when mixed, and many that are poisonous. Homer (Homer 1920), *Odyssey* 4.230.

46 Plato (Plato 1900–1907), *Phaedrus* 274e–275b.

47 *"Les Intempestives parlaient de l'usage critique de l'histoire: il s'agissait de traîner le passé en justice, de couper ses racines au couteau, d'effacer les vénérations traditionnelles, afin de libérer l'homme et de ne lui laisser d'autre origine que celle où il veut bien se reconnaître. À cette histoire critique, Nietzsche reprochait de nous détacher de toutes nos sources réelles et de sacrifier le mouvement même de la vie au seul souci de la vérité. (...) En un sens la généalogie revient aux trois modalités de l'histoire que Nietzsche reconnaissait en 1874. Elle y revient par-delà les objections qu'il leur faisait alors au nom de la vie, de son pouvoir d'affirmer et de créer. Mais elle y revient en les métamorphosant: la vénération des monuments devient parodie; le respect des anciennes continuités devient dissociation systématique; la critique des injustices du passé par la vérité que l'homme détient aujourd'hui devient destruction du sujet de connaissance par l'injustice propre [à] la volonté de savoir"* (Foucault 1971, p. 172).

and things would allow nonhumans to speak through their human representatives, which include all scientists. However, despite his productive incursions in the history of science, Latour does not consider a role for historians in his enlarged assembly: I would then suggest that historians, especially in their Nietzschean and Foucauldian improved version of genealogists, could give a decisive contribution to the deliberations of the Latourian parliament.

Whilst in this renewed body scientists act as essential mouthpieces of things (albeit not the only ones), historians may perform another crucial mediation. This would require nothing else than ratifying what historians have always done: in Western culture, historians are in charge of communicating with the dead. More precisely, historians do not speak to the dead, but rather they make the dead speak. This is not just a ventriloquist's trick, because historians do engage with the deeds of the dead through things.

An immense and expanding hybrid network links the dead, the things, their living orderers and variously integrating, overlapping, and even conflicting ordering techniques. Such a network includes a huge amount and variety of internal connections, which also perform as cross checks. The vastness and the complexity of this network dwarf and ridicule the debates on historical objectivity. Even regardless of its metaphysical implications, the simplistic notion of historical objectivity is but a fig-leave, which covers the obscene reduction of the work of the historian to the assembling of a jigsaw puzzle.

However, other reductions set the course of historiography, such as the shortcut of historical underlying structures, from Thucydides' cycles to Eusebius' heading towards the final judgement, and from Vico's spiralling ascent to the happily convergent evolution of Whig history. Last, but not least, Marx's construction of social conflict as the hidden cypher of history takes also the shape of a historical series of modes of production. Paradoxically, Marx's dynamic view of history turns itself into a confirmation of the historical objectivity (albeit temporary) of the categories of the supposed current mode of production. This reversal not only confirms history's autochthonous and thus most resilient structure, that is, periodization: it also renders even more difficult for us the task of rescuing current categories from the eternal present of neoliberal detemporalization.

Let's consider, for example, the notion of property. Any good legal historian would relieve this category from a banal form of repetition, which is the assimilation of the past to present views. A good legal historian would easily show both continuities and discontinuities in the various historical deployments of the notion of property, provided that these uses would be safely confined within chronological boundaries. Marx himself does not transcend these boundaries, and he only detects in previous stages of the notion of property the anticipation of its subsequent evolution.[48]

On the contrary, a genealogist would detect a more subtle repetition, in which the various reconstructed pasts repeat their various images as construed in the present. In other words, a genealogist would recognize historical reconstructions as differentiating projections onto the past. This recognition would surely improve the epistemic horizon of modern historiography: yet, it would still not transcend this horizon. A genealogist only crosses the cognitive threshold when she acknowledges her own investment in the past, without hiding herself behind the finger of historiographic refinement.

I admit that the choice of synecdochic representatives—the legal historian, the genealogist—is no less risky than Foucault's grammatical subjectivation of genealogy and Péguy's personification of history. In my case, the grammatical individuality of the synecdochic genealogist may make appear (somewhat misleadingly) her investment in the past as the result of individual psychological motivations. I would instead restate the Nietzschean sidestepping of both subject and will, in order to focus on deeds.

---

[48] However, it is fair to recall that in the letter to the editorial board of the Russian journal *Otechestvenniye Zapisky*, written presumably in November 1877, Marx underlines that the key to economic phenomena cannot be arrived at 'by employing the all-purpose formula of a general historico-philosophical theory whose supreme virtue consists in being supra-historical' (Marx and Engels 2010, p. 201).

Deeds, and in this case, genealogies in the plural—rather than a genealogist in the singular—should be then the proper grammatical subjects of my previous sentences. Moreover, genealogies as constellations of deeds would not connect individual subjects, but rather sub-individual and transindividual singularities. However, if one feels uncomfortable with these neologisms devised by Simondon (1989), genealogies' investment in the past may be tentatively expressed in this general form: some parts of us want some of the dead to speak about something.

It is up to us whether the dead will or will not be silenced. However, our intervention well exceeds the sphere of duty: the investment in the past always grants huge returns. The repetition of the past, be it more or less imaginary, never ceases to provide us with a powerful leverage to transform the present.

We rescue the dead not only because they are in danger, as Benjamin anxiously denounces, but also for not losing their precious alliance. Nietzsche knows it well: the dead allows him to speak in the plural, despite his companions are far yet to come. I often do the same, and this paper is no exception.

Conflicts of Interest: The author declares no conflict of interest.

References

Augé, Marc. 1997. *Non-Places: Introduction to an Anthropology of Supermodernity*. Translated by John Howe. London: Verso.

Barthes, Roland. 1957. *Mythologies*. Paris: Seuil.

Benjamin, Walter. 1999. *The Arcades Project*. Translated by Howard Eiland, and Kevin McLaughlin. Cambridge: Harvard University Press.

Bergson, Henri. 1934. Le Possible et le Réel. In *La Pensée et le Mouvant*. Paris: Alcan, pp. 115–34.

Borges, Jorge Luis. 1952. Kafka y Sus Precursores. In *Otras Inquisiciones: 1937–1952*. Buenos Aires: Sur, pp. 126–28.

Borges, Jorge Luis. 1974. *Obras Completas: 1923–1972*. Buenos Aires: Emecé.

Brecht, Bertolt. 1967. Über experimentelles Theater. In *Gesammelte Werke*. Frankfurt am Main: Suhrkamp, Band 15. pp. 285–305.

Croce, Benedetto. 1915. *Zur Theorie und Geschichte der Historiographie*. Tubingen: Mohr.

Deleuze, Gilles. 1966. Renverser le platonisme. *Revue de Métaphysique et de Morale* 71: 426–38.

Deleuze, Gilles, and Félix Guattari. 1972. *L'Anti-Œdipe*. Paris: Les Éditions de Minuit.

Deleuze, Gilles, and Félix Guattari. 1980. *Capitalisme et Schizophrénie 2: Mille Plateaux*. Paris: Éditions de Minuit.

Derrida, Jacques. 1963. Cogito et histoire de la folie. *Revue de Métaphysique et de Morale* 68: 460–94.

Derrida, Jacques. 1967. La structure, le signe et le jeu dans le discours des sciences humaines. In *L'Ecriture et la Différence*. Paris: Éditions du Seuil, pp. 409–28.

Derrida, Jacques. 1967–1968. La pharmacie de Platon. *Tel Quel* 32: 17–59, 33: 4–48.

Eliot, Thomas Stearns. 1920. Tradition and the Individual Talent. In *The Sacred Wood*. London: Methuen, pp. 42–50.

Feyerabend, Paul. 1975. *Against Method*. London: New Left Books.

Foucault, Michel. 1971. Nietzsche, la généalogie, l'histoire. In *Hommage à Jean Hyppolite*. Paris: Presses Universitaires de France, pp. 145–72.

Foucault, Michel. 1972. *The Archaeology of Knowledge*. Translated by A. M. Sheridan Smith. London: Tavistock.

Foucault, Michel. 1984. Des espaces autres. *Architecture, Mouvement, Continuité* 5: 46–49. [CrossRef]

Freud, Sigmund. 1920. *Jenseits des Lustprinzips*. Wien: Internationaler Psychoanalytischer Verlag.

Haraway, Donna. 2003. *The Companion Species Manifesto*. Chicago: Prickly Paradigm Press.

Hegel, Georg Wilhelm Friedrich. 2010. *The Science of Logic*. Translated by George Di Giovanni. Cambridge: Cambridge University Press.

Homer. 1920. *Homeri Opera*. Edited by David B. Monro and Thomas W. Allen. 5 vols. Oxford: Oxford University Press.

Hölderlin, Friedrich. 1966. *Friedrich Hölderlin: Poems & Fragments*. Translated by Michael Hamburger. London: Routledge & Kegan Paul.

Kierkegaard, Søren. 2009. *Repetition and Philosophical Crumbs*. Translated by M. G. Piety. Oxford: Oxford University Press.

Latour, Bruno. 1984. *Les Microbes: Guerre et Paix, Suivi de Irréductions*. Paris: Métailié.

Latour, Bruno. 1991. *Nous N'avons Jamais été Modernes. Essai D'anthropologie Symétrique*. Paris: La Découverte.

Latour, Bruno, and Steve Woolgar. 1979. *Laboratory Life: The Social Construction of Scientific Facts*. Beverly Hills: Sage.

Lucian of Samosata. 1959. How to Write History. In *Lucian*. Translated by K. Kilburn. London: Heinemann, vol. 6, pp. 1–73.

Lyotard, Jean-François. 1979. *La Condition Postmoderne*. Paris: Éditions de Minuit.

Lyotard, Jean-François. 1983. *Le Différend*. Paris: Éditions de Minuit.

Maitland, William. 1888. Why the History of English Law is not Written. In *The Collected Papers of Fredric William Maitland*. Edited by H. A. L. Fisher. Cambridge: Cambridge University Press, vol. 1, pp. 480–97.

Marx, Karl, and Friedrich Engels. 2010. *Marx and Engels Collected Works*. London: Lawrence and Wishart, vol. 24.

Nietzsche, Friedrich. 1878. Menschliches Allzumenschliches. Nietzsche Digital Critical Edition. Available online: http://www.nietzschesource.org/#eKGWB/WS-9 (accessed on 20 March 2018).

Nietzsche, Friedrich. 1887. Zur Genealogie der Moral. Nietzsche Digital Critical Edition. Available online: http://www.nietzschesource.org/?#eKGWB/GM-I-2 (accessed on 20 March 2018).

Nietzsche, Friedrich. 1888. Nachgelassene Fragmente 1888. Nietzsche Digital Critical Edition. Available online: http://www.nietzschesource.org/#eKGWB/NF-1888,14 (accessed on 20 March 2018).

Nietzsche, Friedrich. 1996. *Human, All Too Human*. Translated by R. H. Hollingdale. Cambridge: Cambridge University Press.

Nietzsche, Friedrich. 2006. *On the Genealogy of Morality*. Edited by Keith Ansell-Pearson. Translated by Carol Diethe. Cambridge: Cambridge University Press.

Plato. 1900–1907. *Platonis Opera*. Edited by John Burnet. 5 vols. Oxford: Clarendon Press.

Péguy, Charles. 1932. *Clio, Dialogue de l'Histoire et de l'Âme Païenne*. Paris: Gallimard.

Ranke, Leopold von. 1956. Preface: Histories of the Latin and Germanic Nations from 1494–1514. In *The Varieties of History: From Voltaire to the Present*. Edited by Fritz Stern. New York: Meridian Books, pp. 54–62.

Schmitt, Carl. 1985. *Political Theology: Four Chapters on the Concept of Sovereignty*. Translated by George Schwab. Cambridge: MIT Press.

Serres, Michel. 1977. *La Naissance de la Physique Dans le Texte de Lucrece. Fleuves et Turbulences*. Paris: Éditions de Minuit.

Simondon, Gilbert. 1989. *L'Individuation Psychique et Collective*. Paris: Aubier.

Sklovskij, Viktor. 1991. Art as Device. In *The Theory of Prose*. Translated by Benjamin Sher. Bloomington: Dalkey Archive Press, pp. 1–14.

Stiegler, Bernard. 2010. *Ce Qui Fait que la Vie Vaut la Peine d'Être Vécue: De la Pharmacologie*. Paris: Flammarion.

Stirner, Max. 2000. *The Ego and Its Own*. Edited by David Leopold. Translated by Steve Byington. Cambridge: Cambridge University Press.

Thucydides. 1942. *Historiae*. Edited by Henry Stuart Jones and John Enoch Powell. 2 vols. Oxford: Clarendon Press.

Vaihinger, Hans. 1924. *The Philosophy of 'As If': A System of the Theoretical, Practical and Religious Fictions of Mankind*. Translated by C. K. Ogden. London: Routledge and Kegan Paul.

Valla, Lorenzo. 1517. *De Falso Credita et Ementita Constantini Donatione Declamatio*. Mainz: von Hutten.

Wittgenstein, Ludwig. 1961. *Notebooks, 1914–1916*. Edited by G. H. von Wright and G. E. M. Anscombe. London: Basil Blackwell.

genealogy

MDPI

Article

Using Foucault: Genealogy, Governmentality and the Problem of Chronic Illness

Ann Reich [1,*] and Margo Turnbull [2]

[1] School of Education, Faculty of Social Sciences, University of Technology Sydney,
    Ultimo NSW 2007, Australia
[2] International Research Centre for the Advancement of Health Communication, Department of English,
    The Hong Kong Polytechnic University, Kowloon, Hong Kong 00852, China; margo.turnbull@polyu.edu.hk
*   Correspondence: Ann.Reich@uts.edu.au

Received: 27 February 2018; Accepted: 6 April 2018; Published: 10 April 2018

Abstract: This article explores the unique contribution that Foucault's work on genealogy and governmentality can make to the analysis of contemporary programs of government. The article uses an Australian study of the 'problem' of chronic illness to argue that this perspective offers valuable insights into how 'problems' such as chronic illness have become linked to advanced liberal discourses and practices of self-governing and self-responsibility. These insights are particularly valuable in fields such as primary health care that have a noted shortage of critical and reflective studies that explore the links between people and changing ideas of health and disease. This article details how taking up an analytics of governmentality and political genealogy informed by Foucault, facilitated the tracing of the dominant discourses and practices, and the connections to the day-to-day lives of the clients with chronic diseases. Importantly, this approach opened up a more critical consideration of the ways in which dispersed approaches to governing through programs, such as integrated care, shape and influence the lives of individuals. These dispersed ways of governing are not linear but rather unfold through ongoing relays, connections and the (re)production of discourses.

Keywords: genealogy; governmentality; Foucault; chronic illness; translation; assemblage

1. Introduction

Research inspired by Foucault's work on political genealogy and an analytics of governmentality (Foucault 2007a) has occurred in many disciplines and fields of study. Governmentality writers, such as Nikolas Rose (Rose 1996), Peter Miller (Miller and Rose 2008), Mitchell Dean (Dean 2006, 2007, 2010) and Thomas Lemke (Lemke 2010) to name but a few, have extended Foucault's work, particularly in using it to analyse neo-liberal or what Miller and Rose (2008) call advanced liberal ways of governing in many different areas—the economy, welfare, organisations, bio-health and law. Foucault's governmentality perspective is set out in the lectures he gave at the Collège de France in the Spring terms of 1977–1978 and 1978–1979 (Dean 2010). These lectures were most comprehensively published in French in 2004 (Elden 2007) to coincide with the twentieth anniversary of Foucault's death. The translation and publication of these lectures in 2007 as *Security, territory, population* (Foucault 2007a) generated a new body of scholarship on governmentality and it has been enthusiastically taken up as an analytic approach to investigating the empirical practice of governing.

As a contribution to this *Special issue on political genealogy*, this article focuses on the utility and contribution an analytics of governmentality and genealogy make to a study of chronic illness. The article draws on data from a research study, *Governing chronic illness through integrated care* (Turnbull 2017), which used this approach to understand the ways in which the problem of chronic disease became linked to advanced liberal discourses and practices of self-governing and self-responsibility. The research study[1] traced how a health care program in Australia—HealthOne—was translated in advanced liberal ways to the local lives of clients with chronic illnesses. The analytic perspective used offered a unique view of the contemporary 'problem' of chronic diseases. The broad fields of research that are concerned with chronic diseases and programs of care management tend to be dominated by evaluative and descriptive studies that focus on the need for reform and greater cost effectiveness (Braithwaite et al. 2005; Valentijn et al. 2015; Brown and McIntyre 2014). There is a shortage of critical and reflective studies that focus on "complex strategic relations" (Bacchi 2012, p. 1) that connect people and the changing ideas of health and disease. The insights presented in this article illustrate the potential offered by Foucault's work to empirical studies in many fields, such as health studies.

Taking up an analytics of governmentality and political genealogy informed by Foucault, facilitated a unique tracing of the dominant discourses and practices circulating in the local, national and global contexts and their linkages to the day-to-day lives of the clients with chronic diseases. Importantly, this approach opened up a more critical consideration of the ways in which dispersed approaches to governing, shape and influence the lives of individuals. These dispersed ways of governing are not linear, but rather unfold through ongoing relays, connections and the (re)production of discourses. In particular, notions of translation (Rose 1996, 1998) and assemblage (Murray Li 2007) are used to illustrate how dispersed ways of governing across sites and locations come together around the lives of individuals.

This article begins by discussing an analytics of governmentality and genealogy as a 'method' for analysing, in this case, contemporary, dispersed ways of governing health and disease. The article then focuses on how taking up this perspective facilitated the analysis of contemporary understandings of chronic disease (re)produced within the key policies and texts associated with HealthOne, a state-run integrated, primary health care program located in a metropolitan area of Australia. Importantly, the analytic perspective and genealogical approach used in this study enabled the tracing of the translation and movement of these discourses of health and disease from policy texts and everyday practices of those involved in HealthOne. To illustrate how an analytics of governmentality and genealogy were used and the utility of such an approach, this article focuses on three aspects of the research study—first, the assembling of a crisis and emergence of a programmatic 'solution'; second, the translations of advanced liberal notions of self-responsibility and self-care into the programmatic logic of community-based integrated care (Rose and Miller 1992); and third, the assembling of the patient as a 'client'—the responsible and self-caring chronically ill client—through technologies of government such as education, training and advice.

2. Governmentality and Political Genealogy: Rationalities, Technologies, Translation and Assemblage

Foucault's work on governmentality (Foucault 2007a) and genealogy have been discussed previously in this journal (Knauft 2017). As Knauft (2017, p. 6) suggests, "it is patent that Foucault's notion of genealogy ... has enormous power to recast, upend, and render problematic—though not to 'transcend'—existing accounts of historical progression, influence". As a 'method' for analysing contemporary problems, readings of Foucault's work have revealed that there is no clearly stated, well-defined or prescribed methodology for investigations. There is, however, some guidance on how the perspective can be used to inform an empirical research study. This guidance takes the form of proposing an open system of maxims and injunctions that constitute an ethos of analysis for undertaking a critical and effective form of history (Dean 1994). As Rose states in his additional Foreword to the second edition of *Governing the soul*,

---

[1] Data reported in this article was drawn from the research study, *Governing chronic illness through integrated care* (Turnbull 2017) which was a component of a project funded by the Australian Research Council (ARC). Approval for the study was granted by the University of Technology, Sydney, Human Research Ethics Committee (HREC) on 02/07/2013 (reference code 2013000025). The names of places, programs and research participants have been changed to preserve anonymity.

I am not particularly keen on attempts to derive a formal methodology for this kind of 'history of the present' and it would be misleading to claim this study is the application of any such methodology. Nonetheless, speaking roughly, it is possible to identify a number of dimensions along which this analysis is conducted (Rose 1999a, p. XI).

Rose continues by identifying six dimensions—problematisation, explanations, technologies, authorities, subjectivities, and strategies—which he suggests may be an appropriate analytical grid for some, but not all, problems (Rose 1999a, pp. XI–XII). However, two aspects of Rose's quote above assist in illuminating questions of 'method' as posed by Foucault and critically reflected upon by others. Firstly, the notion of the 'history of the present'; and secondly, that of genealogy, which could be considered a 'method' for undertaking studies framed by an analytics of governmentality perspective.

A *history of the present* is "concerned with that which is taken for granted, assumed to be given, or natural within contemporary social existence, a givenness or naturalness questioned in the course of contemporary" (Dean 1994, p. 35). It is not, as some more traditional historians might view it, a "writing of the past in terms of the present" (Foucault 1977a, p. 31 cited in (Dean 1994), p. 28). Foucault suggests we must avoid this approach to presentism. Rather it is about defining a problem of our time and using a genealogical method to investigate the trajectories of the problem within a history. As Dean (1994) suggests, genealogy can be used to offer unique insights into contemporary social struggles by drawing on the inherent complexity and multiple layers of these 'problems':

> It is a way of analysing multiple, open-ended, heterogeneous trajectories of discourses, practices, and events, and of establishing their patterned relationships, without recourse to regimes of truth that claim pseudo-naturalistic laws of global necessities' (Dean 1994, pp. 35–36).

It is important to highlight that, as has been discussed previously in this journal (Kretsedemas 2017), there are a range of styles of genealogy.[2] Discussion of these different styles are beyond the scope of this article. However, it is of note in the context of this article that when used within an analytics of governmentality, and following Foucault, genealogy and its methods offer a way of analysing liberalism as practices of government rather than as a philosophy or as historical time periods, and to 'understand its plurality, capacity for reinvention and sheer longevity" (Dean 1999, p. 48).

Further, a genealogy of power in this style has a profound (con)textualism and an intimacy with historical circumstances shaped by the specific conditions of locations and particular milieu (Foucault 2007b). It is a move "beyond the limitations of discourse analysis and . . . [to be] more attentive to that which conditions, limits and institutionalises discursive formations" (Tamboukou 1999, p. 216). As Rose (1998) describes it,

> discourse analysis covers a multitude of sins . . . This is because it is not primarily an analysis of text. I'm interested in discourses as they are embedded in practices, as they lead to the emergence of regimes of truth which are connected up with systems of authority, which are operated through very, very specific techniques. This, for me, is a very—if it wasn't a devalued term—materialist kind of analysis, and indeed a very empirical one too (Rose 1998, p. 91).

Discourse analysis in a critical theory approach differs from a Foucauldian genealogy in an analytics of governmentality perspective. The critical theory approach uses the analysis of language to focus on "unmasking the ideological content and highlight the possibility of different emancipatory truths" (Dean 1999, p. 63). In contrast, a Foucauldian genealogy from an analytics of governmentality

---

2 See the following publications for an illuminating discussion of genealogy using two case studies of the government of welfare and poverty, highlighting the differences between the analytical method in the critical theory approach and a Foucauldian genealogy in an analytics of government perspective (Cruikshank 1993; Fraser and Gordon 1994; Dean 1999).

perspective views the language of a problem area, such as welfare dependency, as problematisation, representation and a program of reform. As Tamboukou (1999) suggests,

> Rather than following methodological principles, Foucault's genealogies create a methodological rhythm of their own, weaving around a set of crucial questions ... What is happening now? What is this present of ours? How have we become what we are and what are the possibilities of becoming 'other'? ... Foucault's genealogies do not offer methodological 'certainties'. They persistently evade classification, but they do inspire the writing of new genealogies to interrogate the truths of our world. (Tamboukou 1999, p. 215).

Additionally, this analytics for studies in governmentality rejects the approach to knowledge within the humanities and social sciences that defines it in terms of ideologies, that is, as "the false knowledges with a social formation of legitimation" (Rose 1999a, p. 13). Rather, following Foucault and other writers on governmentality like Rose, there is a focus on the productive role of knowledges, examining the formation of knowledge practices as they have been shaped and what has made them practicable and thinkable. In particular, it is concerned with what Rose describes as 'political' knowledges—"how to govern, what to govern, who should govern and to what ends" (Rose 1999a, p. XIII).

Of particular relevance in this article is an understanding of governmentality not as theory or methodology but rather a research perspective—"an angle of view, a manner of looking, a specific orientation" (Bröckling et al. 2010, p. 15). Taking up this research perspective offers a way of thinking about how governing unfolds through complex linkages between "questions of government, authority and politics, and questions of identity, self and person" (Dean 2010, p. 20). Considering the linkages between political problems and programmatic solutions reveals certain patterns within contemporary approaches to governing. In this article, governmentality opens up a way of thinking about how chronic disease and care are assembled through policies and practices in ways that reflect contemporary "arts of governing"—ways of "employing tactics rather than laws ... arranging things so that this or that end may be achieved through a certain number of means" (Foucault 2007a, p. 99).

In taking up an analytics of governmentality, this article draws on notions related to *how* programs of governing move from a political centre and into the homes and lives of citizens. The concept of advanced liberalism is used, following Rose, O'Malley and Valverde (Rose et al. 2006)—that is, it reflects a "way of doing things" (Rose et al. 2006, p. 84) that allows governing to unfold at a distance. Rose (1999b) described this way of operating as "government at a distance ... distance in both constitutional and spatial senses". This form of liberal rule—at a distance—is entwined "to the activities and calculations of a proliferation of independent authorities ... doctors, ... , managers, planners, parents and social workers. It is dependent upon the political authorizations of authority of these authorities, upon forging of alignments between political aims and the strategies of experts, and upon establishing relays between calculations of authorities and aspirations of free citizens" (Rose 1999b, p. 49).

This complex way of governing at a distance unfolds through multiple relays and connections that draw people and sites together. Key to the sense of coherence associated with such attempts to govern are the political rationalities that are (re)produced through these relays and connections. Political rationalities in this sense refer to the reasoned and accepted ways of thinking about and justifying approaches to governance (Savage 2013). Dominant political rationalities open up opportunities for the emergence of various political technologies or tools that are used to govern—the "techniques, mechanisms, instruments ... the mechanics through which rationalities are put into practice (Savage 2013, p. 86). In this way, rationalities (or ways of thinking) are (re)produced through technologies and techniques that link ways of thinking to actions and behaviours.

The linkages between political rationalities, technologies and techniques allow attempts to govern to move from a source and to be localised within a multitude of sites. Rose (1999b) described these linkages as translation and explained that this connects "one place to another, shifts a way of thinking, from a political centre—a cabinet office, a government department—to a multitude of workplaces, hospital wards classrooms, child guidance centres or homes" (Rose 1999b, p. 51). It is through the 'fragile relays' of translation that discourses, agencies, people and material objects come together at points in time and work to (re)produce and stabilise political rationalities. As Li (Murray Li 2007) observed:

> Governmental interventions that set out to improve the world are assembled from diverse elements—discourses, institutions, forms of expertise and social groups whose deficiencies need to be corrected, among others (Murray Li 2007, p. 263).

Such interventions have no essence or singularity but are somehow made intelligible as they temporarily cohere through the practices that constitute them "only to disperse or realign . . . the shape shifts according to the terrain and the angle of vision" (Murray Li 2007, p. 265).

In this article, this way of thinking about translation and assemblage connects the study of HealthOne to broader shifts in thinking about health, disease and responsibility. The clients of HealthOne were drawn together through the (re)production of discourses that have come to dominate local, national and global ways of thinking about the problem of chronic disease and the types of programs that can address it. By taking up an analytics of governmentality and genealogy, these discourses and ways of thinking and acting are traced through global, national and local policy texts and into the daily lives of clients of HealthOne.

Drawing from data collected as part of the study—*Governing chronic illness through integrated care*, this article examines the emergence of a new program to govern chronic illness in local populations—named HealthOne. Data was collected from local, national and international policy texts, interviews with senior managers and from shadowing a Nurse at the local site on visits to four clients over six months. Observation notes and interview transcripts were analysed together with the policy texts.

Taking up an analytics of governmentality and genealogy allow this 'site of practice' to be traced and dominant discourses recognized. This facilitates a more critical consideration of the ways in which dispersed approaches to governing, shape and influence the lives of individuals.

The following section discusses three aspects of the study's analysis chosen to illustrate the usefulness of analytics of governmentality and genealogy—*Illustration One*—Chronic disease: assembling a crisis and a programmatic 'solution'; *Illustration Two*—Translations of advanced liberal notions of self-responsibility and self-care into the programmatic logic, and *Illustration Three*—Assembling of the patient as 'client'—the responsible and self-caring chronically ill client.

3. *Illustration One*—Chronic Illness: Assembling a Crisis and a Programmatic 'Solution'

This "illustration" focuses on the ways in which a 'crisis' was assembled in the policy texts and discourses of the health field, nationally and internationally, and a programmatic solution emerged. Rather than determining whether elements of these discourses were true or false, following Foucault's (2003, p. 20) interest in problematisation as a "domain of acts, practices, and thoughts that seem to pose problems for politics" (Foucault 2003, p. 20), such analysis draws out the patterns and consistencies embedded and reproduced through texts and everyday practices.

For example, analysis of global health discourses over the past two decades suggests that the 'crisis' of chronic illness emerged from particular regimes of 'truth'. Reports from international bodies such as the World Health Organization (WHO) and national government reports highlighted this crisis. For example, the World Health Organization (WHO) warned that "the global burden of chronic disease is increasing rapidly, and predicts by the year 2020 that chronic disease will account for almost three quarters of all deaths"(Department of Health and Ageing 2009, p. 9). Diseases of greatest concern included diabetes, heart disease, respiratory disease and certain types of cancers. In the USA, reports suggested that in 2010, 86% of health care expenditure was directed towards the management of chronic diseases (Gerteis et al. 2014). Similarly, reports in low- and middle-income countries identified high rates of chronic diseases linked to approximately 80% of deaths in these nations (Slama et al. 2013, p. 83). In 2015, the Australian Government's Department of Health report highlighted the crisis of chronic diseases, which were now the leading cause of "illness, death and disability in Australia, accounting for 90% of deaths in 2011" (Department of Health Chronic Diseases 2016). Australian statistical reports released in 2016 indicated that 75% of Australians over 65 years of age now suffer from one or more of these chronic diseases (Swerissen et al. 2016).

The 'problem' of chronic disease in this crisis became intertwined with economic discourses about costs of long term, complex management, the risk of reduced economic productivity and advanced liberal discources of self-responsibilty—connecting many chronic diseases to lifestyle 'choices' made by individuals. Locating the problem of chronic disease with these economic and self-responsibility discourses, opened up spaces in which very particular programmatic solutions seemed rational and logical—a regime of truth. Importantly, patterns within these programmatic responses reflected advanced liberal ways of governing health and disease through ideas of risk and self-responsibility and dispersed programs of care and education. This way of thinking was evident in international and Australian health policy texts examined, which in recent decades have emphasized the importance of health promotion and preventative interventions for all citizens, including those with chronic diseases. The intended outcomes of these programs that promote self-management included lessening the burden and costs of hospitals on the public 'purse'. For example, in recent Australian policy texts, governments' role in relation to health was described as being to "nudge people towards health-promoting behaviour through better information, evidence-based prevention and health promotion programs" (National Health and Hospitals Reform Commission 2009, p. 62). These programs, which were initiated as a response to the 'crisis', were no longer just about hospitalization. Rather they were mobilized through advanced liberal ways of governing and making the individual 'responsible' for their care. Localized programs, new integrated care models and interventions focused on education, advice and training marked a shift away from the provision of more traditional and expensive medical care. Significantly, these ways of governing through responsibility and self-management were extended beyond general health promotion to those people with serious, long term diseases.

As seen in the following extract from a HealthOne policy text, the emphasis on prevention and community-based approaches is evident in the following program's objectives:

1. Prevent illness and reduce the risk and impact of disease and disability;
2. Improve chronic disease management in the community;
3. Reduce avoidable admissions (and unnecessary demand for hospital care);
4. Improve service access and health outcomes for disadvantaged and vulnerable groups;
5. Build a sustainable model of health care delivery (NSW Government HealthOne NSW 2016).

These objectives focused on the social, economic and political problems associated with chronic disease—prevention, disability, costs of hospital care and sustainability of services.

As seen in the illustration above, an analytics of governmentality foregrounds these dispersed approaches to governing, not in the linear ways implied in the policy texts, but rather by tracing how they unfolded through a succession of alignments, relays and affiliations. Discourses and ideas about problems and policy solutions are (re)produced as they spread from a centre of governing to local sites. This approach to analysis also illuminates the patterns in ways of thinking and talking about problems such as chronic disease, that move back and forth between policy and everyday practices. Through this movement and (re)production certain 'truths' stabilise and become accepted—ideas and ways of thinking about the problem of chronic disease move and disperse. No longer a problem of types of hospital care—what emerged was programs of self-care based in the community.

4. *Illustration Two*—Translations of Advanced Liberal Notions of Self-Responsibility and Self-Care into Programmatic Logic

The second illustration focuses on the ways an analytics of governmentality and genealogy foreground how advanced liberal rationalities and technologies were translated into the programmatic logic of HealthOne. Within the milieu of the global crisis in chronic disease, notions of integrated care with daily life and promoting self-care, rather than expensive hospital care, were (re)produced in HealthOne policy and organisational texts. The texts were littered with terms such as integrated, co-location, holistic and coordinated care. The emphasis was on flexibility and localisation, translating the program across sites and places as responsibility was devolved to local practitioners as the key experts.

For example, the programmatic logic of the programmatic solutions to the problem and crisis of chronic disease was about governing this population of people at a distance (Miller and Rose 2008). The program focused on integrated care—governed through policy texts from a 'policy centre', enacted through by local organisations and practitioners. This is can be seen in the text, *Guidelines for Developing HealthOne NSW Services*, which describes HealthOne services as having come together through the practices of professionals:

> While there is no fixed model for HealthOne NSW services, they are characterised by a motivation to bring health care professionals together to reduce the increasing burden of chronic disease and to focus on those people in the community who need a greater level of coordinated care (NSW Government 2012, p. 6).

The strength of the programmatic logic embedded within HealthOne allowed for flexible configurations of local programs. Despite the variety of models, HealthOne programs were unified by the reproduction of discourses of health and care:

> There is no single model of integrated care that is suited to all settings; Local Health Districts should be guided by their community needs about the configuration that is best suited to each locality. (NSW Government 2012, p. 3).

One model—the virtual model in particular highlights the dispersed nature of HealthOne:

> In the virtual model, a number of separately located providers function as a team through electronic and other forms of communication. Members of a virtual HealthOne NSW may rarely meet face to face. Integration may occur through formalised networks based on explicit governance arrangements and is often underpinned by service level agreements or contracts (NSW Government 2012, p. 22).

These statements of intent, and the linking of the program's integrated care with various models of care, set out what appears as a linear, rational process of governing through programmatic solutions to problems. These policy texts attempted to extract "from the messiness of the social world, with all the processes that run through it, a set of relations that can be formulated as a diagram in which problem (a) plus intervention (b) will produce (c), a beneficial result" (Murray Li 2007, p. 265). In the case of HealthOne, the "programmatic logic" (Rose and Miller 1992, p. 190) sought to govern at a distance through a local integrated program. This relied on the practices of local people and illustrated the translation (Rose 1999b) involved in advanced liberal ways of governing. Governing in this sense is not a rational, linear process, but rather a series of conjunctions and moments in which assemblages come together.

HealthOne was described in interviews with senior managers as suiting local needs as determined by local 'experts':

> ... *that reductionist approach to describing an integrated primary healthcare model or service, we don't fit it because we learnt and I think deliberately have allowed—it must be clinician led at the*

local level. It must suit local circumstances, local needs, local conditions. Therefore, there isn't the one model. (Interview with senior policy maker, 26.10.11).

Here, the program, through a process of translation (Rose 1999b), governs chronically ill people in the local population in advanced liberal ways. The (re)configuring and localising of the programmatic response then links a multitude of workplaces and people as the program is taken up in potentially varying ways. This linking and relaying is neither smooth nor permanent. Captured within the notions of assemblage and translation are a sense of ongoing flux and movement. The neo-liberal economic concerns associated with disease and the provision of care were a recurrent theme in the data. In the heightened 'crisis' discussed above, these discourses became dominant, as indicated in the quote below

the reason all of this happened is because we've reached that kind of—is it the top or the bottom of the bell in terms of all those messages about the health budget is going to actually take the whole State budget in three years if we don't do something. (Interview with senior policy maker, 14.10.11).

The dominant discourses about impending budgetary disaster became linked in the HealthOne program to the lives and homes of its clients in particular, advanced liberal ways. The focus of the daily work of HealthOne was to be these particular practices of care enacted with these clients:

In the end it basically came down to ... better care of people in the community who've got vulnerable, older people, people with complex health conditions particularly around the whole cost blowout of acute system and what can community-based health service delivery do to prevent that? (Interview with senior policy maker, 14.10.11).

Importantly, as this translation took place, discourses of risk and cost were (re)produced and increasingly stabilised. A sense of urgency grew around the need to find people at risk and to engage them in the program:

... we're focusing on the population in a primary health care sense. So we're flushing and we're looking and we're sorting. (Interview with senior policy maker, 14.10.11).

This idea of flushing, looking and sorting through the needs of local populations illustrates the way in which problematisations are localised. Programmatic interventions can thus differ yet maintain linkages to discourses of health and responsibility. This way of sorting through and monitoring populations relied on practices of communication and information sharing between local authorities and experts:

So it gives an opportunity to have a conversation ... So communication, information sharing, understanding of each other's business; that in itself has got to do something about strengthening what we do. (Interview with senior policy maker, 14.10.11).

Here, communication and information sharing were the techniques and technologies for governing the chronic diseases in these populations—rather than the medical techniques of hospital ward rounds, etc. Although local needs differ, the connections to discourses of health and disease were (re)produced and intensified as managers and practitioners talked about what needed to be done in local areas. The localisation is illustrated in the following HealthOne policy text, which set out the problem in terms of access, communication and the need for the education of 'at risk' groups:

[Local government area] was considered an important site for the implementation of HealthOne NSW, as service partners identified [the area] to have:

- One of the highest Culturally and Linguistically Diverse (CALD) populations in the state, particularly refugees;
- Limited access to interpreter services in the area;
- Limited service access by CALD populations, particularly refugees;

- Overstretched health services with long waiting lists or closed books, particularly GPs;
- Poor communication and service coordination between existing service providers;
- Poor health status due to being a significantly disadvantaged community (2013, pers. comm., in meeting documents 8 October).

This (re)contextualisation of the problem of health and illness in local terms reinforces the linkages between risk factors such as cultural and linguistic diversity, disadvantage and the resettlement of population groups, with the *potential* to need costly health care, producing programs of care focusing on integration and community care.

Whilst such discourses are 'depersonalised' in policy texts, as programs translate and disperse out into local communities, problematic populations are defined and identified. In turn, individuals within these groups become a part of a local, national and global 'problem'.

5. *Illustration Three*—Assembling the Patient as a 'Client'—Responsible and Self-Caring

The third illustration focuses on the way in which the 'patient' subjectivity was reassembled as the responsible and self-caring chronically ill 'client'. It utilises data collected from clients of HealthOne, as part of the research study discussed earlier. The lives of these 'clients' were diverse—two had quadriplegia as a result of accidents in adulthood, one suffered from a degenerative neurological disease and the other was an 83-year-old woman with a number of medical conditions affecting her heart and lungs. Whilst their medical conditions were significant, what is of most interest in this research study, was consideration of *how* these people were identified, brought together and assembled as clients of a program that promoted self-management and integrated care.

For the clients of the local program, an entry point into the assemblage was marked by a visit from the local expert at their homes and the knock on the door that announced their arrival. The process of referral and enrolment had been initiated away from the bodies of these people by other 'experts', who had identified their potential for reform and improved management of their health.

In analysing the brochure, the shift in subjectivities was apparent. *Patient* was used in the title and was capitalised. Using the word *patient* in this way linked HealthOne to discourses of medicine and the hierarchical relationships that structure the relations between medical authorities and patients. Within the rest of the text, however, the word *patient* is not used again. Through processes of referral, assessment and enrolment, a new and different subjectivity was emerging for the patient. The process of referral was described in the following terms, with the patient being (re)assembled as a *client*:

- Referrals … are generally made by GPs, Community Health workers and hospital staff.
- Once a referral is received, an assessment will be completed by a Community Health worker.
- HealthOne will be explained to you and your consent obtained to be enrolled as a … client.
- Your GP will be contacted and their consent obtained for their participation. At this point you become a [HealthOne] client (NSW Government n.d.).

This process of referral, assessment and access marks a transition from the subjectivity of *patient* to that of *client*. The subjectivity of the client is active in comparison to that of the patient, who is a passive recipient of care. The subjectivity of the client draws on ideas of activation, engagement and the realisation of *potential*. Networks of experts were connected to discuss and identify patients who had the need and potential to take up the subjectivity of the *client*. The use of the word 'client' activates discourses of choice and responsibility and opens up opportunities for experts to engage with the client in different ways (Mol 2008). Within the bounds of the institution, the doctor or nurse is associated with medical authority and expertise. However, in a program like HealthOne, which seeks to activate the responsible and self-governing client, the expert takes on a subjectivity that works through techniques that seek to engage, guide and educate, rather than through the surveillance associated with the bounded institution. As discourses of choice and responsibility became dominant in the program, a diverse range of experts and professionals came to work with clients on self-development and improvement programs. This work was done by altering the understanding and relationships individuals had with themselves; that is, by "inculcating desires for self-development that expertise itself can guide and through claiming to be able to allay the anxieties generated when the actuality of life fails to live up to its image" (Rose 1999b, p. 88).

This shift in thinking builds an understanding of the client as intrinsically willing and able to choose to engage in projects of development and improvement. Rose (1999b) argued that the implications of rejecting such choices are embodied by the groupings of those who remain outside the "regime of civility", such as the homeless, alcoholics, drug users and lone parents; "an amalgam of cultural pathology and personal weakness" (Rose 1999b, p. 88). The chronically ill client in this case does not, however, sit outside this regime of self-improvement. Being referred and then consenting to enrolment in the program clearly situates the client within relations and practices that help them to make the 'right' choices and accord them the status of the responsible, self-caring client.

6. Conclusions

This article has illustrated the usefulness of an analytics of governmentality and genealogy to the study of contemporary programs of governing. Through the three illustrations provided, this article has shown how this perspective can be used to empirically study problems such as populations of chronic illness. As noted in the introduction to this article, the field of health and care research tends to be dominated by instrumental and process-driven approaches which focus on the evaluation and description of what care is and the potential of restructures and reforms. In contrast, an analytics of governmentality and genealogy using notions of assemblage (Murray Li 2007) and translation (Rose 1999b) draws out the complexity of policy and the "fragile relays, contested locales and fissiparous affiliations" (Rose 1999b, p. 51) that connect policy to everyday practices of care. Programs like HealthOne seek 'regimes of truth' which appear as linear, rational programs, to solve these complex 'problems'. Understanding these as 'regimes of truth' is of value as it opens up opportunities to rethink the underlying "programmatic logic" (Rose and Miller 1992, p. 192). As demonstrated in the illustrations included in this article, taking up this style of genealogy can highlight the "messiness" (Sandberg et al. 2016, p. 117) of everyday practices of care by "tracing their twists, turns, and localized effects" (Peck and Theodore 2010, p. 173). These insights emphasise the importance of critical and reflexive research that can question the close relationships between policy and governing populations at a distance. In this case, studying the translation of integrated care through empirical analysis highlights the complexity of contemporary understandings of chronic illness and the neoliberal economic rationalities that run through it. Further, an analytics of governmentality and genealogy opens up a critical stance on how advanced liberal ways of thinking about chronic disease became embedded in daily practices of a diverse group of professionals and clients in local sites in the community. In so doing it highlights the potential of these 'intellectual tools' for research in many different fields.

Conflicts of Interest: The authors declare no conflict of interest.

References

Bacchi, Carol. 2012. Introducing the 'What's the problem represented to be?' approach. In *Engaging with Carol Bacchi: Strategic Interventions and Exchanges*. Edited by Angelique Bletsas and Chris Beasley. Adelaide: University of Adelaide Press, pp. 21–24.

Braithwaite, Jeffrey, Johanna Westbrook, and Rick Iedema. 2005. Restructuring as gratification. *Journal of the Royal Society of Medicine* 98: 542–44. [CrossRef] [PubMed]

Bröckling, Ulrich, Susanne Krasmann, and Thomas Lemke, eds. 2010. Governmentality: Current issues and future challenges. In *Routledge Studies in Social and Political Thought*. New York: Routledge, vol. 71, pp. 1–33.

Brown, Lynsey J., and Ellen L. McIntyre. 2014. The contribution of Primary Health Care Research, Evaluation and Development-supported research to primary health care policy and practice. *Australian Journal of Primary Health* 20: 47–55. [CrossRef] [PubMed]

Cruikshank, Barbara. 1993. Revolutions within: Self-government and self-esteem. *Economy and Society* 22: 327–44. [CrossRef]

Dean, Mitchell. 1994. *Critical and Effective Histories: Foucault's Methods and Historical Sociology*. London: Routledge, p. 237.

Dean, Mitchell. 1999. *Governmentality: Power and Rule in Modern Society*. London: Sage.

Dean, Mitchell. 2006. Governmentality and the powers of life and death. In *Analysing Social Policy: A Governmental Approach*. Edited by Greg Marston and Catherine McDonald. Cheltenham: Edward Elgar, pp. 19–48.

Dean, Mitchell. 2007. *Governing Societies: Political Perspectives on Domestic and International Rule*. Maidenhead: Open University Press.

Dean, Mitchell. 2010. *Governmentality: Power and Rule in Modern Society*, 2nd ed. London: Sage.

Department of Health and Ageing, ed. 2009. *Primary Health Care Reform in Australia: Report to Support Australia's First National Primary Health Care Strategy*. Canberra: Commonwealth of Australia.

Department of Health Chronic Diseases. 2016. Available online: http://www.health.gov.au/internet/main/publishing.nsf/Content/chronic-disease (accessed on 27 June 2016).

Elden, Stuart. 2007. Rethinking governmentality. *Political Geography* 26: 29–33. [CrossRef]

Foucault, Michel. 2003. Polemics, politics and problematization. In *The Essential Foucault: Selections from the Essential Works of Foucault 1954–1984*. Edited by Paul Rabinow and Nikolas Rose. New York: The New Press, pp. 18–24.

Foucault, Michel. 2007a. *Security, Territory, Population: Lectures at the Collége de France 1977–1978*. London: Palgrave Macmillan.

Foucault, Michel. 2007b. Spaces of security: The example of the town. Lecture of 11th January 1978. *Political Geography* 26: 48–56. [CrossRef]

Fraser, Nancy, and Linda Gordon. 1994. A genealogy of dependency: Tracing a keyword of the US welfare state. *Signs* 19: 309–36. [CrossRef]

Gerteis, Jessie, David Izrael, Deborah Deitz, Lisa LeRoy, Richard Ricciardi, Therese Miller, and Jayasree Jaya. 2014. *Multiple Chronic Conditions Chartbook: 2010 Medical Expenditure and Panel Survey Data*. Rockville: Agency for Healthcare Research and Quality, p. 52.

Knauft, Bruce M. 2017. What is genealogy? An anthropological/philosophical reconsideration. *Genealogy* 1: 5. [CrossRef]

Kretsedemas, Philip. 2017. Genealogy: Inaugural editorial. *Genealogy* 1: 1. [CrossRef]

Lemke, Thomas. 2010. Foucault, governmentality and critique. *Rethinking Marxism* 14: 49–64. [CrossRef]

Miller, Peter, and Nikolas Rose. 2008. *Governing the Present: Administering Economic, Social and Personal Life*. London: Polity.

Mol, Annemarie. 2008. *The Logic of Care: Health and the Problem of Patient Choice*. London: Routledge.

Murray Li, Tania. 2007. Practices of assemblage and community forest management. *Economy and Society* 36: 263–93. [CrossRef]

National Health and Hospitals Reform Commission. 2009. *A Healthier Future for All Australians—Final Report*. Canberra: National Health and Hospitals Reform Commission.

NSW Government. 2012. *Guidelines for Developing HealthOne NSW Services*. Edited by Health. Sydney: NSW Government, pp. 1–25.

NSW Government HealthOne NSW. 2016. Available online: http://www.health.nsw.gov.au/HealthOne/Pages/default.aspx (accessed on 21 July 2016).

NSW Government. n.d. *HealthOne Camara: Information for Patients*. Sydney: Department of Health.

Peck, Jamie, and Nik Theodore. 2010. Mobilizing policy: Models, methods and mutations. *Geoforum* 41: 169–74. [CrossRef]

Rose, Nikolas. 1996. *Inventing Ourselves: Psychology, Power and Personhood*. New York: Cambridge University Press.

Rose, Nikolas. 1998. An interview with Nikolas Rose. *Arena Journal* 11: 83–96.

Rose, Nikolas. 1999a. *Governing the Soul*, 2nd ed.London: Free Association Press, p. 320.

Rose, Nikolas. 1999b. *Powers of Freedom: Reframing Political Thought*. Cambridge: Cambridge University Press.

Rose, Nikolas, and Peter Miller. 1992. Political power beyond the state: Problematics of government. *The British Journal of Sociology* 43: 173–205. [CrossRef]

Rose, Nikolas, Pat O'Malley, and Mariana Valverde. 2006. Governmentality. *Annual Review of Law and Social Science* 2: 83–104. [CrossRef]

Sandberg, Fredrik, Andreas Fejes, Magnus Dahlstedt, and Maria Olson. 2016. Adult education as a heterotopia of deviation: A dwelling for the abnormal citizen. *Adult Education Quarterly* 66: 103–19. [CrossRef]

Savage, Glenn C. 2013. Governmentality in practice: Governing the self and others in a marketized education system. In *Critical Studies in Educational Leadership, Management and Administration: Educational Leadership and Michel Foucault*. Edited by Donald Gillies. Florence: Routledge, pp. 85–105.

Slama, Slim, Louis Loutan, Didier Wernli, Sunoor Verma, and David Beran. 2013. Chronic conditions: Lessons from the front line. *Chronic Illness* 9: 83–86. [CrossRef] [PubMed]

Swerissen, Hal, Stephen John Duckett, and J. Wright. 2016. *Chronic Failure in Primary Medical Care*. Melbourne: Grattan Institute, p. 48.

Tamboukou, Maria. 1999. Writing genealogies: An exploration of Foucault's strategies for doing research. *Discourse: Studies in the Cultural Politics of Education* 20: 201–17. [CrossRef]

Turnbull, Margo Louise. 2017. *Governing Chronic Illness through Integrated Care*. Sydney: University of Technology Sydney.

Valentijn, Pim P., Hubertus J. M. Vrijhoef, Dirk Ruwaard, Inge Boesveld, Rosa Y. Arends, and Marc A. Bruijnzeels. 2015. Towards an international taxonomy of integrated primary care: A Delphi consensus approach. *MC Family Practice* 16: 64. [CrossRef] [PubMed]

genealogy

MDPI

Article

Emancipating Intellectual Property from Proprietarianism: Drahos, Foucault, and a Quasi-Genealogy of IP

Wendyl Luna

School of Humanities and Languages, University of New South Wales, Sydney, NSW 2052, Australia;
wendyl.luna@student.unsw.edu.au

Received: 15 November 2017; Accepted: 15 January 2018; Published: 18 January 2018

Abstract: This paper argues that Peter Drahos undertakes a partial Foucauldian genealogy by emancipating intellectual property (IP) from proprietarianism. He demonstrates the dominance of proprietarianism in IP by drawing sample practices from trademark, copyright, and patent laws, and then seeks to displace the proprietarian dominance with instrumentalism, which reconstitutes IP as a "liberty-intruding privilege." Ironically, despite doing a genealogy, Drahos does not eradicate sovereignty altogether as Michel Foucault insists, but instead determines IP as a "sovereignty mechanism" that has a "sovereignty effect." After explaining what Foucauldian genealogy is, the paper will explain how Drahos undertakes a genealogy of IP, while highlighting the limitations of Drahos' analysis from a Foucauldian perspective.

Keywords: Michel Foucault; Peter Drahos; (quasi-)genealogy; intellectual property/IP

1. Introduction

Although he explicitly references two of Michel Foucault's works and briefly examines his notion of power, it would misrepresent Peter Drahos to say he was inspired by Foucault for his genealogical work of IP. Nevertheless, the minimal Foucauldian inspiration does not prevent it from being said that Drahos undertakes a genealogy. By resisting the common temptation to understand IP as "property" or to view it from a proprietarian perspective, as well as by considering it instead as a "liberty-intruding privilege," Drahos allows us to rethink the notion of intellectual property from an instrumental point of view.

This paper has a twofold aim: first, to show that Foucault's genealogy provides a useful and still relevant approach to analyzing rights and power relations, especially in the specific context of IP; and, second, to explore the difficulties of strictly following genealogical principles in the context of intangible (statutory) rights, such as IP in that they require an acknowledgement of sovereignty as a foundational basis for affirming precisely those rights. Its importance then lies not only in examining Drahos' work from a Foucauldian perspective, but also in pointing out potential responses to the high demands of strictly applying Foucauldian genealogy. Examining Drahos' quasi-genealogy of IP in his book, *A Philosophy of Intellectual Property* (Drahos 2016), this paper demonstrates that, despite falling short of Foucauldian genealogy, Drahos confirms the usefulness of such a genealogy as one of the tools in analyzing regimes beyond those which were the specific subject of study by Foucault (e.g., sexuality or disciplinary society).

I will first briefly outline how Foucault conceives of genealogy, and then examine Drahos' emancipation of IP from the shackles of proprietarianism via instrumentalism as a genealogical undertaking. In lieu of a property rights characterization, Drahos suggests applying the "language of privilege" which, he says, "should form the core of intellectual property theory" (Drahos 2016, p. 2). With this, Drahos validates Foucault's genealogical approach by applying its core principles, although not fully, because he refuses to sever ties with sovereignty as Foucault would demand (Drahos 2016, p. 176). The question to ask Drahos, then, is whether it would be possible to truly liberate IP from proprietarianism if one still clings on to sovereign power in some form.

The paper is divided into three parts: (1) Foucauldian genealogy: otherwise than government; (2) Proprietarianism: the norm in IP; and (3) Drahos' departure from Foucault: a quasi-genealogy. The first part will discuss Foucauldian genealogy through a reading of Foucault's "What is Critique?" to show that it is primarily an immanent critique of the present. Next, I will examine Drahos' genealogy of IP, which consists of determining proprietarianism as the dominant norm in IP, as well as displacing it with instrumentalism. The final section will explain why Drahos' genealogy of IP is a quasi-genealogy. Even though his genealogy may well be considered Foucauldian, he undertakes Foucauldian genealogy only partially. For, despite displacing successfully the dominant proprietarian view in IP with an instrumental one, he, unlike Foucault, refuses to "cut off the head of the king."

2. Foucauldian Genealogy: Otherwise Than Government

Much has already been said about Foucauldian genealogy, and it is useful to explore what others have said to provide context before engaging directly with Foucault himself. While stressing that Foucault's genealogy is closely linked to his questioning of the present, Colin Gordon argues that in order to specify the singularity of Foucault's genealogical work, it must be compared with other genealogical works of Cassirer, Hayek, Adorno, and other genealogists (Gordon 1986, p. 78). Likewise, the title of Rudi Visker's book, *Michel Foucault: Genealogy as Critique*, already gives us a hint as to how he understands Foucault's genealogy. Its utilization of quotation marks, he says, is "an exemplary expression of a model of critique" (Visker 1995, p. 2). Furthermore, he argues that Foucault's use of quotation marks, which he says should neither be exaggerated nor taken seriously (Visker 1995, p. 2), structures his critique of subjectivity, power, and the pretentious claims to scientificity of the so-called "sciences" such as psychoanalysis and the human sciences (Visker 1995, p. 110). Like Visker, Colin Koopman gives his book the same title, whose "central aim," he says, is to explain that genealogy is a "philosophical-historical critique of the present" (Koopman 2013, p. 5).[1] While acknowledging his indebtedness to Foucault, he nonetheless seeks to revise Foucault, as well as reconstruct his "problematization" of modernity. Joseph Tanke is another Foucauldian scholar who deals with Foucault's genealogy of modernity. Scrutinizing Foucault's philosophy of (visual) art that deals with the paintings of such artists as Velázquez, Manet, and Magritte, he claims that this Foucauldian corpus forms a different "strand in the historical ontology of ourselves," constituting a significant part of Foucault's critique of modernity (Tanke 2009, pp. 4–6).

Finally, *Foucault and the History of Our Present* (Fuggle et al. 2015) is a rich collection of essays, which explain Foucault's "history of the present", not by reiterating what he said, but by identifying those interstices out of which new forms of subjectivities and struggles may be illumined. In her essay, for example, Judith Revel explains that the "modern attitude" Foucault elaborates in "What is Enlightenment?" comprises two attitudes ((a) critical-historical; and (b) experimental), which together make his genealogy an immanent critique of the present.[2] This brief, non-exhaustive survey shows that, in spite of the many interpretations of Foucauldian genealogy, a common theme emerges: genealogy is a form of critique. To elaborate such a critique and to add something to this already rich literature on Foucauldian genealogy, I propose to examine Foucault's "What is Critique?" Considering this text should not only give a clearer idea about what Foucault means by critique and/or genealogy but should also illuminate why Drahos' genealogy of IP may be described as Foucauldian, albeit partially.

---

[1] Critical reviews of Koopman's book, to which he replies (Koopman 2014), appear in *appear in 2014. Foucault Studies* 18: 238–60. See (Allen 2014; Mendieta 2014; Olson 2014).

[2] Revel writes: "We never exit from history, but we always experiment inside it. That is, we invent from the very inside of a present state of historical determinations of an already-there of history" (Revel 2015, p. 23).

In the lecture addressed to the French Society of Philosophy on 27 May 1978, which would become known widely as "What is Critique?", Foucault gives his threefold definition of "critique": general, historical, and analogical; in this section, I will focus on Foucault's historical definition of critique. Generally speaking, critique is captured by what he calls the "critical attitude," which he defines as a mode of "thinking, speaking and acting" (Foucault 2007a, p. 42). Likewise, in general terms, critique or critical attitude is a type of relationship one has with things, other people, and one's self. Foucault argues that critique is essentially different from, or in stark contrast to, government or the art of governing others. As such, critique may be said to be otherwise than government.

Peculiar to the West, Foucault traces the roots of the art of governing others to the Christian pastoral that advances its own notion of governing others; namely, that everyone needs to be governed or directed by an able person to salvation. In Foucault's account, this art of governing others saw an expansion into spheres beyond religion in the fifteenth century for two reasons. The art of governing spread first because of secularization. This means that such an art is not a question of saving souls anymore, and is no longer done exclusively by the priest, but extends beyond the religious sector to the secular part of society. The second reason for the expansion is that, while it was previously confined to the church, the art of governing others could then be accomplished in different areas, such as governing children, families, cities, and others. Hence, the art of governing which, in Foucault's analysis, Christianity started during the medieval times, multiplied or proliferated in the fifteenth or sixteenth century because the arts of governing and the institutions of government themselves diversified.[3]

What is more interesting than the proliferation of the arts of governing is that any art of governing, according to Foucault, is always accompanied by its counter-movement, which I call the refusal to be governed in a certain way or the refusal to follow an existing form of "power." Moreover, he says that it is with the refusal to be governed in a certain way that one can align or locate the critical attitude. Two movements can then be juxtaposed: on the one hand, the art of governing; and, on the other hand, the refusal to follow this form of governing. Foucault argues that the art of governing and the refusal to be governed in a certain way are two sides of the same coin, and are inseparable; as such, the refusal is always tied to a particular form or art of governing. Whereas the fundamental question of the art of governing is "how to govern," the question of its counter-movement is "how not to be governed *like that*."[4] If the two are always tied together, and if the art of governing has multiplied, then it would be safe to say that the refusal to be governed in a certain way has also multiplied, even though Foucault does not explicitly say this in his lecture. Having identified its beginnings, Foucault determines the historicity of critique. From this, one can say that Foucault's historical definition of critique is such that it pins down to a certain period in history the proliferation of the critical attitude or the refusal to be governed in a certain way.

Foucault presents three points that anchor, if not determine, critique historically (Foucault 2007a, pp. 45–47). The first historical point of the critical attitude or refusal to be governed in a certain way is the defiance or opposition against the authority of the Church over the interpretation of scriptures. This refusal to be governed by what the magisterium says about scriptures seeks to go back to the "truth" or real meaning that is embedded in scriptures. This makes critique or the refusal to be governed in a certain way to manifest as exegesis or biblical hermeneutics, which, unlike eisegesis, allows the text to speak for itself as it were, hence a much better way of approaching or interpreting the Bible. The second historical point of this critical attitude is found in the refusal to obey unjust laws. This refusal enables people to come up with fundamental and inalienable rights that all governments

---

[3] After giving the lecture, Foucault says during the panel discussion: "[T]he history of the critical attitude, as it unfolds specifically in the West and in the modern Western world since the 15th–16th centuries must have its origin in the religious struggles and spiritual attitudes prevalent during the second half of the Middle Ages, precisely at the time when the problem was posed: how should one be governed, is one going to accept being governed like that?" (Foucault 2007a, p. 69).

[4] Foucault writes: "[T]his governmentalization [i.e., the art of governing or how to govern], which seems to me to be rather characteristic of these societies in Western Europe in the 16th century, cannot be dissociated from the question 'how not to be governed?'" (Foucault 2007a, p. 44).

must recognize, making critique a legal issue. This second point also indicates that the art of governing has limits and that it has no absolute authority. The final historical point is the refusal to submit to the authority of dogmatism. This refusal opposes a particular authority of dogmatism, and submits to it only if one discovers that it is just and reasonable. Critique, then, is found wherever there is an unreasonable, unjust, and corrupt status quo. The refusals are each connected to a particular form of governing at all times. With Foucault's three examples of different refusals against existing forms of "power," critique is defined historically. It is very interesting to see that the critical attitude can be found even outside the province of philosophy, as if Foucault is saying that it is not exclusively a problem for philosophy.

If one examines Foucault's definition of critique, however, she finds that it is quite narrow, because it is identified only as a refusal to be governed in a certain way. Moreover, one has reason to ask whether Foucault is correct in saying that this critical attitude began as a reaction to the Christian pastoral, and then carried over through the 15th and 16th centuries up to our times. A question can be raised: is there no critical attitude in the East? One can also ask whether there was no critical attitude before the refusal to follow the Christian pastoral. Henri Gouhier, who was one of the interlocutors during the panel discussion, actually wondered whether it is possible to trace Foucault's account of the critical attitude to the Socratic method, saying: "there is a critical ferment due to Socratic thought" (Foucault 2007a, p. 73). What if, to use Foucault's language, these critical attitudes or different refusals are actually dispersed and disconnected? He himself acknowledged at the beginning of his lecture that the critical attitude peculiar to the Western tradition is "condemned to dispersion, dependency and pure heteronomy" (Foucault 2007a, p. 42). Therefore, there are two contrasting Foucauldian ideas of critical attitude: one which is dispersed or heteronomous, and the other which can be historically unified or connected.

It would appear difficult to make sense of the critical attitude as both dispersed and unified. The different critical attitudes occurring at different times in the history of the West only seem to be historically unified or connected because Foucault, the historian-philosopher, tries to connect these dispersed objects. This is perhaps not faithful to the historiography or the approach to history he proposes in *The Archaeology of Knowledge* (Foucault 2002); namely, that dispersed objects are to be respected as they are, and accounted for precisely as dispersed objects. It is highly unlikely that our current refusals to follow unjust forms of governing today (or at any time) are mere reprisals of the critique or critical attitude of the past (even before the Christian pastoral). Our criticism of Foucault's historicizing the critical attitude, therefore, is this: in contrast to seeing critique as that which can be historically connected, critique is considered not as a continuation of the critical attitude of the past, but one that is done with respect to any unjust, unreasonable, and corrupt status quo or current art of governing.

Whether or not Foucault is right in historicizing the critical attitude, one can still agree with him that many forms of governing are stifling, and there will always be a refusal or critical attitude that is tied up with each of these forms. If the art of governing stifles or subjugates individuals, the refusal to be governed in a certain way de-subjugates and empowers them. It is worth quoting Foucault at length:

> [I]f *governmentalization* is indeed this *movement through which individuals are subjugated* . . . I will say that *critique* is the *movement by which the subject* gives himself the right to *question truth* on its effects of power and *question power* on its discourses of truth . . . *critique* will be the art of *voluntary insubordination*, that of reflected intractability. *Critique* would essentially insure the *desubjugation of the subject in the context of* . . . *the politics of truth.* (Foucault 2007a, p. 47; emphases mine).

The quotation above is a good summary of what I have been trying to say so far: critique or critical attitude is the process by which one de-subjugates or frees oneself from oppressive and stifling forms of governing (i.e., a "voluntary insubordination"). It is to question, or hold as suspect, both "truth" and "power"; namely, "truth" that produces power, and "power" that articulates truth. Not subscribing to the correspondence theory of truth, Foucault argues that "truth" is a product of power relations. It is malleable, ephemeral, contingent, and dependent on various forces, such as institutions. If it were to question "truth," then critique questions not only those "truths" that are held to be true, but also those that produce and have an effect on power. On the other hand, there is a kind of "power" that expresses truth and, while doing so, subjugates individuals. This conception of power seems to be different from the notion of power that Foucault talks about in his other works, such as *The History of Sexuality*, where he conceives of power as that which is constituted, supported, and conditioned by force relations. Power, in this sense, is not something negative, but productive and positive.[5] It is important to take note of this positive sense of power because, as we will see, Drahos shares the same view. In his lecture, however, the "power" that Foucault has in mind is something negative: it stifles and subjugates individuals.

It might be thought that Foucault is inconsistent here, because he presents a seemingly contradictory notion of power in "What is Critique?" However, if we follow his idea found in *The History of Sexuality*, that the power that subjugates is merely an effect of the positive "power" that is constituted and conditioned by the various power relations, then the former is not foreign to the latter. There is therefore no contradiction on Foucault's part. He is using the same "grid" of power to analyze the critical attitude. Nevertheless, we have these forms of governing that are "powerful" (those that express and define "truth") and "truthful" (those that produce "power") and, as such, they are stifling and subjugating. In opposition to these stifling, "powerful", and "truthful" forms of governing, the critical attitude relates itself to them, and seeks to free itself from them.

The remainder of Foucault's lecture explains how his notion of critique is similar to Kant's understanding of *Aufklärung*[6] (Foucault 2007a, pp. 47–58), as well as how his "historical-philosophical" critique may be conducted (Foucault 2007a, pp. 58–67). It would be instructive to determine how exactly this critique is conducted, as well as examine the connection between Foucault and Kant, which would be the analogical definition of critique, but I do not have space to do that here. What I have said about critique, though, is sufficient to explain why it is a genealogy. Critique is genealogy precisely because it determines singularities and contingencies. Here is Foucault: "what is proposed instead is a *genealogy*, that is, something that attempts to restore the conditions for the appearance of a singularity born out of multiple determining elements of which it is . . . the effect" (Foucault 2007a, p. 64; emphasis in the original). In other words, critique as genealogy determines those singularities and contingencies that constitute who or what we are.

There are things and/or events that make truths about ourselves or impose truths on us (e.g., sexuality) and, according to Foucault, these are the same sorts of things that one refuses to believe to be true. Therefore, she rejects whatever she has been made or forced to accept, especially those "truths" about herself. In "What is Enlightenment?", Foucault elaborates what he means by critique, describing it as both the historical analysis of the limits imposed upon us, and an experiment as to the possibility of going beyond them (Foucault 2007b, p. 118). This means that, in doing genealogical critique, one needs to undertake, first, a historical inquiry into those things or events that make her what she is at present, and then determine other possible subjectivities that she can constitute for herself. Otherwise than government, Foucauldian genealogy is an immanent critique of the present. We will see that this is exactly what Drahos accomplishes in critiquing IP. By identifying proprietarianism

---

5 For example, in *The History of Sexuality*, vol. 1, Foucault writes: "By power, I do not mean 'Power' as a group of institutions and mechanisms that ensure the subservience of the citizens of a given state. By power, I do not mean, either, a mode of subjugation which, in contrast to violence, has the form of rule. Finally, I do not have in mind a general system of domination exerted by one group over another" (Foucault 2008, p. 92).

6 Foucault writes: "I would have the arrogance to think that this definition . . . is not very different from the one Kant provided: not to define critique, but precisely to define . . . the *Aufklärung*" (Foucault 2007a, p. 47). On the following page, he writes: "What Kant was describing as the *Aufklärung* is very much what I was trying before to describe as critique, this critical attitude which appears as a specific attitude in the Western world starting with what was historically, I believe, the great process of society's governmentalization" (Foucault 2007a, p. 48).

as the dominant norm in IP and replacing it with instrumentalism, Drahos undertakes Foucauldian genealogy to a certain but significant extent.

3. Proprietarianism: The Norm in IP

Before discussing how for Drahos proprietarianism becomes the dominant norm in IP, let me first contextualize his work. His book, *A Philosophy of Intellectual Property*, was published in 1996 shortly after the signing of the Agreement on Trade-Related Aspects of Intellectual Property Rights, commonly known as TRIPS. Signed on 15 April 1994 by one hundred and eleven countries at the GATT[7], TRIPS is an international agreement that regulates and promulgates minimum standards of various forms of intellectual property such as patents, trademarks, and copyright for member-nations of the WTO. Drahos explains that TRIPS was initiated by developed countries, particularly the US, to economically coerce developing countries to implement intellectual property laws. He writes: "By helping its multinational clientele to achieve *dominium* over the abstract objects of intellectual property the US goes a long way towards maintaining its *imperium*. TRIPS at one level is very much a story about the continuation of US hegemony" (Drahos 1995, p. 16; emphases in the original).[8] Once a country joins TRIPS, any member nation is able to make a complaint to the WTO if that country is not complying with the requirements of TRIPS.[9] By linking membership of WTO with adoption of TRIPs, the more powerful developed nations effectively coerced the developing nations to recognize intellectual property rights, most of which were generated and owned by companies originating in the developed countries. Particular examples include the protection given to pharmaceutical composition patents and computer software generally.

Another attempt to further the globalization and "proprietarianization" of IP identified by Drahos in his various works can be seen in the ambitious Trans Pacific Partnership (TPP). The TPP had its origins in a trade agreement in 2005 between four countries in the Pacific region: Brunei Singapore, New Zealand, and Chile, known as the Trans-Pacific Strategic Economic Partnership Agreement. From 2008, various other countries indicated a desire to join that agreement. The end result was the TPP between 12 nations occupying the Pacific Rim including the US, Japan, Canada, Singapore, and Australia, and covering more than 40% of the world's population. Importantly, from a geo-political perspective, China was not a participant of the TPP. The TPP does contain provisions allowing for further countries to join, and a number of other countries had expressed interest in becoming part of it.

The TPP was signed by all 12 countries on 4 February 2016, and was hoped to be ratified by all of them by 4 February 2018, following which, it would come into effect. Rather ironically, in 2017, the Trump administration of the United States withdrew from the TPP, citing the potential damage to local US manufacturing industries associated with lowering of tariff barriers, among other things. The remaining 11 nations are continuing efforts to proceed with the TPP (now renamed Comprehensive and Progressive Agreement for Trans-Pacific Partnership), but with the relevant IP aspects suspended, pending the hoped-for re-engagement of the United States at a later time. Many of these controversial IP provisions were insisted upon by the United States. With its departure from the TPP, the other countries have decided to suspend the IP provisions for now, but have continued with a partial implementation of the TPP, having reached a revised agreement in November 2017.

Although no longer the powerhouse it would have been, due to the US' departure, the TPP process, like TRIPS, aptly demonstrates Drahos' consistent thesis that IP has become a commodity with the IP-rich developed nations exercising their economic power to encourage developing nations

---

[7]   GATT stands for General Agreement on Tariffs and Trade.

[8]   In another work, Drahos and Braithwaite write: "The case of intellectual property shows the US state and international business mobilising the mechanism of coercion to get developing countries to sign TRIPs" (Drahos and Braithwaite 2001, p. 124).

[9]   In their book, Drahos and Braithwaite explain that the US takes advantage of TRIPS: "The minute that TRIPS came into force the US began to use the WTO dispute resolution mechanism to obtain compliance with its provisions. It remains to date the biggest litigator under TRIPS" (Drahos and Braithwaite 2002, p. 113).

to enshrine and perpetuate the proprietarian approach to IP in their local laws. In this sense, it is important to undertake a genealogical analysis of IP for two reasons: first, in order to determine the dominant norm, the identification of which would make it possible to develop forms of resistance and alternatives; and, second, in order to be cognizant of the way power morphs and continues to dominate certain aspects of our lives. In light of this, we now describe the characteristic features of proprietarianism which, according to Drahos, have come to dominate IP.

In contrast to the narrower, natural rights-based notion of proprietarianism advocated by Jeremy Bentham and John Locke, Drahos understands proprietarianism in a broader sense, defining it as a creed which asserts "that the possessor should take all, that ownership privileges should trump community interests and that the world and its contents are open to ownership" (Drahos 2016, p. 235). He further explains that this proprietarian creed consists of three core beliefs: the moral priority of property rights over other rights and interests, the first connection thesis, and the existence of a negative commons (Drahos 2016, p. 235). To elaborate, because it deems property as foundational, proprietarianism according to Drahos prioritizes property rights or interests over others.[10] The first connection thesis of proprietarianism states that the person who establishes first a connection to an economically valuable object becomes entitled to property or ownership of that object. This can be fulfilled by exercising control over a certain object which, in turn, is guaranteed by first possession rules. The proprietarian belief in the existence of a negative commons means that things are not automatically owned, but are open to ownership by any individual. Taken together, all three beliefs are for Drahos constitutive of proprietarianism. Having explained his own general conception of proprietarianism, Drahos then clarifies how it has infiltrated IP. He shows this not through an extensive empirical investigation, but through a discussion of what he calls "proprietarianism in action," drawing examples from trademark, copyright, and patent laws (Drahos 2016, pp. 236–47). Although it is doubtful that proprietarianism could be characterized completely by these sample practices, we grant that they not only constitute the characteristic features of proprietarianism, but also demonstrate Drahos' contention that proprietarianism has dominated IP law and practice.

In present-day trademark practice, according to Drahos, there is a tendency to prioritize trademark proprietors more than consumers. Because of the growing need for modernization and commercialization, addressing the "needs of the market," trademarks, he says, "become tradeable entities in their own right that serve the interests of their owners" (Drahos 2016, p. 238). Instead of serving consumer and public interests, which used to be the case, trademark proprietors are served first. This significant change in trademark practice, according to Drahos, is brought about by the expansion of the meaning of sign (which now includes colors, movements, shapes, scents, and sounds), the main purpose of which is to protect not the consumers' interests, but those of the traders. It makes sense that a trademark is a badge of origin, indicating the source of the product and enabling the consumer to make assumptions about quality, characteristics, and reputation, perhaps across a range of products to which the trademark is applied. Nonetheless, these attributes are problematic for him, given his assertion that consumer and public interests are increasingly set aside in the modern approach to trademarks.

In its original conception, to be granted a trademark was to be granted a statutory privilege, which privilege was to be exercised within the purpose and intent of trademark law. However, Drahos argues, over time, a trademark has evolved (better yet, devolved) as just another species of commercial property, no different from any other type of property. The trademarks have abandoned their statutory privilege, and joined the indistinguishable host of property rights. As examples of this abandonment, Drahos cites the relatively recent commercial phenomena of trademark licensing and assignment. In these situations, something which was originally conceived as original statutory privilege acquires

---

[10] Drahos explains: "[Proprietarianism] is a creed and an attitude which inclines its holders towards a property fundamentalism. The consequence within normative theory is that property interests are continuously given a moral primacy" (Drahos 2016, p. 234).

the ability to be alienated to someone else unconnected with the original source or reputation, through licensing or outright sale. He essentially says that when someone is allowed to license or sell the trademark, the primary purpose and function of the trademark as a badge of origin is lost, because the person now using or owning the trademark is not the original source of the trademark. He is correct because, as the franchising model shows, the franchisor or the original owner of the trademark (origin and reputation) grants multiple unrelated parties the right to use the trademark in exchange for a substantial fee. Given the prevalence of licensing and assignment of trademarks, there certainly appears to be some validity to Drahos' argument that the original consumer-oriented purpose of indicating true source or origin has been lost. However, the vast majority of trademarks continue to be used and applied by the original "privileged" holder, and thus, one may say that while there has been a dilution in the original purpose of a trademark, as explained by Drahos, the original purpose of indicating original source continues for many trademarks today.

Turning to copyright, Drahos gives the example of the "sweat of the brow" doctrine to demonstrate how copyright proprietarianism is at work. Illustrated by the United States case of *Jeweler's Circular Pub. Co.* vs. *Keystone Pub. Co.*, the sweat of the brow doctrine simply states that if one puts enough effort into creating something, even something which merely involves the laborious collection of data or facts, it may be protectable by copyright in the US at least. This proprietarian approach to copyright is problematic for Drahos, because it favors privatization of reports of facts, with little or no creative element. He writes: "Copyright proprietarianism in the form of the 'sweat of the brow' doctrine potentially transfers these public domain reports into private hands" (Drahos 2016, p. 242). Consequently, these supposedly "public" domain reports, which are now protected by copyright, enable the "owner" to commercialize this new private property through licensing it to others and extracting payment. As in the case of trademark discussed above, this proprietarian approach "privileges" copyright proprietors, because it enables them to protect something which otherwise would not have been protectable, and for which they can charge a fee. Subsequent cases, in the US and elsewhere, have denied or cast doubt on the validity of the sweat of the brow doctrine on the basis that the relevant material does not meet the copyright requirements of originality and creativity. However, as Drahos points out, the march of proprietarianism continues with the creation of a sui generis database protection right (in place of copyright protection) in some jurisdictions, which explicitly protects such public domain reports and other data compilations involving significant effort. In many ways, this is an even worse outcome from Drahos' perspective because a new proprietary right is created from nothing, as opposed to being created out of the modification of the privilege doctrine on which intellectual property was originally based, nullifying any possibility of arguing for a return to the original roots of the property right (i.e., privilege).

Finally, Drahos explores the field of patents, and explains that, traditionally, discoveries themselves were not patentable, only inventions with an industrial application (Drahos 2016, p. 244). Whereas discovery consists of revealing or unveiling something already existing in the world, invention arises when something new is created which has a useful effect for industry. The observance of the distinction between discovery and invention, according to Drahos, helped shape the traditional goal of the patent system, which was meant to improve skills within current industries and/or create new industries or technical fields. However, with the advent of proprietarianism, the distinction between discovery and invention is blurred, if not abolished. The proprietarian approach to patent, he says, argues that discovery should be "the subject of a patent right," because the process of discovering "can be [as] costly, labour-intensive and economically valuable" as an invention (Drahos 2016, pp. 245–46). In this cost-based justification, one sees a similar approach to that taken in relation to granting copyright protection for laborious (if rather uncreative) data compilations under the sweat of the brow doctrine. Discovery, then, like invention, becomes patentable from the proprietarian perspective. With the proprietarian influence, biological materials, such as genes, newly discovered plant and animal species, including those that are bred by growers or breeders, may now be granted patent rights or plant breeders rights in some jurisdictions, although, since Drahos wrote, this window is gradually closing, due to various court decisions and legislative changes around the world narrowing the field of patentable subject matter. According to Drahos, if proprietarianism continued to dominate the patent system, it would not be long until every piece of abstract information belonging to the public domain would be held privately by a select few. To Drahos, this would be problematic, because it would betray the true function of the patent system, which is meant to protect not useful ideas (e.g., a discovery), but a method of manufacture (e.g., patentable invention). Something that was potentially publicly available for use by anybody now becomes captured under the individual control of the patent owner who can then prevent others from using it without permission and payment.

It is now easy to understand why Drahos is critical of the proprietarian approach to intellectual property. He rejects proprietarianism because it prioritizes the rights of proprietors of intellectual property over the rights of the public, as well as espouses the privatization of such abstract objects as intellectual property, which he says poses a threat to "the core value of negative liberty" (Drahos 2016, p. 248). In describing intellectual property rights, he complements the classical formulation of negative rights that merely includes rights to "life, liberty and property" (Drahos 2016, p. 248). Intellectual property rights to him are not just negative rights, but are also "liberty-inhibiting privileges" (Drahos 2016, p. 250). This means that they allow the person who has the privilege to exercise it to inhibit the freedom of others to do things protected by the privilege. Unlike tangible assets, such as land or equipment, IP rights do not impact in a physical way, being incorporeal, but they impact any activity of any person that is within the scope of the abstract object (i.e., the subject matter of the particular intellectual property). As such, the inhibition of liberty can potentially apply on a global basis, rather than a territorial one, as would be the case for physical property, such as land or an item of equipment. It appears though that the distinction between the classical conception of property as negative rights and Drahos' broader notion of intellectual property rights as liberty-inhibiting privileges is marginal. For, it may be true that negative rights are themselves rights, whereas intellectual property rights may be viewed as "privileges" (at least in the original and Drahos' conception of it) and have more global importance than, say, ownership of a piece of land; nevertheless, both share the same "negative" quality of freedom restriction that enables its owner to interfere with the activities of others with respect to the (intellectual) property in question. Arguably, the only difference between the two is that the territorial effect is limited physically in the case of land, while the territorial effect for intellectual property is limited to the scope of the relevant IP. Thus, both intellectual property and other sources of rights have a territorial limitation, even if the nature of that territorial limitation differs, given the differing nature of the relevant property (abstract or otherwise).

In lieu of the proprietarian approach to intellectual property, Drahos posits instrumentalism, which has a twofold characteristic: (a) humanistic; and (b) naturalistic. Instrumentalism is humanistic, because it seeks to improve the human condition and experience by maximizing not just physical, but also human capital. It is naturalistic, because it conceives of intellectual property rights as natural rights or privileges which must be exercised responsibly, and seeks to eliminate the idea of property as a mere economic right or commodity free of any responsibility to consider others. Drahos applies the term instrumentalism because he argues that IP should be considered as an instrument to improve the human condition, rather than being an end in itself or a source of unqualified rights for the holder. Thus, IP is to return to its original roots as a privilege with which comes responsibilities as well as rights, and the responsibilities are to exercise the privilege in a way which benefits not only the holder, but also the public. Considering intellectual property rights as privileges to Drahos entails more responsibility for their owners for, following Hohfeld, there is a correlativity between duties and privileges (Drahos 2016, pp. 173, 248). Having described how for Drahos proprietarianism has become dominant in characterizing the nature and operation of IP, I am now going to explain how his approach to genealogy falls short of Foucault's methodology.

4. Drahos' Departure from Foucault: A Quasi-Genealogy

As mentioned, Drahos briefly examines Foucault's analysis of power, consisting merely of two pages (Drahos 2016, pp. 175–77). It would be counterproductive to overemphasize the importance of these two pages, since it is not Drahos' intention to expound Foucault's notion of power, much less give a detailed account of what power is in general. Though not exhaustive, Drahos' treatment is not an unfaithful reading of Foucault's analysis. On the contrary, Drahos gives an accurate interpretation of Foucault's notion of power. His two-page analysis may seem somewhat insignificant, but it still sheds light on and plays an important part in his genealogy of IP.

Drahos' analysis of Foucault's notion of power appears to be a small digression from his discussion of "Power of Abstract Objects" in chapter 7, which explains the unique relationship between intellectual property and power *in general*. Written under the section "Property and Private Sovereignty," it seems to be an elaborate addendum to his well-reasoned position in support of Morris Cohen's argument for private property as "a form of sovereignty over others" (Drahos 2016, p. 172) using Wesley Hohfeld's thesis of correlativity between right and duty (Drahos 2016, p. 173). I will not go into the details of Drahos' presentation of Cohen's argument, but will simply suggest that his analysis of Foucault can be better understood when placed in the context of this discussion.

Drahos correctly points out that Foucault does not endorse the traditional juridical conception of power. This is consistent with the commonly held understanding, Cutrofello's in particular, of Foucault's project as "a sustained attempt to formulate a nonjuridical model for Kantian critique" (Cutrofello 1994, p. x). In contrast to the juridical (i.e., negative) conception of power, says Drahos, Foucault conceives of it "in terms of flow and network concepts" (Drahos 2016, p. 175). He identifies quite accurately that Foucault's notion of power is not one which links power to sovereignty or a "top-down" model, but rather is that which views power as "exercised" in and through a number of means (Drahos 2016, p. 175).[11] Foucault's conception of power may then be said to be "positive", since it is neither restrictive nor obstructive, unlike its traditional juridical counterpart. The problem with the nonjuridical conception of power, according to Drahos, is that it fails to give a satisfactory answer to the question of how individuals harness power: "The analytical shift to conceiving of power as a polycentric phenomenon has still to confront and explain how individuals harness power" (Drahos 2016, p. 176). The "best" (that is, for Drahos, inadequate) explanation that this positive, fluid, and net-like conception of power could give is that there are mechanisms that enable individuals precisely to harness power.[12]

It is not clear in his text, but Drahos seems to suggest that there has to be more to individuals harnessing power than simply being enabled by empowering mechanisms. This is what he writes: "[A]n important question remains to be answered: how do agents within the relevant network harness power flows? Clearly, individual agents have to harness power in order to exercise it" (Drahos 2016, p. 175). In other words, for Drahos, before individuals can even exercise power, they must possess it in the first place. His observation is correct, and his criticism of Foucault justified. It may sound clichéd but, to paraphrase Theodore Roosevelt, one can only do what one has.[13] However, if Drahos is seeking to account for that "more" in individuals' harnessing of power, in my understanding he fails, because he relies solely on the mechanism of intellectual property for his

---

[11] For an interesting debate on Foucault's notion of power, see Charles Taylor and Paul Patton's essays (Taylor 2014a, 2014b; Patton 2014a, 2014b) that have been re-published in David Owen's edited work, *Michel Foucault* (Owen 2014). Patton (2014a) rectifies Taylor (2014a) misconception of Foucault's notion of power first by pointing out that power for Foucault "creates subjects" and, second, by distinguishing "power to" from "power over." The ability to create subjects and the idea of "power to" to Patton determine the positive sense by which Foucault understands "power." Drahos captures this "positive" sense of Foucault's notion of power in his brief commentary on Foucault.

[12] Drahos writes: "[T]he answer to this question has to be given in terms of mechanisms that allow the individual agent (A) to concentrate to some degree the flow of power so that A can affect B in a manner contrary to B's interests" (Drahos 2016, p. 175).

[13] Quoting a certain Squire Bill Widener, Theodore Roosevelt writes: "Do what you can, with what you've got, where you are" (Roosevelt 1916, p. 350).

explanation. As such, he puts himself in an awkward position because he subjects himself to his own criticism of Foucault. Being focused on one sovereignty mechanism (i.e., intellectual property), his explanation for how individuals harness power appears to be less convincing than Foucault's more general account of power mechanisms.

Nevertheless, having identified an inadequacy in Foucault's nonjuridical analysis of power, in the later sections, Drahos offers his own account of the way individuals harness power.[14] Surprisingly, at this juncture of his argument, he claims that his "analysis converges nicely with Foucault's" (Drahos 2016, p. 175). Indeed, his and Foucault's analyses converge for, whereas Foucault considers law to be "an instrument of power," Drahos identifies property as "a law-dependent mechanism of power" (Drahos 2016, p. 176). This means that law and property are, for Foucault and Drahos, respectively, two of the many forms that power or sovereignty assumes and through which it continues to dominate our lives. Their convergence becomes even more apparent when, having adopted "Foucault's emphasis on mechanisms of power" (Drahos 2016, p. 176), Drahos claims that property is a "sovereignty mechanism," which to him is one way by which individuals acquire power.[15] From this, it would not be difficult for him to draw the conclusion that "intellectual property not only is a sovereignty mechanism but it [also] has a sovereignty effect in social systems" (Drahos 2016, p. 185).

As soon as an alliance between Drahos and Foucault is forged, however, it is broken because, although he subscribes to Foucault's account of the "mechanisms of power," Drahos avoids the most important goal of Foucault's genealogy of power; namely, the displacement of sovereignty. Drahos is well aware that the purpose of Foucault's account is not only to show that the juridical conception of sovereignty is flawed but, more importantly, to displace it. However, he explicitly chooses not to follow Foucault mainly because, as I have said, he refuses to sever ties with sovereignty: "Here our analysis *parts ways with Foucault's*, for he is seeking to replace the juridical-political theory of sovereignty ... The approach being advocated here adopts Foucault's emphasis on mechanism of power, but *retains the link to sovereignty*" (Drahos 2016, p. 176; emphases mine). Instead of metaphorically "cutting off the head of the king" as Foucault attempts to do (Foucault 2008, p. 89), Drahos wants to keep the Leviathan alive which, he says, now morphs into intellectual property that has a sovereign effect.[16]

What this shows is that, despite acknowledging the convergence between his and Foucault's analyses, and in spite of adopting Foucault's strategy, Drahos is ultimately at odds with Foucault's conception of power, and the sources of power. Instead of following Foucault, he deliberately espouses the juridical conception of power, which is the very conception Foucault put into question. In continuing to subscribe to the traditional juridical conception of power, Drahos places himself in a precarious position. Despite this, one can still appreciate the value of Drahos' genealogy of IP, which consists precisely of detecting the transformation of sovereign power itself. Ultimately, however, one cannot say that Drahos is faithful to the spirit of Foucauldian genealogy. For, to do so would never result in the preservation of sovereignty in any form. Of course, Drahos explicitly noted that he was departing from Foucault on this point.

A number of Foucault's followers support our claim, contending contra Drahos that the end result of genealogy should be the decentering, if not the total elimination, of the juridical conception of power. Drawing from Foucault's conception of power "without the king" (Foucault 2008, p. 91), they would say that genealogy has no other goal except to forego any analysis of power that is based

---

14 From page 192 onwards, Drahos (Drahos 2016) gives the example of pharmaceutical companies. He explains that they have vaster "threat power" than land owners precisely because of their ownership of patents over certain drugs, which is much more extensive than the ownership of a piece of land. For Drahos, the mere ownership of abstract objects such as copyright, trademark or patent therefore enables their owners to harness power.

15 Here is Drahos: "Our purpose here is not to give a general description of the mechanisms that can be utilised to harness power. Rather the purpose is to show that property is one such mechanism, what we might call a sovereignty mechanism" (Drahos 2016, p. 175).

16 Drahos writes: "Thus we should not follow Foucault when he suggests that we should 'eschew the model of Leviathan in the study of power' (Foucault 1980, p. 102). Instead we need to recognise that, through mechanisms of power, Leviathan changes its shape and produces progeny, which ultimately come to threaten its supremacy" (Drahos 2016, p. 177).

on law and/or sovereignty, or to topple down any power that has held us captive and has never been questioned up until now. David Owen, for example, claims that genealogy is a form of critique that enables "us to free ourselves from a condition of aspectival captivity" (Owen 2014, p. 58). The idea of genealogy emancipating us from captivity is also captured by Martin Saar when he argues that "the critical aim of genealogy ... [consists] in installing a devaluating, delegitimizing vocabulary within genetic descriptions of existing norms and values" (Saar 2014, p. 77). The language of "freedom from," devaluation or de-legitimization used by these Foucauldian scholars to describe genealogy is very consistent with Foucault's immanent critique of the present explained above, which seeks to determine the dominant norm, analyze it historically, and investigate ways by which to go beyond it.

For his part, Drahos could respond by saying, what he is doing in IP is consistent with Foucauldian genealogy. He may not have the same goal of discarding sovereignty as Foucault, but he nonetheless still undertakes an important aspect of Foucauldian genealogy. As we have seen, he starts off by analyzing the status of IP and, having determined that it has long been dominated by proprietarianism, he seeks to emancipate IP from it. Similar to what Foucault does to the juridical notion of power that he seeks to displace, Drahos not only shows how proprietarianism has remained unchallenged in IP but, more importantly, displaces it with his notion of instrumentalism. From this, one can deduce that for Drahos, what is crucial for any genealogical work is not so much the displacement of sovereignty, as analyzing its dominance and effecting a transformation of its goals and purposes. There is therefore a parallelism between Foucauldian genealogy and Drahos' genealogy of IP. Drahos not only emulates Foucault by determining intellectual property as a sovereign mechanism but also undertakes Foucauldian genealogy by applying its core principles. A question still remains: would it really be possible to emancipate IP from proprietarianism if one still clings on to sovereign power?

The short answer is, no. It is impossible to truly emancipate IP if one continues to adhere to a sovereign, juridical notion of power as Drahos does. For, obviously, one remains captive to a dominant form of power. In doing genealogy, while laudable, it is nonetheless insufficient to "simply" determine a dominant norm, analyze it historically, and propose a new norm that would replace it. Drahos has simply replaced one master with another, very similar, master (or perhaps masters, in the form of "sovereignty mechanisms"). As Saar argues, it is not by creating new or neutral norms that constitutes genealogy (Saar 2014, p. 67). As we have seen, this is exactly what Drahos does; in lieu of proprietarianism, he posits the instrumental view for IP. With this, his genealogy of IP falls short of Foucault's methodology, with the result that Drahos' approach, as I have argued, may be considered a quasi-genealogy. For, although it identifies and analyzes the dominant proprietarian norm historically, it maintains its link with sovereign power. In order for it to be a full-fledged genealogy, it must sever ties from sovereignty. Cutting off the head of the king is the only way by which one can emancipate IP, but perhaps this would demand too much from Drahos or any genealogist of IP for that matter. One can sympathize with Drahos when he argues that IP, as a creation of law, is such that it can never be independent from law and, ultimately, the sovereign. The best that a genealogy of it can do is to identify how the sovereign morphs, and determine the form it assumes.

Cutting off the head of the king in the context of IP, therefore, at its most extreme could mean the dissolution or abandonment of the whole concept of IP itself. A less extreme version might involve the replacement of existing laws with new laws or norms, which vary widely from region to region or country to country, according to the needs and attitudes of the citizens of that place, rather than a uniform system which favors the few at the expense of the many. Drahos and others might argue that without law and sovereignty, IP loses substance. That is, an underlying Leviathan is essential to the creation and maintenance of a workable scheme of IP. On this view, the necessity of maintaining sovereignty in the specific, concrete context of IP demonstrates that Foucauldian genealogy may be too ambitious a project or that the standards it sets may be too high to accomplish. It is one thing to prescribe a theoretical model, and another to implement it in the real world with its existing power relations and, in the specific case of IP, trade and regulatory globalization. Foucauldian scholars may defend Foucault, saying it was never Foucault's intention to be prescriptive, but to be descriptive instead, recognizing that each application must be considered in its particular context. Nevertheless, when brought down to the rough grounds of IP law and practice, Foucault's exhortation to cut off the head of the king falls on deaf ears in view of the overwhelming political, trade, and intellectual dominance of the developed nations now enshrined in the various global and regional treaties. Foucault would not ignore these realities, as he did not in the various genealogical studies he undertook. Instead, he would exhort us to resist these structures as best we can, with a view to improving outcomes, despite even partial decapitation of the errant sovereign not being possible.

5. Conclusions

Foucault's genealogy is an immanent critique of the present; immanent, because it never leaves the domain of history, but ascertains and surpasses any limit imposed upon us by means of historical analysis and experimentation, thereby undertaking critique from within the present itself. Drahos' genealogy of IP may be correctly described as Foucauldian in that it seeks to emancipate IP from the dominant proprietarian view, determining thus a norm-limit in IP, as well as postulating a way of moving beyond it through the instrumentalist view of intellectual property. In his work that examines the origins, purpose, and current state of intellectual property, Drahos finds that it was originally grounded in the language of privilege, with attendant duties on the privilege holder. He carefully identifies the transfer of power away from the public and in favor of owners, showing that, over time, intellectual property has devolved into mere proprietarianism, becoming just another category of property. Having identified these power relations, he proposes a recharacterization of IP to seek to reinstate its legacy as privilege—bestowing both power and responsibility. Despite this, his approach explicitly falls short of Foucauldian genealogy, and hence, may only be understood as a quasi-genealogy, by maintaining its link to sovereignty, and seeking to keep the Leviathan alive. Cutting off the head of the king would be the final step to making it a full-fledged genealogy, but perhaps it is impossible for any genealogy of IP to do so as IP will always be based on law, and law is the hand, if not the head, of the king.

Acknowledgments: I would like to thank the Australian Government Research Training Program Scholarship for the support given to me. My heartfelt gratitude goes to my supervisor, Paul Patton, who commented on parts of the paper. Thanks also to Marie Rose Arong for her comments and to the reviewers for their helpful feedback. Finally, I am very grateful to Christopher Bevitt who was my sounding board while writing the paper and from whom I learned a great deal about IP.

Conflicts of Interest: The author declares no conflict of interest.

References

Allen, Amy. 2014. The Normative and the Transcendental: Comments on Colin Koopman's Genealogy as Critique. *Foucault Studies* 18: 238–44. [CrossRef]

Cutrofello, Andrew. 1994. *Discipline and Critique: Kant, Poststructuralism, and the Problem of Resistance*. New York: State University of New York Press.

Drahos, Peter. 2016. *A Philosophy of Intellectual Property*. Acton: ANU eText. First published 1996; Aldershot: Ashgate/Dartmouth, Available online: https://www.researchgate.net/publication/304514536_A_Philosophy_of_Intellectual_Property (accessed 11 October 2017).

Drahos, Peter. 1995. Global Property Rights in Information: The story of TRIPS at the GATT. *Prometheus* 13: 6–19. [CrossRef]

Drahos, Peter, and John Braithwaite. 2001. The Globalisation of Regulation. *The Journal of Political Philosophy* 9: 103–28. [CrossRef]

Drahos, Peter, and John Braithwaite. 2002. *Information Feudalism*. London and Sterling: Earthscan.

Foucault, Michel. 1980. Two Lectures. In *Power/Knowledge: Selected Interviews and Other Writings 1972–1977*. Edited by Colin Gordon. New York: Pantheon Books, pp. 78–108.

Foucault, Michel. 2002. *The Archaeology of Knowledge*. Translated by A. M. Sheridan Smith. London and New York: Routledge.

Foucault, Michel. 2007a. What is Critique? In *The Politics of Truth*. Edited by Sylvère Lotringer. Los Angeles: Semiotext(e), pp. 41–81.

Foucault, Michel. 2007b. What is Enlightenment? In *The Politics of Truth*. Edited by Sylvère Lotringer. Los Angeles: Semiotext(e), pp. 97–119.

Foucault, Michel. 2008. *The History of Sexuality: The Will to Knowledge*. Translated by Robert Hurley. Camberwell: Penguin Books, vol. 1.

Sophie Fuggle, Yari Lanci, and Martina Tazzioli, eds. 2015. *Foucault and the History of Our Present*. Basingstoke and New York: Palgrave Macmillan.

Gordon, Colin. 1986. Question, Ethos, Event: Foucault on Kant and Enlightenment. *Economy and Society* 15: 71–87. [CrossRef]

Koopman, Colin. 2013. *Genealogy as Critique: Foucault and the Problems of Modernity*. Bloomington and Indianapolis: Indiana University Press.

Koopman, Colin. 2014. Genealogy, Methodology, & Normativity beyond Transcendentality: Replies to Amy Allen, Eduardo Mendieta, & Kevin Olson. *Foucault Studies* 8: 261–73. [CrossRef]

Mendieta, Eduardo. 2014. On Left Kantianism: From Transcendental Critique to the Critical Ontology of the Present. *Foucault Studies* 18: 245–52. [CrossRef]

Olson, Kevin. 2014. Genealogy, Cryptonormativity, Interpretation. *Foucault Studies* 18: 253–60. [CrossRef]

Owen, David. 2014. Criticism and Captivity: On Genealogy and Critical Theory. In *Michel Foucault*. Edited by David Owen. Farnham and Burlington: Ashgate, pp. 47–61, Originally published as 2002. *European Journal of Philosophy* 10: 216–30. [CrossRef]

Patton, Paul. 2014a. Taylor and Foucault on Power and Freedom. In *Michel Foucault*. Edited by David Owen. Farnham and Burlington: Ashgate, pp. 121–37, Originally published as 1989. *Political Studies* 37: 260–76. [CrossRef]

Patton, Paul. 2014b. Foucault's Subject of Power. In *Michel Foucault*. Edited by David Owen. Farnham and Burlington: Ashgate, pp. 145–56, Originally published in French as 1992. *Sociologie et Sociétés* 24/1. The first English version appeared in 1994. *Political Theory Newsletter* 6: 60–71.

Revel, Judith. 2015. 'What Are We At The Present Time?' Foucault and the Question of the Present. In *Foucault and the History of Our Present*. Edited by Sophie Fuggle, Yari Lanci and Martina Tazzioli. Basingstoke and New York: Palgrave Macmillan, pp. 13–25.

Roosevelt, Theodore. 1916. *An Autobiography*. New York: Macmillan.

Saar, Martin. 2014. Genealogy and Subjectivity. In *Michel Foucault*. Edited by David Owen. Farnham and Burlington: Ashgate, pp. 71–85, Originally published as 2002. *European Journal of Philosophy* 10: 231–45. [CrossRef]

Tanke, Joseph. 2009. *Foucault's Philosophy of Art: A Genealogy of Modernity*. London and New York: Continuum.

Taylor, Charles. 2014a. Foucault on Freedom and Truth. In *Michel Foucault*. Edited by David Owen. Farnham and Burlington: Ashgate, pp. 89–120, Originally published as 1984. *Political Theory* 12: 152–83. [CrossRef]

Taylor, Charles. 2014b. Taylor and Foucault on Power and Freedom: A Reply. In *Michel Foucault*. Edited by David Owen. Farnham and Burlington: Ashgate, pp. 139–43, Originally published as 1989. *Political Studies* 37: 277–81. [CrossRef]

Visker, Rudi. 1995. *Michel Foucault: Genealogy as Critique*. Translated by Chris Turner. London and New York: Verso.

MDPI

St. Alban-Anlage 66

4052 Basel

Switzerland

Tel. +41 61 683 77 34

Fax +41 61 302 89 18

www.mdpi.com

Genealogy Editorial Office

E-mail: genealogy@mdpi.com

www.mdpi.com/journal/genealogy

www.ingramcontent.com/pod-product-compliance
Lightning Source LLC
Chambersburg PA
CBHW051315020426
42333CB00028B/3359